Mary Batchelor's Everyday Book

D0893055

Here is a book to warm the heart and deepen faith – a book it does you good to read.

Mary Batchelor's Everyday Book is packed full of stories of real people, past and present. Scientists, statesmen, writers, sportsmen, entertainers, all have their place in this unique collection of daily readings, each linked to a particular date.

The total impact of so many people who have, in their own way, done 'something beautiful for God' is both stirring and enriching. Here are the good news stories. Here is faith and hope and love, within the reach of every one of us.

MARY BATCHELOR'S EVERYDAY BOOK

A LION BOOK

Tring · Belleville · Sydney

Copyright © 1982 Mary Batchelor

Published by
Lion Publishing
Icknield Way, Tring, Herts, England
ISBN 0 85648 723 6
Lion Publishing Corporation
10885 Textile Road, Belleville, Michigan 48111, USA
ISBN 0 85648 723 6
Albatross Books
PO Box 320, Sutherland, NSW 2232, Australia
ISBN 0 86760 569 3

First edition 1982
This revised paperback edition 1984

Cover photographs: Sonia Halliday Photographs
(below left) and Lion Publishing

Typeset by First Page Ltd, Watford
Printed and bound in Great Britain by Cox and Wyman, Reading

Contents

Foreword   7
January   9
February   40
March   69
April   100
May   130
June   161
July   191
August   222
September   253
October   283
November   314
December   344

Acknowledgements   375
Sources   376
Index   379

Foreword

Where food is concerned, 'a little of what you fancy does you good'. I hope very much that, in the same way, the selections in this book will be both enjoyable and health-giving.

Stories are the staple diet – stories of people throughout the world, from Bible times to the present day. They come in all shapes and sizes, with a variety of beliefs and temperaments, yet all have in common a trust in God and a love for Jesus Christ. This love has driven them to put right the wrongs of society, compose music, make scientific discoveries or care for the sick. It has caused some to relinquish freedom and life itself.

Choice of material has been very much a matter of personal taste or the chance discovery of people and stories too good to miss out. This may help to explain why some great and important Christians have been omitted and little-known ones included. With so many facts and dates to juggle with, I may well have made some mistakes, for which I apologize.

The aim of the book is to link every entry to the date on which it occurs, by using some relevant anniversary. This has sometimes led to a crop of martyrs or musicians, for example – rather as knitting with rainbow wool produces a dense patch of one colour from time to time. But the overall effect is one of great variety and contrast – twentieth-century footballers rubbing shoulders with medieval mystics.

During the book's preparation, I have met with great courtesy and patience – even from the busiest and most eminent contemporary Christians whose stories I have asked to tell. Many other people have helped me, but I must single out for special thanks the staff of the public library of Stockton-on-Tees (Lesley and Melanie in particular), and my own family, who have given enthusiastic help.

I hope that the book gives readers even a fraction of the fun and delight that it has brought me.

Mary Batchelor

1 January

Bible beginnings

'Do you not know?
Were you not told long ago?
Have you not heard how the world began?
It was made by the one who sits on his throne
    above the earth and beyond the sky . . .
The Lord is the everlasting God;
    he created all the world.'
From *Isaiah 40*

'When anyone is joined to Christ, he is a new being; the old is
gone, the new has come.'
From *2 Corinthians 5*

'We wait for what God has promised: new heavens and a new
earth, where righteousness will be at home.'
From *2 Peter 3*

PRAYER FOR A NEW YEAR
Thank you, Lord, for all the new beginnings that you give to
us. Thank you for this new year. We go into it with you.
Amen

2 January

Gladys Aylward died at the beginning of January 1970.

Gladys Aylward, cockney parlourmaid, became a missionary in China, travelling there – and often working – alone. The film about her, *Inn of the Sixth Happiness,* made her famous in her lifetime, all over the world.

'Here's me'

The bedroom was plainly furnished, with washstand, basin and jug. Gladys, the new maid, sat on the edge of the bed and surveyed her small store of belongings: a Bible, a *Daily Light* book of devotional readings, and about three and a half old pence. It seemed impossible to think of getting to China, yet she was absolutely sure that God had called her to go and tell the people there about him. She couldn't pass exams. She hadn't been accepted by a missionary society, but still she knew she must go. She put her few possessions together, laid her hand on them and prayed.

'Oh God. Here's me. Here's my Bible. Here's my money. Use us, God. Use us!'

'Gladys!' a voice called. The mistress wanted to see her and Gladys hurried downstairs.

'I want to pay your fare here,' the lady of the house explained.

When Gladys returned to her room, she had ten times more money than when she had prayed a few minutes before. Of course God could send the money if he wanted her to go! She would begin to save in earnest.

See also 12 January

3 January

J.R.R. Tolkien was born on 3 January 1892.

J.R.R. Tolkien was Professor of English at Oxford University for over thirty years. He began to 'create' Middle Earth, the world of *The Hobbit* and *Lord of the Rings*, many years before, when he was in military hospital recovering from trench fever in the First World War.

An Inkling

'In a hole in the ground there lived a hobbit. Not a nasty, wet hole, filled with the ends of worms and an oozy smell, nor yet a dry, bare, sandy hole with nothing in it to sit down on or to eat: it was a hobbit-hole, and that means comfort.'

The little group of men who met on Thursday evenings in the shabby sitting-room at Magdalen College, Oxford, settled down to listen as Professor Tolkien began to read from his handwritten manuscript. Four or five of them were there: C.S.Lewis, in whose room they met, his brother Warnie, Tolkien and one or two others. They called themselves the 'Inklings', a good name for people with glimmerings of ideas set down in ink. Any of the group who had written a new poem or story would read it out to the rest.

They listened delightedly as Tolkien read on about Bilbo Baggins, Gandalf the wizard and Gollum, in his strange underground home. When in due course *The Hobbit* was published, Lewis wrote a glowing review: 'No common recipe for children's books will give you creatures so rooted in their own soil and history as those of Prof. Tolkien – who obviously knows much more about them than he needs for this book.'

Lewis spoke truly. Soon the Inklings were listening to what they called 'the new Hobbit'. It took eleven years to write, because every detail of history, geography and language was as carefully thought out and recorded as if it actually existed. 'It's more than good,' was Lewis's verdict. 'The only word I can use is great.'

'But how the public will take it, I can't imagine,' his brother added.

See also 10 January, 16 June, 29 and 30 November

4 January

Nick Page became a Christian at the age of ten. He committed his life to Jesus, at home, after a Billy Graham meeting. Nick ran a phone-in and interview programme for London commercial radio, then joined the BBC in 1979. He became well known as the host of a regular Sunday morning show on Radio 2.

In the nick of time

Having a 'brown sugar voice', as someone has described it, may be a big help in broadcasting, but it isn't the whole answer. Nick Page has to be able to think – and pray – on his feet, coaxing the shy or stemming the talkative, channelling what is said into interesting and worthwhile listening for his audience. Outside broadcasts can give plenty of technical headaches.

Easter – from Jerusalem

A special broadcast from the Garden Tomb, and minutes before it was due to begin, radio contact was completely dead. One of the hundreds of pilgrims in the party was a BBC employee on holiday. She realized the problem and set off to trace the long cable its full length. She found a place where it crossed the path the pilgrims walked. A junction had come apart. She swiftly mended it – not a moment too soon.

Easter – from Rome

Nick and his team were perched on the parapet of St Peter's. He had managed to talk and interview above the noise of the multitudinous little bells around him. But ten minutes before the end of the broadcast, the big bell of St Peter's itself was due to ring out. It would be impossible to speak above its deafening roar. Nick put on a record and hoped and prayed that the bell would end before his record did, when he was due to talk. It did – just in time!

5 January

5 January is the Feast Day of St Simeon the Stylite who died in AD 459.

Simeon, the son of a shepherd, lived at a time of luxury and self-indulgence. He set an example by his simple, self-denying way of life and his love for others. He was nicknamed 'Stylites' – from the Greek word for pillar. The base of his pillar can still be seen amid ruins in Syria.

Up the pole

People flocked to see Simeon in his remote monastery, seeking his advice, asking for his prayers. Soon he had no time or privacy for his own prayers and meditation. So, to get away from it all, he went to the desert, built a pillar and began to live on top of it. At first it was not very high. But as time went by he kept adding to it until he was sixty feet up.

His attempts to rise above it all failed completely. Simeon became a talking point and pilgrims – everyone from the emperor down – flocked to gaze at the saint and to ask his advice. In spite of his odd behaviour, Simeon seems to have been both kind and sensible. Although he wished to avoid crowds, he was helpful and sympathetic to all who came, and many became Christians through his loving words.

6 January

Epiphany means 'showing'. Jesus was first 'shown' to people outside Israel when the Wise Men came to worship him. In *The Man Born to be King*, Dorothy L. Sayers pictures Mary, Joseph and the baby staying at the home of a shepherd and his family when the Magi arrive.

'Hail, Jesus, King of the World!'

ZILLAH (*running in from outside*): Oh, Mother! Mother!

WIFE: What's up now? . . .

ZILLAH: Kings – three great kings! riding horseback. They're coming to see the Baby.

WIFE: Kings? Don't talk so soft! Kings indeed!

ZILLAH: But they *are*. They've got crowns on their heads and rings on their fingers and servants carrying torches. And they asked Dad, is this where the Baby is? And he said Yes, and I was to run ahead and say they were coming.

JOSEPH: She's quite right. I can see them from the window . . .

WIFE: Bless me! And supper not cleared away and everything upside down . . . Zillah . . . find a clean bib for Baby Jesus.

ZILLAH: Here you are, Mum. One of the kings is a very old gentleman with a long beard and . . . scarlet cloak, the second's all in glittering armour – and . . . the third's a black man with big gold rings in his ears and the jewels in his turban twinkling like the stars . . .

JOSEPH: Take heart, Mary. It's all coming true as the Prophet said: The nations shall come to thy light, and kings to the brightness of thy rising.

MARY: Give me my son into my arms.

WIFE: To be sure . . . Mercy me, here they are . . . Come in, my lords, come in. Please mind your heads. I fear 'tis but a poor lowly place.

CASPAR: No place is too lowly to kneel in. There is more holiness here than in King Herod's Temple.

MELCHIOR: More beauty here than in King Herod's palace.

BALTHAZAR: More charity here than in King Herod's heart.

CASPAR: O lady . . . the nations of the earth salute your son, the Man born to be King. Hail, Jesus, King of the Jews!

MELCHIOR: Hail, Jesus, King of the World!

BALTHAZAR: Hail, Jesus, King of Heaven!

See also 12 April, 14 and 16 December

7 January

The Russian Orthodox Church celebrates Christmas on 7 January.

To the Orthodox Christians, Christmas is the 'Little Feast'; Easter is seen as the 'Great Feast'. Perhaps Steve Turner, the author of this poem, thinks the same.

Christmas is Really For the Children

Christmas is really
for the children.
Especially for children
who like animals, stables,
stars and babies wrapped
in swaddling clothes.
Then there are wise men,
kings in fine robes,
humble shepherds and a
hint of rich perfume.

Easter is not really
for the children
unless accompanied by a
cream filled egg.
It has whips, blood, nails,
a spear and allegations
of body-snatching.
It involves politics, God
and the sins of the world.
It is not good for people
of a nervous disposition.
They would do better to
think on rabbits, chickens
and the first snowdrop
of spring.
Or they'd do better to
wait for a re-run of
Christmas without asking
too many questions about
what Jesus did when he grew up
or whether there's any connection.

See also 25 September and 10 December

8 January

Jim Elliot was killed on 8 January 1956.

His death was not in vain. His colleagues returned to the tribe, and today Auca Christians form part of the worldwide church.

'Perhaps today is the day'

Jim Elliot and his wife, Elisabeth, went as Bible translators to the Indian tribes of South America. But Jim's real longing was to bring the good news of the gospel to the Aucas, a wild and savage tribe known for their killings and their hostility to white people. The project began with flights in a small mission plane over Auca territory, dropping gifts and making friendly overtures. Then, in January 1956, five men, including Jim, set out to land on the tribe's territory and meet the Aucas face to face. They knew a few scraps of the language and went armed with gifts. All five were murdered by the Aucas.

This is an extract from Jim's last pencilled note to his wife, four days before his death.

'We saw puma tracks on the beach and heard them last night. It is beautiful jungle, open and full of palms . . . Sweat with just a mosquito net over me last night. Our hopes are up but no signs of the "neighbours" yet. Perhaps today is the day the Aucas will be reached . . . We're going down now . . . prayer in our hearts – '

JIM ELLIOT'S PRAYER
God, I pray thee, light these idle sticks of my life and may I burn for thee. Consume my life, my God, for it is thine. I seek not a long life, but a full one, like you, Lord Jesus.

9 January

Bible wisdom – about tact

'Don't visit your neighbour too often; he may get tired of you and come to hate you.'

'Singing to a person who is depressed is like taking off his clothes on a cold day or rubbing salt into a wound.'

'A man who misleads someone and then claims that he was only joking is like a madman playing with a deadly weapon.'

'You might as well curse your friend as wake him up early in the morning with a loud greeting.'

From the *Book of Proverbs*

PRAYER
Lord, help me to see the world from other people's
viewpoint, not just my own. Show me what my jokes or
thoughtless behaviour can do to them. Give me the tact that
springs from love. Amen

10 January

The Penny Post was introduced in England on 10 January 1840.

Even before postage became cheap, Christians used letter-writing as a way to share their faith and encourage one another. St Paul himself started the ball rolling! His letters form one third of the New Testament.

Forgiving is easy!

'I really must digress to tell you a bit of good news. Last week, while at prayer, I suddenly discovered – or felt as if I did – that I had forgiven someone I had been trying to forgive for over thirty years. Trying, and praying that I might. When the thing actually happened – sudden as the longed-for cessation of one's neighbour's radio – my feeling was "But it's so easy. Why didn't you do it ages ago?" So many things are done easily the moment you can do them at all. But till then, sheerly impossible, like learning to swim . . . It also seemed to me that forgiving (that man's cruelty) and being forgiven (my resentment) were the very same thing . . . by heavenly standards . . . forgiving and being forgiven are two names for the same thing. The important thing is that a discord has been resolved, and it is certainly the great Resolver who has done it. Finally, and perhaps best of all, I believed anew what is taught us . . . no evil habit is so ingrained nor so long prayed against (as it seemed) in vain, that it cannot, even in dry old age, be whisked away.'

From *Letters to Malcolm, Chiefly on Prayer*, by C.S. Lewis

See also 27 January, 27 February

11 January

Alan Paton was born on 11 January 1903.

Alan Paton, a Christian and ardent enemy of apartheid in his own country of South Africa, makes his views plain in his life and by his books. The most famous of these is *Cry, The Beloved Country*.

Breaking down the barriers

'In my own country where there are many races, and where race difference is established and maintained by law, it is difficult for many members of the so-called superior groups to serve those of the so-called inferior groups. For every white man who would help an old black woman to cross a busy street, there would be some who would not; though perhaps some of those would wish that they *could* do so. But once the barrier is crossed, the whole personality becomes richer and gentler. There is only one way in which man's inhumanity to man can be made endurable to us, and that is when we in our own lives try to exemplify man's humanity to man.'

From *Instrument of Thy Peace*, by Alan Paton

PRAYER
Lord, help us to cross the barriers that exist in *our* society in order to show love and kindness to others. May we not follow the crowd by being cruel or uncaring to any individual or group we meet today. For Jesus' sake. Amen

12 January

God is still God

Gladys Aylward sat at the edge of the Yellow River, in despair. She had trekked over the mountains from her 'home town' of Yangcheng, in charge of over 100 children and teenagers, escaping from the fast-advancing Japanese armies. It had been unbelievably hard. The small children had grown tired and fretful, and they often had to beg for food. Somehow Gladys had kept them going, carrying the little ones, singing to keep their spirits up, longing for the time when they would arrive at the river and cross into greater safety.

Now they had been by the bank for two nights. All boats had been safely moored on the opposite side, where no Japanese could commandeer them. There was no possible way to get everyone across.

'Why doesn't God open the Yellow River like he did the Red Sea for Moses?' one teenager asked Gladys.

'That was a long time ago,' she replied, 'and I'm not Moses.'

'But God is still God,' the girl persisted.

She was right, of course, and Gladys prayed again, imploring God to meet their need. She lay down exhausted, but was soon stirred to action by the excited cries of the children. A Chinese Nationalist officer was approaching. He asked her some questions about the forlorn crowd of refugees, then promised, 'I'll get a boat for you.'

He went to the water's edge and whistled. In response, a boat pulled away from the opposite shore and made its way towards them. The children were rowed across in relays. Yes, God *was* still God!

See also 2 January

13 January

George Fox, founder of the Society of Friends (Quakers),
died on 13 January 1691.

A faith to live by

Young George Fox would not be satisfied. He was disgusted by the empty and outward form of religion of his time. He determined to find a faith that he could live by. None of the preachers he went to London to hear seemed to help him. The ministers round Fenny Drayton in Warwickshire, where he lived, were no better. One advised him to cheer himself up with psalms and tobacco; another flew into a rage because George accidentally trod on his flower-bed.

'When my hopes in them and in all men were gone,' he wrote later, 'so that I had nothing outwardly to help me, nor could tell what to do, then, oh then, I heard a voice which said, "There is one, even Christ Jesus, that can speak to thy condition", and when I heard it, my heart did leap for joy.'

One day, when Fox was travelling through Lancashire, preaching his new-found faith, he saw the strange hump of Pendle Hill.

'I was moved by the Lord to go atop of it,' he recounted. 'There, atop of the hill . . . the Lord let me see in which places he had a great people to be gathered.'

True to the vision, Fox began to find a great band of followers, prepared to face imprisonment and confiscation of goods, in order to live according to the faith they too had found.

PRAYER
Thank you, Lord Jesus, that you are able to meet the individual needs and condition of us all. Please meet my need today. Amen

See also 9 July

14 January

Albert Schweitzer was born on 14 January 1875. He was awarded the Nobel Peace Prize in 1952.

The things we owe to others

Albert Schweitzer was a brilliant man, outstanding as a musician, theologian, philosopher and doctor of medicine. But he did not aim to get to the top in any of these professions. Instead, he chose to spend his life in the mission hospital at Lambarene, in the African jungle, caring for the sick and poor. There he created a haven of love and tranquillity. In his writing he recognized that the qualities he possessed were his only because others, in turn, had passed them on to him.

'One other thing stirs me when I look back on my youthful days, the fact that so many people gave me something or were something to me without knowing it. Such people entered into my life and became powers within me. We all live spiritually by what others have given us in the significant hours of our life. Much that has become our own in gentleness, modesty, kindness, willingness to forgive, in veracity, loyalty, resignation under suffering, we owe to people in whom we have seen these virtues at work.

'If we had before us those who have been thus a blessing to us and could tell them how it came about, they would be amazed to learn what had passed over from their life to ours.'

From *Schweitzer, Hero of Africa*, by Robert Payne

PRAYER
Thank you, Father, for all who have unconsciously set us a positive example by their lives. Help us to follow in their footsteps. Amen

See also 4 September

15 January

Martin Luther King Jr was born on 15 January 1929.

'My feet hurt'

Mrs Rosa Parks had done a hard day's work at the sewing factory, as well as shopping for the family. She was thankful to sink into a seat on the bus taking her home to Montgomery, Alabama. She had been careful to sit near the back, in the section reserved for negroes, according to the rules laid down by the Montgomery City Bus Line.

At the next stop, more people climbed on and the driver ordered Mrs Parks to give up her seat to a white passenger. Mrs Parks usually obeyed but, as she later said, 'I was just plain tired and my feet hurt.' She sat tight. The driver called the police, and Mrs Parks was arrested and taken to the courthouse.

It was the last straw for the black population of Montgomery. Not only were negroes segregated and made to give up seats to whites, but they had to pay their fare at the front of the bus, then get off and enter by the back door. Often the bus would drive off while they made their way to the back, leaving passengers who had paid their fare stranded in the road. And the way they were treated on the buses was only one example of the discrimination they experienced in every part of life.

The idea of a bus boycott was suggested. No negro would travel by bus until the authorities changed their laws. Martin Luther King, the young negro minister, led the protest – first with prayers, then with action. The date was December 1955. The great, non-violent civil rights movement of American negroes had begun.

See also 16 January, 4 April

16 January

Innocent victim

It was no new thing for Dr Martin Luther King to be arrested on trumped-up charges, since he had begun to lead the peaceful movement for negro rights. The sentence was prison or a fine, and eager friends had always paid the fine. One day, Dr King decided to go to prison instead. This is part of his statement to the judge:

'Your Honour, you have no doubt rendered a decision which you believe to be just and right. Yet, I must reiterate that I am innocent ... I have been the victim of police brutality for no reason ... In spite of this I hold no animosity or bitterness in my heart towards the arresting officers ... These men, like all too many of our white brothers, are the victims of an environment blighted with more than three hundred years of man's inhumanity to man as expressed in slavery and segregation ...

'Last night my wife and I talked and prayed over the course of action that I should take ... It was our conclusion that I could not in all good conscience pay a fine for an act that I did not commit and above all for brutal treatment that I did not deserve ...

'I also make this decision because of my deep concern for the injustices and indignities that my people continue to experience ... Last month in Mississippi, a sheriff, who was pointed out by four eyewitnesses as the man who beat a Negro to death with a blackjack, was freed in twenty-three minutes. At this very moment, in this State, James Wilson sits in the death house condemned to die for stealing less than two dollars ... The Negro can no longer silently endure ... because we are commanded to resist evil by God that created us all ... The time has come when perhaps only the willing and non-violent acts of suffering by the innocent can arouse this nation to wipe out the scourge of brutality and violence inflicted upon negroes who seek only to walk with dignity before God and man.'

From *My Life with Martin Luther King,* by Coretta King

See also 15 January, 4 April

17 January

Bible wisdom – about lazy people

'The lazy man turns over in bed. He gets no farther than a door swinging on its hinges.'

'Some people are too lazy to put food in their own mouths.'

'The lazy man stays at home; he says a lion might get him if he goes outside.'

'No matter how much a lazy man may want something he will never get it. A hard worker will get everything he wants.'

'Never get a lazy man to do anything for you; he will be as irritating as vinegar on your teeth or smoke in your eyes.'

'Lazy people should learn a lesson from the way ants live. They have no leader, chief or ruler, but they store up their food during the summer, getting ready for the winter. How long is the lazy man going to lie in bed? When is he ever going to get up? "I'll just take a short nap," he says; "I'll fold my hands and rest a while." But while he sleeps, poverty will attack him like an armed robber.'

From the *Book of Proverbs*

18 January

Noel Streatfeild, author of *Ballet Shoes, Caldicot Place,*
White Boots and many other books, also writes about
herself – under the name of Victoria – as a vicar's daughter.
In January one year, almost the whole family caught 'flu.

Good intentions

'Victoria . . . was worried that her father might be neglected, so
she slipped into the kitchen when no one was about and started to
prepare what she thought would please him: tea, toast cut in
fingers, and a boiled egg set on a tray covered with the best tray
cloth, on which she pinned a spray of winter jasmine. She was
hurrying out of the kitchen with this offering, trying to get it
upstairs before her mother came down, when she ran straight into
her. The egg fell off the tray and smashed on the kitchen floor
and the tea splashed over the best tray cloth . . . The children's
mother, barely convalescent, saw this accident as a last straw.

'"Really Vicky! I would have thought a great girl like you would
try to help, not to hinder. And why is this flower pinned on to my
nice cloth?"

'Victoria's mouth set in an ugly line.

'"It's for Daddy. *I* care if he's looked after, even if nobody else
does."

'Her mother could have slapped her.

'"He's asleep and he's only to have liquids. I wish you would
ask before you do these things. There's plenty for you to do if you
want to help."

'Victoria, also barely convalescent, looked more mulish than
ever.

'"All right, I'm asking now."

'Somehow her mother kept her temper.

'"Then take that tea to Miss Herbert."'

From *A Vicarage Family*, by Noel Streatfeild

PRAYER
Thank you, Lord, that you understand us through and
through. You know about the times when we try to help
and please and things go wrong. Don't let us give up
because others misjudge us. Amen

See also 19 January

19 January

Left out

After the confirmation [of Victoria's older sister, Isobel], Aunt Penelope stayed on at the vicarage for a day or two and on Saturday afternoon she had invited her goddaughter out to tea:

'Going out to tea in those days meant going to a café and eating innumerable cream buns, and was a much-loved treat . . . Whatever Aunt Penelope's reason, at the last moment she invited Louise to tea too – which meant leaving Victoria alone at home. No one had ever behaved like that before and all three sisters were shocked. Victoria was wounded in a way she had never been before. To be left behind by one's aunt! It was unthinkable.

'Her father and mother were out and so was Miss Herbert. Victoria took Spot into the garden and while he sniffed round the lawn, she climbed up a cedar tree. She had thought she wanted to be alone to cry, but no tears came. Aunt Penelope's behaviour had hurt her, but that her parents had not interfered and said, "You can't leave Victoria out", cut her to the quick. But it was not her hurt she thought about but her future.

'"This is something I am never going to forget. I'll always see myself on this day, and remember how it felt when people were cruel and I was thirteen."'

From *A Vicarage Family*, by Noel Streatfeild

PRAYER
Father, please comfort all who feel left out and neglected.
Help us not to make favourites of some people, but to show
kindness and be thoughtful to all. Amen

See also 18 January

20 January

20 January is Inauguration Day in the USA.

American singer Pat Boone began his career at the height of rock and roll's popularity in the fifties. He sang ballads and Country Music. He now also sings with his wife Shirley and their four daughters.

Royal command

'People are still awed by royalty. Nobody stirs excitement or demands respect on every level of life like a king . . . I know. I've sung for kings and queens and presidents several times, and I can tell you it's an exhilarating, fascinating, strange – and frightening – experience. No matter how many times you tell yourself, "they're just people like I am" . . . your heart pounds, your normal behaviour is suspended . . . '

'But what about an intimate meeting with God, the Lord of heaven and earth? . . . Does an ordinary human being have the right to even imagine such a thing?

'"And so, dear brothers, now we may walk right into the very Holy of Holies where God is, because of the blood of Jesus . . . let us go right in, to God himself."

'I tremble, anticipation mixed with awe . . . he [Jesus] welcomes us, he died so that we could have this incredible privilege, and I will go in.'

From an interview with Pat Boone in *New Music*

21 January

On 21 January 1952, the Bethlehem Chief of Police, two archaeologists and two soldiers of the Arab Legion took possession of the Dead Sea caves and their rich hoard of ancient manuscripts. Some of the scrolls, which document life in a Jewish religious community, throw light on the Gospel records and the biblical scrolls themselves confirm the truth and reliability of the Bible as we have known it.

Treasure

Muhammed the Wolf was looking after goats down by the shores of the Dead Sea. The water was dull blue, the hills around yellow, brown and dull purple. The whole scene was lifeless, and Muhammed, a teenage Bedouin, was bored. He climbed listlessly up the cliff to rescue a straying goat, then noticed a cave he had not seen before. Idly he picked up a stone and hurled it into the mouth of the cave.

A moment later, he heard the sound of something breaking. Frightened, he took to his heels, returning later with a friend to explore. They clambered into the cave and there discovered some tall clay jars. It was one of these that Muhammed's stone had broken. When they took off the lids there was a nasty smell, coming from some dark oblong lumps inside the jars. They carried the oblong lumps outside to look at them in the daylight, and found that they were lengths of linen coated with pitch. Inside these wraps were manuscripts, sewn together and covered in strange writing. The boys decided to keep their finds and sell them on their next trip to Bethlehem.

It was many months and many adventures later that the manuscripts' true worth was recognized. The Dead Sea Scrolls, as they are called, contain nearly the whole of the Old Testament in copies dating from 1,000 years earlier than any manuscripts previously found. Years of patient piecing together and deciphering have been required to yield to scholars their full treasure.

22 January

On 22 January 1977, Pat Seed was given only a few months to live.

Pat Seed is a journalist, married, with two teenage children. When she was told that she was dying, she decided to use the time left to raise the million pounds then needed to buy the hospital that had been treating her an X-ray body scanner, for the early detection of cancer. She had amazing success and – miraculously – five years later was pronounced free from all cancer symptoms herself. Pat sums up: 'In place of fear I put my hand trustingly into His. I had trod the path along which He chose to lead me.'

One in a million

'If only a million people would give 75p,' Pat had remarked to a friend, 'we'd be home and dry.'

The friend, Julie – also suffering from cancer – remembered. One day, she rang Pat and outlined her scheme to encourage that kind of giving. Everyone likes badges to wear, so why not produce a million badges, selling at 50p each, and saying 'I'm one in a million'? Pat's only objection was that the badges would cost too much to make. One million badges would cost nearly £20,000. That seemed to be that. But Julie and her husband volunteered to pay the cost – they'd be paid back if the scheme worked.

The badges sold like hot cakes. Mayors were photographed in local papers wearing them and the whole work-force in a local factory bought them. Julie's husband had a badge made in gold for his wife to wear. Sadly, she did not wear it for long. She died of cancer. But she – like Pat, and many others – helped to bring the chance of a cure for thousands of others in the Christie Hospital at Manchester.

23 January

Thursday October Christian

In 1814, the British ship *Tagus* discovered an island not on the charts. To the sailors' amazement, a canoe from the island drew alongside and they were hailed in English.

'Who are you?' the captain asked.

'Thursday October Christian,' the young man replied.

He and his companion were taken on board to breakfast with the captain. Before eating, 'they both rose and one of them pronounced in a pleasing tone, "For what we are going to receive, the Lord make us truly thankful."'

Soon there were explanations. In 1790, Fletcher Christian and his fellow mutineers had landed on the tiny island after setting their rightful captain adrift in the ship's longboat with some of the crew. They felt safe from the long arm of the law and hoped to spend happy and peaceful lives in their 'new Eden'.

Plenty went wrong. The record of the months that followed tells of treachery, murder, drunkenness and conspiracy. After three years, only four white men survived, and none of the coloured companions they took with them.

So how had these young men learned their courteous and Christian manners? Two Bibles had come ashore with the mutineers. They had made all the difference.

POSTSCRIPT
Fletcher Christian gave his son his unusual name because he had been born on a Thursday in October. Later, they realized that since they had crossed the international date-line to reach Pitcairn, he *should* have been Friday October! They tried to change his name, but the old one stuck.

See also 6 November

24 January

William Barclay died on 24 January 1978.

Plain truth for plain people

William Barclay was an outstanding scholar in Classics and Divinity. After being the minister of a parish in Scotland, he taught at Glasgow University and became Professor of Divinity and Biblical Criticism. But the books he wrote make the New Testament come alive for ordinary people.

'Because I need simple things myself, I can talk simply to others,' he wrote.

How can I start to pray?

'Once someone asked a wise man how to set about praying. The wise man said: "Just take a chair and put it opposite you and think to yourself that God is sitting on that chair and just talk to him in the way that you would talk to your closest friend."'

Does God answer prayer?

'Someone has said that God has four answers to prayer. Sometimes he says Yes. Sometimes he says No. Sometimes he says Wait. Most of all he says If. He says, "I will help you *if* you will do everything you can to help yourself". Prayer is not an excuse for being lazy and for pushing all the work off on to God: prayer is a way to finding the strength and ability to do things along with God that we could never have done by ourselves.'

From *Prayers for Young People*, by William Barclay

25 January

25 January is St Paul's 'Red Letter Day' in *The Book of Common Prayer.*

Conversion

The midday sun burned bright and hot as Paul and his little band of companions pressed wearily on towards Damascus, the city of their destination. There, Paul's official papers would give him permission to deal with a few more troublesome Christians. Suddenly, a light more blinding and brilliant even than the noon sun, struck Paul full on the face. He fell to the ground, blinded and overpowered in mind as well as body.

As he lay, shocked and silent, he heard a voice:

'Paul, why are you persecuting me?'

Memories of men and women, old and young, carried off to prison by his orders, flashed into Paul's mind. They had not cursed him or struggled, but had gone, often to death, with calmness and courage: Christians arrested only for their faith. Which one of them was speaking to him now? But already he guessed the answer to that question.

'Who are you, Lord?' he asked.

'I am Jesus, whom you are persecuting.'

Now Paul knew for certain that the Christians he had tried to silence had been telling the truth. Their Jesus was not dead but alive, and if alive he must indeed be the Son of God and Lord of all – Paul's rightful Master too.

'What do you want me to do, Lord?' Paul humbly asked.

'Tell others what you have seen and who you have met. Open *their* eyes and turn them too from darkness to light.'

Dazed and still blind, Paul got up from the ground and, helped by his men, walked unseeing into Damascus. He had been given his orders. From now on he would obey his true Lord. He was to travel throughout the Roman Empire, preaching the good news of new life in Jesus Christ.

Many years later he was able to say truthfully, 'I did not disobey the vision I had from heaven.'

Adapted from *Acts 9*

PRAYER
Lord Jesus, may we hear you speaking to us through the
Bible, through your servants and through the happenings of
daily life. May we, like Paul, obey you always. Amen

26 January

Today is the Feast Day of Polycarp.

Polycarp was Bishop of Smyrna (modern Izmir in Turkey).
He was martyred for his faith in AD 156.

'Eighty-six years have I served him'

'We want Polycarp! Get Polycarp!' the crowds shouted.

The Christians were the people that everyone loved to hate. The Roman rulers were worried by them too. All kinds of strange tales were going around about what these Christians did when they met together. There was one way to test their right to be left in peace. Were Christians willing to take the oath of allegiance to the emperor? Everybody else did – just sprinkled a pinch of incense and repeated 'Caesar is Lord' – to show loyalty to the Roman authorities.

So the old man Polycarp, for many years a respected bishop in the city of Smyrna, was dragged before the police captain and ordered to take the oath of allegiance. The captain felt pity for the old man and wanted to save him from the death penalty that was passed on those who refused.

'What possible harm can there be in saying "Caesar is Lord" and offering incense to save yourself?' he asked persuasively.

But Polycarp stood firm. He recognized that behind this ceremony was the belief that Lord Caesar was divine. For him there could be only one Lord – Jesus Christ his Master.

'Have some respect for your age,' the captain pleaded. 'Swear by the divinity of Caesar. If you take the oath I will let you go.'

Polycarp replied, 'Eighty-six years have I served him and he has done me no wrong; how then can I blaspheme my Saviour and King?' So he went to his death.

27 January

Forgiveness – the Bible way

'Praise the Lord, my soul! All my being, praise his holy name! Praise the Lord, my soul, and do not forget how kind he is. He forgives all my sins.'

From *Psalm 103*

'Let us praise God for his glorious grace, for the free gift he gave us in his dear Son! For by the death of Christ we are set free, that is, our sins are forgiven.'

From *Ephesians 1*

'If we confess our sins to God . . . he will forgive us our sins and purify us from all our wrongdoing.'

From *1 John 1*

'Be kind and tender-hearted to one another, and forgive one another, as God has forgiven you through Christ.'

From *Ephesians 4*

'Jesus said, "When you pray . . . forgive anything you may have against anyone, so that your Father in heaven will forgive the wrongs you have done."'

From *Mark 11*

PRAYER
Our Father in heaven, forgive us the wrongs we have done,
as we forgive the wrongs that others have done to us. For
Jesus' sake. Amen

See also 10 January, 27 February

28 January

On 28 January 1980, Rita Nightingale received a pardon
from the king of Thailand.

Sentence – twenty years

'Just sit down,' the British Consul advised Rita, on his second
visit to her prison in one week. She felt sure it must be bad news –
perhaps from home in England. But she was quite wrong.

'Something unheard of has happened,' he told her. 'The king
of Thailand has granted you a free pardon.'

Rita could hardly believe it, even when she saw the headline in
the *Bangkok Post* he had brought as proof. It was nearly three years
since she had been put in this stinking, primitive jail – with a
sentence of twenty years to serve. She had refused to lighten her
sentence by pleading guilty – she knew she was utterly innocent.

The nightmare had begun one January day at Bangkok
Airport. The guards had said, 'Step this way', and examined her
luggage, but she had not been worried. Even when they pulled
out the incriminating packets of brown heroin granules from her
hold-all, she remained unruffled. Her boy-friend would vouch
for her innocence, so she gave the guards his address.

On the afternoon of the flight, she had gone out, leaving her
cases at the boy-friend's flat. At the last minute, he decided not to
fly with her and introduced her to two other men who would
accompany her instead. When, after inquiries, all three denied
any knowledge of the drugs, Rita realized with mounting horror
that she was the victim of a plot to smuggle drugs. Her boy-friend
had made her the plant. She was under arrest.

Continued on 29 January; see also 6 February

29 January

Free – to go to prison!

In that filthy, overcrowded Thai prison, Rita gave up hope. Some American missionaries visited her, but got no response. Rita wanted nothing to do with a God who had landed her in this mess.

But when, one day, she heard the familiar soft Lancashire accents of her home town, she broke down and cried bitterly. She was homesick, helpless and hopeless. Her visitor, a Mrs Livesy – who had broken her journey to Australia specially to visit Rita – had barely two minutes' conversation with her, but before leaving she gave Rita some booklets.

In her misery, alone again, Rita read one called *The Reason Why*. It told her the reason why Jesus came to die.

'Every word was for me,' Rita says. 'I prayed there and then, asking Jesus for his forgiveness and gave my life to him.'

Thanks to the king of Thailand, Rita is free now: free to go to prison of her own accord, to try to bring comfort and hope to those she calls 'forgotten people' – the men and women in prisons. To her, they are no more guilty than the rest of us, for we *all* need God's forgiveness whether innocent or guilty by the laws of the land. God's love and forgiveness are great enough to reach the 'worst' as well as the 'best' people. Rita visits prisons with this message, and an understanding born of personal experience.

See also 28 January, 6 February

30 January

King Charles I was executed on 30 January 1649.

Nothing common, nothing mean

It was a freezing January morning. The king was wearing two shirts so that he should not shiver and be mistaken for a coward. He stepped from a window of the palace at Whitehall on to the scaffold that had been made ready. It was two o'clock in the afternoon. Large ranks of soldiers separated him from the crowd of his subjects who stood watching their king. Only those nearest him could hear his last words.

'I go from a corruptible crown to an incorruptible crown,' he told his chaplain, 'where no disturbance can be, no disturbance in the world.' He then handed to Bishop Juxon a jewel made from a single onyx. He asked that it should be given to the Prince of Wales, then in hiding in Holland, with the message, 'Remember'.

The masked executioner raised his axe and, as Charles's head left his body, 'There was such a groan by the thousands then present', one spectator wrote, 'as I never heard before and desire I may never hear again.'

After his death, some reckoned Charles a martyr and saint; others believed his execution had secured democracy for England. But all recognized that on the scaffold Charles had acted bravely.

'Nothing in his life became Charles like the leaving of it,' one person commented. And the poet Andrew Marvell, who lived through the event, wrote:

> He nothing common did or mean
> Upon that memorable scene,
>   But with his keener eye
>   The axe's edge did try;
> Nor called the gods with vulgar spite
> To vindicate his helpless right;
>   But bowed his comely head
>   Down, as upon a bed.

31 January

On 31 January 1980, Dr Billy Graham preached to an
audience of undergraduates in Oxford.

Billy Graham, the American evangelist, has been preaching
worldwide for over thirty years – to a total of nearly 90
million people. Ernest Shippam, head of the Chichester firm
making meat and fish pastes, was at his 1954 Harringay
Crusade.

Moment of truth

Ernest Shippam may have had problems in his personal life, but
he was a good employer. He had begun a programme for better
conditions in his factory, and decided to include a 'bit of religion'
for his staff. He planned to take a group of them to hear Billy
Graham at London's Harringay arena. So he and his wife went to
one of the meetings first, to try it out.

He admitted: 'I found the set-up quite infuriating as everyone
looked so happy. Nothing is more upsetting than to be among
people who are obviously happy while you yourself are feeling
unhappy and frustrated. As we entered the arena, I saw a vast text
hung up and that too rubbed me up the wrong way. The hymns
were by no means what a good and staid Anglican was used to.'

He remembers little of the service except for Billy Graham's
last words: 'If Jesus Christ could carry his cross to Calvary for
you, can't you trust him with everything you've got?'

In that moment, Ernest Shippam felt he was seeing his whole
life for what it was – rotten through and through. It was now or
never. He had to trust Jesus Christ with everything – his business,
his marriage, the future. He and his wife went forward in
response to the closing appeal. As he went he discovered that 'it is
not possible to give God anything except your sin'.

Ernest Shippam does not believe that mass evangelism is the
only route to being 'born again', but it is one that God uses. And
Billy Graham is one man the Holy Spirit speaks through in order
to bring people to a close encounter with Christ.

1 February

1 February is the Feast Day of St Ignatius, who died in
AD 107.

God in his heart

Ignatius' surname was Theophorus, which means 'one who
carries God in his heart'. Tradition has it that he was taken to
Rome in chains and sentenced to be thrown to the wild beasts
because of his Christian faith. In the Middle Ages, the legend
grew that Ignatius was the child chosen by Jesus in the story told
by the Gospel writers. Here is Mark's account:

'After going indoors, Jesus asked his disciples, "What were you
arguing about on the road?"

'But they would not answer him, because on the road they had
been arguing among themselves about who was the greatest.
Jesus sat down, called the twelve disciples, and said to them,
"Whoever wants to be first must place himself last of all and be
the servant of all." Then he took a child and made him stand in
front of them. He put his arms round him and said to them,
"Whoever welcomes in my name one of these children, welcomes
me; and whoever welcomes me, welcomes not only me but also
the one who sent me."'

From *Mark 9*

2 February

Six weeks after the birth of her baby, Mary took Jesus to the temple in Jerusalem, to present him to God, according to Jewish regulations. From about AD 350, a feast was held by Christians in Jerusalem to commemorate this event. It was known as 'Meeting' – because it was then that Simeon and Anna met Jesus. The church in the East and the West adopted the custom, and in the seventh century it became known as Candlemas. Candles are blessed and distributed to the congregation before the service. While the *Nunc Dimittis* (Simeon's Song) is being sung, the candles are lit and carried round the church in procession. It is a celebration of the coming of Jesus, the true Light, into the world.

The light has come

'Joseph and Mary . . . took the child to Jerusalem to present him to the Lord . . . When the parents brought the child Jesus into the Temple . . . Simeon took the child in his arms and gave thanks to God: "Now, Lord, you have kept your promise, and you may let your servant go in peace. With my own eyes I have seen your salvation . . . A light to reveal your will to the Gentiles and bring glory to your people Israel."'
From *Luke 2*

'This was the real light – the light that comes into the world and shines on all mankind.'
From *John 1*

'"I am the light of the world," Jesus said. "Whoever follows me will have the light of life and will never walk in darkness."'
From *John 8*

'The light has come into the world, but people love the darkness rather than the light, because their deeds are evil.'
From *John 3*

3 February

George Thomas was brought up in a Welsh mining village and enabled to stay at school through the sacrifice of his brother and widowed mother. He was a schoolteacher and Methodist lay preacher. When he retired from the House of Commons in June 1983, members of all parties acknowledged his fine leadership and example and hailed him as one of the great Speakers in Parliament's history. George Thomas himself was never ashamed to confess his Christian faith as the key to his actions in every part of life.

The fight for justice

The Member of Parliament for Cardiff Central listened patiently and kindly as the two elderly ladies poured out their tale of woe. It was their home. The two sisters had lived all their lives in the same house, caring for their parents until their death. Now, because of the system of leasehold, whereby a house reverted to the ground landlord or owner after ninety-nine years, the sisters would be turned out and left homeless. They were also faced with a bill for £400 for repairs which the landlord considered necessary to bring the property up to standard.

Mr Thomas took the case to the landlord himself, arguing that the sisters could not pay the money anyway, and persuading him that the whole community would be up in arms against him if he evicted them. The landlord agreed to drop his claim and allow the ladies to pay rent and stay put.

This was no isolated incident. George Thomas vowed he would put an end to the iniquities of leasehold. Through his constant campaigning, the Leasehold Reform Bill was finally passed by parliament. Now all leasehold owners in Britain have the opportunity to buy their property freehold and at a fair price.

4 February

Dietrich Bonhoeffer was born in Germany on 4 February 1906.

Bonhoeffer was exiled from Berlin for speaking out fearlessly against the Nazi regime. He was abroad on a lecture-tour when the Second World War broke out, but insisted on returning to his native land to work for the church and against Hitler. He was arrested in 1943, imprisoned at Buchenwald and hanged. His last words – a message to a friend – were, 'This is the end – for me the beginning of life.'

God's guiding hand

Much of Dietrich Bonhoeffer's fresh thinking about the Christian faith is found in the letters he wrote from prison. Here is an extract from one:

'Please don't ever get anxious or worried about me, but don't forget to pray for me – I'm sure you don't! I am so sure of God's guiding hand and I hope I shall never lose that certainty. You must never doubt that I am travelling my appointed road with gratitude and cheerfulness. My past life is replete with God's goodness, and my sins are covered by the forgiving love of Christ crucified. I am thankful for all those who have crossed my path, and all I wish is never to cause them sorrow, and that they, like me, will always be thankful for the forgiveness and mercy of God and sure of it. Please don't for a moment get upset by all this, but let it rejoice your heart.'

See also 5 February, 27 July

5 February

These prayers were written by Dietrich Bonhoeffer, in prison, and are dated Christmas 1943.

Morning

O heavenly Father,
I praise and thank thee
For the peace of the night.
I praise and thank thee for this new day.
I praise and thank thee for all thy goodness and faithfulness
  throughout my life.
Thou hast granted me many blessings:
Now let me accept tribulation from thy hand.
Thou wilt not lay on me more than I can bear;
Thou makest all things work together for good for thy children.

Evening

Grant me a quiet night's sleep beneath thy tender care,
And defend me from all the temptations of darkness.
Into thy hands I commend my loved ones
  and all who dwell in this house;
I commend my body and soul.
O God, thy holy name be praised.

From *Letters for Fellow Prisoners*

See also 4 February, 27 July

6 February

The reason why

There was dust in summer and mud in winter. Young Robert Laidlaw would set out on horseback for a sales trip lasting five or six days. He took orders for his hardware firm from all over the north of New Zealand.

As he rode, he thought about the new mail order scheme that had begun in America. Transport was difficult there too. He chatted about the idea with the farmers who rode companionably beside him. Mail order seemed to be just what they needed.

So, at twenty-three, he gave in his notice and began to compile his first catalogue. It was not just market research and business flair that encouraged Robert Laidlaw to take the risk. He had been a Christian for six years and he prayed about every decision he made. He believed God was in this new venture with him.

He chose the trade name of Laidlaw Leeds – with the slogan, 'Laidlaw Leeds – Others follow'. The new business was an immediate success, and within three months new premises were needed. In time Laidlaws became the biggest department store in Auckland.

When a special evangelistic mission was held in Auckland in 1913, Robert Laidlaw arranged for all his 200 staff to attend. He told them that as he could no longer chat to each individually about the Christian faith, he would write a booklet explaining the reason why he was a Christian. The result was *The Reason Why* – a sixty-four-page tract that has been translated into many languages and shown many thousands the way to become a Christian.

1913 is a long time ago and an old-fashioned tract might not be expected to appeal today. Yet Rita Nightingale, ex-night-club receptionist, serving sentence in a Thai prison on a drugs charge, found peace and new life in Jesus Christ through reading *The Reason Why*.

See also 28 and 29 January

7 February

A memorial service for Joyce Grenfell was held on 7 February 1980 at Westminster Abbey.

Joyce Grenfell was best known for her dramatic monologues on stage and television. At her memorial service, Geoffrey Howard White said: 'Joyce Grenfell was the most spiritually-minded person I have ever met. She spent one hour each day with her Bible and what she called her "holy books" and took what she learned from God in that hour into her very busy day.'

Singing to the troops

During the last year of the Second World War, Joyce Grenfell travelled to fourteen different countries, entertaining the troops. Sometimes she would sing out in the open, competing with wind or rain, encouraging men who were tense, awaiting battle. But her more poignant memories were of army hospital visits. One day they arrived at a hospital that had once been an Italian monastery, where serious casualties were arriving hourly from the battle zone. The scene was horrific. Joyce blanched at the thought of entertaining men in such condition.

'You can't possibly want us here today. Shall we go away?' she asked the sister in charge. But instead the sister asked her to move the piano into one corner and sing quietly for a few soldiers at a time.

Before leaving England, Joyce had selected cheerful dance songs and romantic numbers to bring with her, but she discovered that it was the sad, gentle songs about home that the men loved and asked for. On this occasion a young soldier with fair hair and a Devon accent beckoned her over and asked if she would sing a song about a mother. For a moment Joyce was stumped. Then she remembered a lullaby and sang that softly for him.

'You learn as you go,' was her comment, 'and you stop being afraid of sentiment.'

Before the tour began, Joyce had been warned that she would only be able to keep fresh for eight weeks. But she found that the rewards were more than enough to keep her going, and although she grew very tired, she discovered that there was a spiritual source of strength on which she could always draw.

See also 8 February

8 February

After Joyce Grenfell's death, the book *Joyce* was published containing some of her monologues and many memories of her contributed by friends, relatives and those who worked with her on radio, stage and television. Two sisters describe Joyce's kindness to them when they were children and their widowed mother was in hospital.

A practical fairy godmother

The winter was bitter, and Rachel and Janie with their brother and two sisters were taking care of themselves. Joyce would arrive with surprise meals, often on her way to the theatre. Rachel describes one freezing afternoon:

'Joyce dropped in like an unexpected angel with a ready-cooked shepherd's pie in an insulated bag.' She was on her way to the theatre, looking very glamorous, and had a car waiting for her in the street. 'But she popped on a pair of pink rubber gloves and gave our kitchen bin a quick wipe-out. "You'll find, Rachel, that a little drop of Jeyes, every day, keeps it nice".'

At Christmas, their mother gave Joyce the little money she had to buy the children presents. Janie longed for a party dress but knew it cost far too much. When she woke up on Christmas morning, the most beautiful navy organza dress was hanging beside her stocking. Joyce had cut out the label to hide the fact that it had come from an expensive shop. She loved to do good by stealth.

PRAYER
Thank you, Lord Jesus, for all who give to others with imagination and thoughtfulness for their needs. Help us to give without show or self-congratulation, as you taught us to do. Amen

See also 7 February

9 February

Fyodor Dostoyevsky, the Russian writer, died on 9 February 1881.

Love every leaf

'Love will teach us all things: but we must learn how to win love; it is got with difficulty: it is a possession dearly bought, with much labour and in a long time; for one must love not sometimes only, for a passing moment, but always ... Love all God's creation, the whole of it and every grain of sand. Love every leaf, every ray of God's light! Love the animals, love the plants, love everything. If you love everything, you will perceive the divine mystery in things ... And you will at last come to love the whole world with an abiding, universal love.'

From Father Zossima's discourse in *The Brothers Karamazov*, by Fyodor Dostoyevsky

PRAYER
Lord, teach us how to love. Give us a love that is more than feelings. Show us how we can behave in loving ways. May we treat everything you have created with consideration, gentleness and unselfishness. Teach us to love one another, for that is even harder. Thank you for loving us *always* in Jesus Christ. Amen

10 February

Bible wisdom – about jealousy

'Peace of mind makes the body healthy, but jealousy is like a cancer.'

'Don't be jealous of violent people or decide to act as they do because the Lord hates people who do evil but he takes righteous men into his confidence.'

'Don't be envious of evil people and don't try to make friends with them.'

'Don't be envious of sinful people, let reverence for the Lord be the concern of your life.'

'Anger is cruel and destructive but it is nothing compared to jealousy.'

From the *Book of Proverbs*

'Pilate knew very well that the Jewish authorities had handed Jesus over to him because they were jealous.'
From *Matthew 27*

'We must not be proud or irritate one another or be jealous of one another.'
From *Galatians 5*

'Where there is jealousy and selfishness, there is also disorder and every kind of evil.'
From *James 3*

'Love is not jealous.'
From *1 Corinthians 13*

11 February

Galileo Galilei, the astronomer, was born at Pisa in Italy in
February 1564.

The starry messenger

Unfriendly critics wondered that Galileo could see anything
through his new telescope, even though it magnified objects
1,000 times. But Galileo, peering determinedly through it at the
night sky discovered amazing things. For the first time it was
possible to see mountains and valleys on the moon and shadows
cast by sunlight. He discovered 'a myriad of stars planted
together in clusters' – what we know as the Milky Way.

One night in 1610, Galileo was looking at Jupiter and saw three
tiny stars – two to the left and one to the right of the planet. Next
night, all three could be seen to the right. Since they moved, he
knew they could not be stars but must be satellites in orbit round
Jupiter.

Galileo wrote a book – *The Starry Messenger* – telling of his
findings. He firmly believed too that the earth moved round the
sun.

To his first readers his conclusions were startling. The church
considered herself to be the guardian of all knowledge and the
church maintained that the earth stood still, at the very centre of
God's universe. In vain Galileo maintained that he was a staunch
Christian. He was branded a heretic and his later years were
dogged by opposition, personal tragedy and illness. Although he
was finally forced to recant and say that the earth did not move
round the sun, Galileo's dying words were, 'Yet it still moves'.

PRAYER
Help us never to fear the truth. Teach us to discern between
scientific theory or Christian tradition and the truth. Thank
you that Jesus Christ is truth. Amen

See also 25 May

12 February

Abraham Lincoln was born in a Kentucky log cabin and never had a whole year of schooling in his life. He learned to read by spelling his way through the Bible. He was a giant of a man, strong, absolutely honest and upright. He worked for the emancipation of slaves, and succeeded in his struggle to keep the States united. He had a deep religious faith.

Death of a president

The bitter Civil War between the northern and southern states was over. Abraham Lincoln sat with his wife in the box at Ford's Theatre in Washington, enjoying a comedy. He had already determined that he would treat the conquered rebel states with generosity and forgiveness. He would not hear of some senators' calls for hangings and confiscation of property.

'Enough lives have been sacrificed,' Lincoln insisted. 'We must extinguish our resentments if we expect harmony and union.'

He and his wife chatted happily during the interval and talked of travel when the duties of the White House were over.

'There is no place I should so much like to see as Jerusalem,' the president said. Then the curtain went up for the second half of the performance and the lights dimmed.

But an unobserved watcher had been noting exactly where the president sat. As the second act began, he noiselessly opened the door of the box and fired point-blank at Lincoln. Lincoln rose in his chair, then sank back, head drooping and eyes closed.

The assassin, a handsome young actor called John Wilkes Booth, who bitterly opposed Union, pushed past the rest of the party in the box, leaped over the rail and made his escape. The president was carried across the street to the home of a tailor. Next morning he died.

See also 13 February

13 February

In November 1863, Abraham Lincoln was present at
Gettysburg when a cemetery was dedicated for the 3,600
Union soldiers who had died there in one of the worst
battles of the Civil War. This quotation is taken from his
famous speech.

Dedication

'Fourscore and seven years ago our fathers brought forth on this
continent a new nation conceived in liberty and dedicated to the
proposition that all men are created equal. Now we are engaged
in a great civil war testing whether that nation . . . can long
endure. We are met on a great battlefield of that war. We have
come to dedicate a portion of that field as a final resting-place for
those who here gave their lives that that nation might live. It is
altogether fitting and proper that we should do this. But in a
larger sense we cannot dedicate, we cannot consecrate, we
cannot hallow this ground. The brave men, now living and dead,
who struggled here have consecrated it far above our poor power
to add or detract . . . It is for us the living rather to be dedicated
here to the unfinished work which they who fought here have
thus far so nobly advanced . . . We here highly resolve that these
dead shall not have died in vain, that this nation under God shall
have a new birth of freedom and that government of the people,
by the people, for the people, shall not perish from the earth.'

See also 12 February

14 February

The greatest is love

No one knows much about St Valentine. He lived in the third century after Christ and was probably a bishop in Italy. He died for his faith during a period of fierce persecution.

There is nothing to connect him with the sending of valentines or any of the other customs that go with his day. But there is an old English tradition that 14 February is the day when the birds choose their mates. Choosing a valentine may be linked to that belief, and the saint's day is probably pure coincidence.

This is how St Paul describes Christian love:

'Love is patient and kind; it is not jealous or conceited or proud; love is not ill-mannered or selfish or irritable; love does not keep a record of wrongs; love is not happy with evil but is happy with the truth. Love never gives up; and its faith, hope and patience never fail. Love is eternal. These three remain: faith, hope and love; and the greatest of these is love.'

From *1 Corinthians 13*

15 February

On 15 February 1819, Louis Braille went as a pupil to the
Royal Institute for Blind Children in Paris.

Tragedy at Coupvray

The saddler's sign had hung outside the workshop of the Braille
family in the village of Coupvray for more than a century. Louis's
grandfather had started the business. At five years old, Louis
would watch his father cut and trim the leather for saddles and
harnesses.

One day, the workshop was empty and the child went in. The
curved blade of the saddler's knife gleamed temptingly and Louis
grasped it with small hands, trying to cut the leather as his father
did. But the knife slipped, and the blade pierced his eye. The
doctor could not save the boy's sight and worse was to follow. The
infection that was set up spread to the other eye. Louis was totally
blind.

His father determined to help him learn. The village priest –
once a Benedictine monk – taught him the Christian faith and the
village schoolmaster did what he could to help. There is a story
that his father took a piece of wood and drove in upholsterer's
nails to form the letters of the alphabet so that Louis could learn
their shape by touch.

In Paris, some years before, Valentin Hauy had been sickened
by the sight of a group of ragged, blind musicians, exhibited for
the amusement of a crowd at the fair. To be blind meant being
illiterate, the butt of others' ridicule, and Hauy determined to
help educate the blind. Hauy eventually founded a school in
Paris, and when Louis Braille was ten years old, he won a
scholarship to go and study there. He set off on the twenty-mile
journey from Coupvray, determined to learn all he could.

Continued on 16 February

A system that works!

Louis Braille was a star pupil. He scooped every prize at the Royal Institute for Blind Children – whatever the subject. He was enthusiastic to test the newly-devised alphabet for the blind introduced by Captain Barbier. Instead of the raised letters previously used, this so-called 'night writing' used dots punched out on cardboard to form the leters.

At twelve, Louis suggested improvements, and from that day began work to produce a less cumbersome and more comprehensive system of reading for blind people. Busy at school-work by day, he persevered with his new alphabet by night and in the holidays. By the time he was fifteen, he had arrived at an entirely new and simplified system, which he continued to refine and improve. By using a combination of six dots, he could provide sixty-three permutations. Now it was possible to express mathematical symbols and musical notes too. No subject was out of bounds for blind readers.

The boys at the institute were delighted with the work of their genius companion. Though the authorities and jealous rivals criticized and discouraged Louis, the blind people themselves recognized that a new age had dawned for them. But it was twenty years before Braille's system was officially recognized.

Louis took setbacks and insults with gentleness and good will. His Christian faith sweetened all his circumstances. As he lay dying at the age of forty-three, he begged that the box containing debts owing to him should be burned. He did not want his friends to be worried about repayment.

POSTSCRIPT
One hundred years after Braille's death, his remains were taken from the village graveyard and buried with ceremony at the Pantheon in Paris. Braille's alphabet has been adapted to Chinese, African and Slavonic languages and is in use all over the world.

See also 15 February

17 February

On 17 February 1977, Ugandan radio announced the death
in a car accident of the Archbishop of Uganda, Janani
Luwum.

'He is not here – he is risen!'

There were many who did not believe the story of the accident.
They knew that President Amin hated Christians, and they knew
too how fearless the archbishop had been. The government
promised that his body would be handed over for burial at the
cathedral the following Sunday, so preparations were made for
the service and huge crowds gathered. At the last minute, it was
announced that he had been buried in his home village instead.
The radio also forbade the holding of any memorial service at the
cathedral.

But the order was ignored. Instead of being intimidated by this
outburst of Amin's hatred and cruelty, all the Christians present
determined to take their stand as loyal followers of Christ. It took
an hour for the huge congregation to leave the cathedral. As they
came out, they were still singing. They gathered round the empty
grave prepared for Luwum's coffin. The retired archbishop
stepped forward and spoke to the crowd.

'When we see an empty grave it reminds us of when the angels
spoke to the women at the empty grave of Jesus at that first
Easter.' Then he cried out, 'He is not dead, he is risen!' And the
crowd knew that he spoke too of their beloved archbishop.

POSTSCRIPT
Janani Luwum's coffin was left in the village church
overnight. Christians opened it and the bullet-wounds in his
face proved that he had been murdered by Amin and had
met a martyr's death.

18 February

Martin Luther died on 18 February 1546.

Martin Luther lived from 1483 to 1546. He became a monk and also lectured at Wittenberg University. He went to extreme lengths in his anxiety to find personal salvation before discovering from the Bible that God forgives on the basis of faith alone. His preaching and writings brought him into conflict with both church and state, and he was outlawed till his death. One of his great achievements was to translate the Bible into German.

'My Katie'

Luther was forty-two before he married, but he entered as enthusiastically into marriage as he did into every other event of life.

He certainly needed a wife. He admitted that his bed had previously been unmade 'from one end of the year to the other, so that finally the bed clothes and straw decayed with the sweat. I never noticed. I was working so hard I simply used to fall down on it at night and know no more till morning.'

Katherina soon put things right. She also grew fruit in the little orchard, kept fish in the pond, reared pigs, hens and ducks, as well as keeping the house tidy. But she did not succeed in persuading Luther to banish his little dog to the courtyard. And her husband littered the house with his writings and papers. He invited everyone to come to stay – students, orphans, refugees.

Katie, who was a skilled nurse, often had a house full of invalids when the plague raged. She took in women friends to have their babies at her home in peace. She tried in vain to stop the 'Herr Doctor' from giving all their possessions away – though once, at least, she succeeded. Luther wrote to a friend: 'I am sending you a beaker for a wedding present. P.S. Sorry, Katie's hidden it.'

What Luther said about Katie

'My Katie is in all things so obliging and pleasing to me that I would not exchange my poverty for all the riches of Croesus.'
'I would not exchange Katie for all France and Venice, because God has given her to me – and other women have worse faults.'

See also 18 April, 31 October

19 February

Shrove Tuesday comes at about this time of year. It is the day before the season of Lent begins.

'Shrove' comes from the verb 'to shrive' or to give absolution from sin. On Shrove Tuesday, sins were confessed and absolution given in preparation for the solemn season of Lent.

One last treat

For hundreds of years – till nearly the end of the last century – the 'pancake bell' rang loud and persistently on Shrove Tuesday. It reminded everyone that:

it was time to go to church – to confess their sins;

it was time to down tools – Shrove Tuesday was a holiday;

it was time to start making pancakes.

In days gone by, everyone made the most of Shrove Tuesday. After all, Lent would begin next day and all kinds of pleasures would be forbidden for the next six weeks. Any eggs, butter and other good things left in the larder were made into pancakes so that everyone could enjoy one last treat and no forbidden foods would be left as a temptation during Lent.

Anyone could ring the church bell on Shrove Tuesday, so there was great demand to 'have a go', and the pancake bell got little rest. Holidays and feasts were few and far between and always came by courtesy of the Christian festivals.

PRAYER
Thank you, Lord, for the fun and festivities as well as the solemn parts of our Christian faith. Help us to keep the right balance between the two. Amen

---

Bible wisdom – about being generous

'Be generous and you will be prosperous. Help others and you will be helped.'

'Be generous and share your food with the poor. You will be blessed for it.'

From the *Book of Proverbs*

'Give to others, and God will give to you. Indeed, you will receive a full measure, a generous helping, poured into your hands – all that you can hold. The measure you use for others is the one that God will use for you.'

From *Luke 6*

'Love your enemies and pray for those who persecute you, so that you may become the sons of your Father in heaven. For he makes his sun to shine on bad and good people alike, and gives rain to those who do good and to those who do evil.'

From *Matthew 5*

'God loves the one who gives gladly . . . He will always make you rich enough to be generous at all times, so that many will thank God for your gifts.'

From *2 Corinthians 9*

'God gives generously and graciously to all.'

From *James 1*

21 February

Eric Liddell, Olympic gold medallist, died on 21 February 1945.

Eric Liddell went as a missionary to China and in 1943 was interned in Japan with other British, American and so-called 'enemy nationals'. There he died of a brain tumour, exhausted too by his tireless and cheerful service to all in the camp.

Never on Sunday?

Jesus said: 'What does our Law allow us to do on the Sabbath? To help or to harm?'

The thin, bronzed man in the multi-coloured shirt carefully collected each hockey stick from the teenage players and examined them for wear. There'd be no new ones – they were lucky to have even these in the camp. Eric bound them up carefully with strips torn from his own precious sheets.

When they were first interned with their families, the teenagers had been hopelessly bored. With no privacy and nothing to occupy their time, they had wandered aimlessly round the camp perimeter at nights, with no outlet for their energies. So Eric Liddell organized hockey, rounders and baseball as well as chess and indoor activities. There was never any trouble with teenage high spirits after that. Except on one occasion.

Eric, true to the principles that had made him famous in the 1924 Olympic Games, refused to organize games on Sundays. The boys and girls rebelled against the restriction and arranged their own hockey match. It ended in a disastrous free-for-all. Eric said nothing, but the next Sunday he went with them and refereed their match. He put their genuine need for exercise, and the peace and well-being of relationships throughout the camp above his own treasured observance of Sunday for the sole worship of God.

See also 11 July

22 February

On 22 February 1913, Eric Gill was received into the Roman Catholic Church.

Eric Gill became a carver in stone and wood, but he began as an engraver and 'letterer'. He designed a type-face, still used by printers, called after him 'Gill Sans'. An example of his stone-carving can be seen in London, outside Broadcasting House and in the *Stations of the Cross* at Westminster Cathedral.

The stamp of truth

Eric Gill did not see himself as an artist if that meant being a hot-house plant – kept apart from the harsh realities of life. He believed that he was a 'maker of things that people wanted'. His lettering, type-designing, engraving and stone-carving were all means of serving God and his fellow men and of earning a living.

Everything that he made had to bear the stamp of truth and integrity. He told his pupils that to carve in stone they must 'think stone'. They must not copy an artefact in one medium and make it in another.

But as a Christian Gill also longed to make a unity of life. He aimed to make 'a cell of good living in the chaos of our world'. He wanted to bring the separated fragments of home and school, earth and heaven together and make them into a whole.

PRAYER
Forgive us, Lord, for changing with our circumstances, behaving in different ways according to whether we are at home or at work, with our family or our friends. Make us true to you and to our real selves so that our lives may be cells of good living in the world today. Amen

23 February

Lent is the season in the church's calendar between Ash Wednesday and Easter Saturday and is a reminder of the forty days of Christ's fasting and temptation in the wilderness.

Jack o'Lent

Jack o'Lent was a figure, looking like a man, set up during Lent for everyone to pelt with stones. In Cornwall, the figures were paraded round towns and villages on Ash Wednesday before being burned on bonfires. Charles Causley, a Christian poet, puts his own interpretation on Jack o'Lent.

Where are you running to, Jack o'Lent,
Your yellow coat so ruined and rent?
I'm going to the sea-shore as fast as I can
To try and find the Galilee man.

What will you have from him, Jack o'Lent,
Before your thirty of silver is spent?
I'll have some fish and I'll have some bread
And some words to cure the pain in my head.

How long will it take you, Jack o'Lent,
Your legs all crooked, your body all bent?
With the help of prayer and the help of praise
It'll take me forty nights and days.

Should you not find him, Jack o'Lent,
What will then be your intent?
I'll find the hungry and find the poor
And scatter my silver at their door.

What will you do then, Jack o'Lent,
If nobody takes a single cent?
I'll go to the rope-maker cunning and old
And buy me a collar against the cold.

Where will your lodging be, Jack o'Lent,
If house and home give no content?
I'll climb as high as heaven's hem
And take my rest on a sycamore stem.

What can we do for you, Jack o'Lent,
If in the fire the tree is pent?
Take the fire and take the flame
And burn the curse from off my name.

What shall we do then, Jack o'Lent,
If all to ashes you are sent?
Take the cinders you can see.
Cross your brow. Remember me.

24 February

In February 1958, author and broadcaster Mary Craig was told that her son was 'not normal'.

A way through

'Children like that shouldn't be allowed on public transport,' Mary Craig heard a woman on the bus remark as she caught sight of Mary's little son, Paul. She felt deeply hurt. Paul suffered from Höhler's syndrome, or gargoylism, a rare disease with no treatment or cure. He could do nothing for himself – he had to be changed and fed like a baby, and he did not even recognize his parents. But his energy was boundless and caring for him along with two normal sons exhausted Mary.

Yet, when a nurse friend volunteered to give her a break, Mary did not take a rest but went to help at a Sue Ryder home, where survivors from Nazi concentration camps lived. Here she encountered suffering far exceeding her own. Those people's courage and joyful faith in God cured her of her bitterness and self-pity.

At length, a place was found for Paul for two years in a special home. Soon after he went, Mary found that she was pregnant again. When another son was born, he was diagnosed as suffering from Down's syndrome, or mongolism. The night after his birth Mary felt herself slipping back into despair and darkness. That she should suffer twice! Then she had a unique experience of God.

'It seemed to me that suddenly I was held firm, safe from further falling and a voice was saying, "There is a way through but you must find it outside yourself. Remember I am here in the darkness. You are never alone."' Thoughts of her friends from the concentration camps came into her mind, and over everything she saw the cross of Christ, shedding light and peace. She remembered that the joy of Easter followed the suffering of Calvary.

25 February

In February 1981, a report reached Keston College in Kent, England, that Nikolai Grigorievich Bobarykin had been arrested and sentenced to six years' strict regime and five years' exile.

Nikolai was a deacon in a Russian Pentecostal church in northern Caucasus before his arrest. Pentecostalists in Russia have been persecuted for their faith since the 1930s. Many trekked as far as Siberia only to face loss of jobs and arrest there too. It is not only parents who suffer. Their children are openly insulted – threatened in class and bullied outside school.

With only the hills to hear

It was nearly Easter and the Christians in Frunze, Kirghiz Republic, longed to celebrate, but the church was strictly forbidden to hold any kind of service. At night, the KGB would even shine their torches in at the windows of their homes to make sure that they were not holding prayer meetings or studying the Bible together.

Nikolai was a young man then, and he and his friends determined to plan an open-air Easter service to avoid discovery. They left the town quietly, inconspicuously, in twos and threes at most. The older ones followed at a slower pace, steadily covering the ten kilometres or so to their agreed destination. It was a blazing hot day. Not a single green tree broke the landscape of bare rock outcrops and hills.

But for the Christians there was freedom to praise and worship God. Only the hills and God himself could hear their joyful singing, and their laments at the persecution they suffered. Tired, but renewed and exhilarated, they turned homewards to the city – and the watchful eyes of their persecutors.

26 February

26 February is American singer Johnny Cash's birthday.

After a childhood of poverty and hardship – picking cotton and hauling five-gallon water jugs for work-gangs – Johnny Cash joined the US Air Force. Then he went to Memphis, Tennessee, and found success through a Sun Records' audition. Now a Country and Western star, Johnny has become a legend in his own lifetime.

Prisoners

One night, Johnny Cash woke up in jail in Georgia and didn't remember how he got there. It was enough to give anyone a jolt. The pressures of touring, recording, working for radio and television had become too much. He had taken to tranquillizers and stimulants as the only way to survive. But the habit brought its own train of disaster and Johnny ended up that night in jail.

Life itself seemed a bit like a prison to Johnny. *Time* magazine had summed up the message of his songs in a similar way: they seemed to be saying, 'Life both in and out of prison is a kind of sentence to be served'.

Johnny had great sympathy with those who were literally inside. His compassion for convicts is expressed in many of his songs. He has sung in many of the big prisons in the USA, including San Quentin. He is strongly critical of the whole prison system.

'You put them in like animals,' he said, 'and tear the souls and guts out of them, then let them out worse than when they went in.'

But after his own experience of prison, Johnny found freedom – not only from the Georgia jail, but from his personal prison of drugs and despair. He found the freedom which Jesus Christ can give.

BIBLE VERSE
'Jesus said . . . "If the Son sets you free, then you will be really free."'
From *John 8*

27 February

Corrie ten Boom was arrested by the Gestapo at the end of February 1944.

Corrie ten Boom and her sister, Betsie, were sent to a German concentration camp during the Second World War because they had given refuge to Jews in Holland. Betsie died as a result of the ill-treatment they received there. After her release, Corrie travelled widely to preach the message of God's love and forgiveness in Jesus Christ.

'Love your enemies'

Suddenly Corrie caught sight of him in the congregation at Munich – the former SS man who had been their guard at Ravensbruck camp. Somehow she managed to go on speaking, but scenes of horror and anguish from those past days crowded into her mind. It was not for herself she cared – she remembered poor Betsie, ill, frail, yet made to strip while those mocking guards examined their helpless prisoners. Now the leader of them was here in church.

After the service he came up the church towards her, smiling broadly and with outstretched hand.

'Thank you for your message,' he said, 'Jesus has washed my sins away.'

Corrie looked at him, unable to lift her hand from her side. She had *preached* forgiveness, but how could she show it to the very person who had humiliated and hurt her beloved sister? For a long moment she paused, then prayed silently, 'Lord Jesus, forgive me and help me to forgive him.' But still she could neither smile nor raise her hand – it seemed bound to her side. 'Give me *your* forgiveness,' she prayed, 'I cannot forgive him on my own.'

As she took his hand, Corrie felt an amazing current passing from herself to him and love filled her heart. So, she concluded, 'I discovered that when God tells us to love our enemies, he gives, along with the command, the love itself.'

See also 10 and 27 January

28 February

Dr Denis Burkitt was a surgeon in Africa for twenty years. He served there in a government post, in answer to God's call. He became world-famous when he discovered and successfully treated a childhood cancer now named after him as Burkitt's Lymphoma. He has since turned his brilliant medical detective mind to Western diseases and their prevention.

The carton and its contents

When we go to see a doctor, his chief aim is to heal our bodies. He may inquire how we are feeling because it is increasingly recognized that grief, depression or mental tiredness can affect the whole person, and therefore produce physical symptoms. But very few, says Dr Burkitt, think about spiritual health – how we are coping with our relationship with God, with guilt or bitterness, or with fear of death.

Dr Burkitt believes that doctors – like the rest of us – have their priorities wrong. All too frequently, we make the mistake of lavishing all our care and effort on maintaining the 'container' – our bodies – while the 'contents' are left to take care of themselves. The real truth is that the carton matters less than what it contains.

He points out that Jesus never made that mistake. He cured men's spirits as well as their minds and bodies. And he did it in the right order, as the story below illustrates.

Jesus' example

'Some people brought to Jesus a paralysed man, lying on a bed. When Jesus saw how much faith they had, he said to the paralysed man, "Courage, my son! Your sins are forgiven." . . . [Then] he said to the paralysed man, "Get up, pick up your bed and go home!"'

From *Matthew 9*

PRAYER

'May the God who gives us peace make you holy in every way and keep your whole being – spirit, soul and body – free from every fault at the coming of our Lord Jesus Christ.'

From *1 Thessalonians 5*

See also 29 February (even if it isn't Leap Year)

29 February

Dr Burkitt's experiences in Africa gave him the clue to Western disease and ill-health. As well as caring for people's spiritual well-being, he has brought physical health to very many people by his revolutionary advice on healthy eating.

Prevention is better than cure

If people keep falling from a dangerous cliff-top, there are two possible actions to take, reasons Dr Burkitt. One is to station a fleet of ambulances at the foot of the cliff, to ferry the casualties to hospital; the other is to fence off the cliff so that accidents are prevented. Most medical students learn how to deal with the results of illness and disease, rather than learning how to prevent them.

When Dr Burkitt returned to England after many years in Africa, he was interested in the ideas of a former naval surgeon, who believed that many diseases could be prevented if more roughage or fibre was introduced into the diet.

Dr Burkitt began some detective research, painstakingly comparing the incidence of certain diseases in the West with that in the countries he had worked in for so long. Such diseases as appendicitis, cancer of the colon and rectum, heart disease – all very common in the West – are practically unknown in less developed countries. There, the diet is high in fibre, which has been gradually processed out of the foods eaten in richer countries. Dr Burkitt believes that the fibre, discarded as useless, has an important function in keeping us healthy and preventing many diseases.

Here is his recipe for adopting a diet which will 'fence off the cliff-top' and avoid the need for an ambulance:

Double your *starch* intake
Double your *fibre* intake (found in bran, oatmeal,
    wholemeal bread, vegetables)
Halve your *sugar* intake
Halve your *salt* intake
Cut your *fat* intake *by one third*

See also 28 February

1 March

For the first three weeks of March 1976, Eunice Diment,
Bible translator in the Philippines, was held by kidnappers.

The Bible comes alive

Eunice struggled from sleep to write to the Chief of Philippine
police at her kidnappers' dictation:

'Dear Colonel,
Kindly send us food supplies for the daily sustainment of ours:
1 sack good rice
20 packages American loaf bread
1 big tin Ovaltine
1 bottle Lady's Choice preserves
1 bottle peanut butter
10 kilos white sugar.'

She must have been half-asleep, Eunice decided, or she would
never have included peanut butter – she hated it!

Alone, guarded by armed guerillas, Eunice needed more
than food – so she was grateful that a box of clothes and medicines delivered by a negotiator also included a copy of the
Psalms. As she read eagerly the words came alive.

'Have mercy upon me, O Lord; for I am weak; O Lord, heal
me; for my bones are vexed.'

Her bones were certainly 'vexed' from sleeping on the floor –
and so was her soul! She knew how the psalmist felt.

Negotiations repeatedly broke down. Her mission could not
afford the ransom. Was she willing to accept death from her
captors if that should come? At first, her answer was 'No'. Then
she read, 'My heart is fixed, O God, my heart is fixed. I will sing
and give praise.' This was her answer. It was not for her to worry
over the final outcome but to praise God, whatever his plan.
And in doing so she found peace and release from worry.

Release from her kidnappers came later.

2 March

John Wesley died on 2 March 1791.

John Wesley, who transformed England by his preaching, often described himself in Old Testament words as 'a brand plucked from the burning'.

Fire!

Little Hetty was asleep in the attic room of the thatched rectory where Samuel and Susanna Wesley lived with their large family. She woke to find a piece of blazing thatch on her bed, and raised the alarm. The fire spread quickly. The maid carried the baby, and Samuel Wesley shepherded the children out into the street. Mrs Wesley, expecting another baby in a few weeks, struggled through the flames to join them.

As they huddled on the pavement in the February cold, where a crowd had collected, they saw a small figure crouched on the window-sill of the nursery. Six-year-old John was trapped.

His father tried to get into the house again but the flames drove him back. Despairing, he fell to his knees, praying that God would receive the child's soul. But neighbours refused to be beaten. Someone shouted 'Fetch a ladder!' But that would take too long.

Then a large, broad man beckoned to his small companion and went towards the wall below the window. Bracing himself, he told his friend to climb on his shoulders and lift the boy down. At the second attempt, John was snatched from the ledge and lowered to safety.

At that instant, the roof fell in and the house burned down completely. His father called to the neighbours to kneel by the roadside and give thanks to God. His mother felt convinced that God had some great future for John.

'I do intend to be more particularly careful for the soul of this child, that thou hast so mercifully provided for,' she promised God.

See also 20 and 28 June, 24 July

3 March

George Herbert, the poet, was buried in the churchyard at
Bemerton on 3 March 1633.

'Musick at midnight'

Twice a week George Herbert would go to the cathedral at
Salisbury and on his way home he would call on some friends for
an informal session of music-making. One day, walking to
Salisbury, 'he saw a poor man with a poorer horse that was fallen
under his load; they were both in distress and needed help; which
Mr Herbert perceiving, put off his canonical coat and helped the
poor man to unload and after to load his horse: the poor man blest
him for it: and he blest the poor man: and was so like the good
Samaritan that he gave him money to refresh both himself and
the horse; and told him that as he loved himself he should be
merciful to his beast. Then he left the poor man and at his coming
to his musical friends at Salisbury they began to wonder that Mr
George Herbert, which used to be so trim and clean came into
that company so soiled and discomposed; but he told them the
occasion: and when one of the company told him he had
disparaged himself by so dirty an employment, his answer was,
that the thought of what he had done would prove musick to him
at midnight – "and though I do not wish for the like occasion
every day, yet let me tell you, I would not willingly pass one day of
my life without comforting a sad soul or showing mercy; and I
praise God for this occasion: and now let's tune our instruments."'

Adapted from Izaak Walton's *Life of Mr George Herbert* published in 1670

PRAYER
Thank you, Lord, for the enjoyment we have from music and
poetry. May they also inspire us to be practical, like George
Herbert, and to relieve misery and need wherever we find it.
Amen

See also 4 March, 8 August

4 March

George Herbert, of noble birth and gifted for high office, gave up his ambitions and became a poor clergyman in the little village of Bemerton, where he died before he was forty. The scientists of his age were experimenting to find the philosopher's stone, which they believed would turn all base metals into gold. Another name for this so-called 'tincture' was the 'elixir'. In his poem of that title, Herbert claims to have found the secret of turning the basest and dullest task into an act of golden worth.

The Elixir

Teach me, my God and King,
In all things thee to see,
And what I do in anything
To do it as for thee . . .

All may of thee partake;
Nothing can be so mean,
Which with this tincture, 'for thy sake,'
Will not grow bright and clean.

A servant with this clause
Makes drudgery divine;
Who sweeps a room, as for thy laws,
Makes that and the action fine.

This is the famous stone
That turneth all to gold;
For that which God doth touch and own
Cannot for less be told.

See also 3 March

5 March

Gerhard Kremer, better known by his Latin name of Geradus Mercator, was born in Flanders on 5 March 1512.

Mercator was a man of many talents – mathematician, engraver, instrument-maker and geographer. He is most famous for his map-making. Mercator had a strong religious faith which led at one time to his arrest and imprisonment. When he was freed he settled in Germany where many of his family had lived. He also published a Harmony of the Gospels. He died in 1594.

'You will certainly get there'!

Look at a map of the world in a school-type atlas and compare the sizes of Greenland and South America. Greenland looks bigger. Now compare them on a globe and the relative sizes seem to be reversed. The globe, of course, is correct. South America is actually nine times larger than Greenland. The atlas is based on what is known as Mercator's projection.

Mercator was a skilled and painstaking map-maker and the apparent 'mistakes' are not the result of his ignorance. He had already made fine globes of the world in which he had corrected longstanding errors in cartography. But now he recognized the great need that existed for a map to help sailors. So Mercator produced his Great World Map, published in 1569.

To make this map he 'stretched' the earth in both directions and 'flattened' the globe, in order to provide a map from which mariners could easily chart a course. To help them further, he invented an easy-to-read italic writing to take the place of the illegible script usually used for maps.

He explained the characteristics of his new map for the benefit of the sailors who were to use it:

'If you wish to sail from one part to another here is a chart, and a straight line on it, and if you follow this line carefully you will certainly arrive at your destination. But the length of the line may not be correct. You may get there sooner or may not get there as soon as you expected, but you will certainly get there.'

Four hundred years later, sea charts are still prepared on Mercator's projection.

6 March

John Newton had not always been the saintly and respected clergyman of his later years. And he never forgot it. When he was very old he said, 'My memory is nearly gone but I remember two things: that I am a great sinner and that Christ is a great Saviour.'

Amazing grace!

'Oh! I have reason to praise God for that storm: for the apprehension I had, first of sinking under the weight of all my sins into that ocean and into eternity. Then I began to think: I attempted to pray and my first half-formed prayers were answered.'

That was how John Newton described the storm that changed his life when he wrote about it later to his wife.

His life had been hard, his mother dying when he was six. At eleven, he joined his father's ship and later was press-ganged into the navy. He deserted ship because conditions were so bad and was severely punished. He became involved in the slave-trade, then jumped ship again and spent a year in Sierra Leone, sick and degraded, bullied by an African woman.

At last, a message from England arrived and he returned, experiencing the terrifying storm on his journey back. That storm shocked Newton into facing his own sin and finding a Saviour. The rough sailor who had been the slave of every kind of evil, became the slave of Christ and gave his life to preaching the good news that had set *him* free.

Amazing grace! how sweet the sound
That saved a wretch like me!
I once was lost, but now am found,
Was blind, but now I see.

John Newton

See also 11 April

7 March

On 7 March 1780, Edward Jenner presented the king of England with his book on smallpox vaccination.

Sixty million people died from smallpox in Europe in the eighteenth century. In ten years, nearly 250,000 died from it in London alone. Inoculation with smallpox virus was practised but could result in serious illness or death.

A dairymaid with cowpox

It all began when Edward Jenner, a young apprentice doctor, heard a dairymaid who was being treated for a skin eruption, say, 'It can't be the smallpox because I've had cowpox.'

'Just an old wives' tale,' doctors commented, 'like carrying a potato to get rid of rheumatism.' But Jenner determined to try out the theory. This just might be the key to preventing the world's greatest scourge.

Sometimes cows developed blister-like spots on their udders, and the girls who milked them developed similar blisters on their hands and felt off-colour for a few days. If Jenner could prove that a dose of cowpox made the sufferer immune to smallpox, he could inoculate using the mild cowpox virus and so save patients from the danger of contracting deadly smallpox.

All he needed to carry out his research were some outbreaks of cowpox, and he eagerly followed up every case at farms nearby. He collected the cowpox vaccine, inoculated volunteers with it, then later inoculated with smallpox virus. None of those inoculated with cowpox reacted to the smallpox. They *were* immune!

Jenner was a Christian and he believed that God might use him to wipe out this terrible disease. His theory took years to confirm and the medical men of his time took a great deal of persuading. But thanks to Jenner and cowpox, what was once the world's worst killer disease has now been officially eradicated.

See also 13 March

8 March

The Missionary Aviation Fellowship (MAF) began work in Sudan in March 1948.

MAF was founded in 1947, and its pilots and planes help to meet the needs of missionaries and tribespeople in some of the least accessible parts of the world.

Air rescue

Dick Crossman was drilling for water in Lowelli, a remote, isolated place in southern Sudan. He planned to live there as a missionary. One day, as he worked, he heard a warning shout from one of his Sudanese helpers, and looked up to see a heavy section of iron from the rig hurtling towards him. It smashed across Dick's leg, crushing and breaking his ankle.

It was a Sunday morning when the telegram arrived for Stuart King, in charge of the MAF base at Malakal, some 250 miles away. He read 'Dick Crossman seriously hurt with broken ankle at Lowelli. Please come immediately.'

Stuart cancelled the family trip to church and rushed to fetch a pilot. They located Lowelli on the map, stopped just long enough to snatch up sandwiches, then made for the airstrip, prepared the aircraft and were soon airborne into the hot sky. They flew for an hour and a half over desolate, flat, swampy grassland, then circled a lonely mission station to pick up a doctor.

Once near Lowelli, they could spot Dick's drilling rig and even make out his tent close by. They landed and ran to the tent. Dick looked at them with enormous relief.

'I've been waiting three days to hear the sound of that plane,' he said.

They soon had him on board and flew on another 800 miles into Kenya, taking him to hospital in Nairobi. Dick's leg was saved. MAF had been in time.

9 March

A naturalist writes in March 1773.

Gilbert White was born in 1720 in the Hampshire village of Selborne, where his grandfather was vicar and where he in turn became curate. He was a keen naturalist in an age which regarded such study as eccentric. His *Natural History of Selborne* fully and delightfully documents the birds, animals and plants of the area.

'The Lord God made them all'

'A willow-wren had built in a bank in my fields. This bird a friend and myself had observed as she sat in her nest; but were particularly careful not to disturb her, though we saw she eyed us with some degree of jealousy. Some days after as we passed that way we were desirous of remarking how this brood went on; but no nest could be found, till I happened to take up a large bundle of green moss, as it were, carelessly thrown over the nest, in order to dodge the eye of any impertinent intruder.

'The flycatcher . . . builds every year in the vines that grow on the walls of my house. A pair of these little birds had one year . . . placed their nest on a naked bough, perhaps in a shady time, not being aware of the inconvenience that followed. But an hot, sunny season coming on before the brood had half fledged, the reflection of the wall became insupportable, and must inevitably have destroyed the tender young, had not affection . . . prompted the parent-birds to hover over the nest all the hotter hours, while with wings expanded, and mouths gaping for breath, they screened off the heat from their suffering offspring.'

PRAISE
'Lord, you have made so many things!
  How wisely you made them all!
  The earth is filled with your creatures . . .
May the glory of the Lord last for ever!
May the Lord be happy with what he has made!' Amen
From *Psalm 104*

See also 11 May

10 March

The Evangelical Alliance Relief Fund (Tear Fund) helps to meet need in all parts of the world through gifts to local Christians, or by sending helpers to the area. Cliff Richard gives concerts in aid of Tear Fund and many of his fans also support the work.

Contrasts

Cliff believes that everyone should be compelled to spend some time in an area of real poverty. His opportunity came on the way home from an Australian concert tour.

'In Australia I'd been impressed by one of man's most spectacular creative achievements [the Sydney Opera House]; in Bangladesh I watched an eighteen-month-old baby die of starvation because its parents couldn't afford to feed it . . . I left behind my stage suits and smart gear and kept with me a toothbrush, spare pair of jeans and a guitar: just that was enough to put me in a class apart. People in Bangladesh don't have spare anything . . .

'That first morning I must have washed my hands a dozen times. Whenever we stopped, I made a beeline for the communal tap or the well; I didn't want to touch anything, least of all the people. Everyone in those camps, even the babies, were covered in sores and scabs.

'I was bending down to one little mite, mainly for the photographer's benefit [Tear Fund was making a soundstrip for publicity purposes], and trying hard not to have too close a contact, when someone accidentally stood on the child's fingers. He screamed out and, as a reflex, I grabbed hold of him, forgetting all about his dirt and his sores. I remember now that warm little body clinging to me and the crying instantly stopped. In that moment I knew I had an enormous amount to learn about practical Christian loving but that at least I'd started.'

From *Which One's Cliff?*, by Cliff Richard

See also 19 and 20 August

11 March

Bible wisdom – about money

'Some people pretend to be rich but have nothing. Others pretend to be poor but own a fortune.'

'Riches will do you no good on the day you face death. Those who depend on their wealth will fall like the leaves of autumn, but the righteous will prosper like the leaves of summer.'

'Your money can be gone in a flash as if it had grown wings and flown away like an eagle.'

From the *Book of Proverbs*

'If your riches increase, don't depend on them.'

From *Psalm 62*

'Jesus . . . said, "How hard it is for rich people to enter the Kingdom of God! It is much harder for a rich person to enter the Kingdom of God than for a camel to go through the eye of a needle."'

From *Luke 18*

'Command those who are rich in the things of this life not to be proud, but to place their hope, not in such uncertain things as riches, but in God, who generously gives us everything for our enjoyment. Command them to do good, to be rich in good works, to be generous and ready to share with others.'

From *1 Timothy 6*

12 March

Geoffrey Smith, who lives in Yorkshire, is well known in Britain for his television gardening programmes and his books on gardening. Here he shares some personal recollections:

Planted in the memory

'Recently I visited a garden which houses a notable collection of clematis. Amongst all the lovely pictures revealed by each turn of the path there is one engraved deep in my recollection. A clematis planted at the foot of a twenty-foot high purple-leaved beech had climbed up through the branches and overlain the dark canopy with pure white flowers. A moment to be hoarded in the memory, polished by being frequently recalled.

'There is a lane in Norfolk which is buried under an overhanging canopy formed by beech leaves on either side. For almost a mile the trees hold company with the lane, branches interlaced as if protecting it from the sharp eye of the sun. In winter just a delicate twig tracery, in spring a pale green haze, deepening with June to moss green shade. Loveliest of all seasons is the autumn as the leaves turn copper – aflame, as if all the sunlight of summer had been stored and was being reflected back to its source . . .

'Surely the love of beauty so firmly rooted in all mankind could never be other than God-given. No accidental chemical combination could have produced this appreciation. All things beautiful are made by God who gave us the ability not only to appreciate loveliness but also to recall it at will. Almost every day of my life as a gardener some new association is added to the ever-increasing store held in my memory.'

13 March

On 13 March 1789, a paper by Dr Edward Jenner was read to the Royal Society. He was elected a Fellow of the Royal Society later that year.

No cuckoo!

For centuries country folk had known that cuckoos used other birds to hatch their eggs for them. But who sent the original fledgelings packing? Jenner determined to find out. He could take all the time in the world, for life moved at a leisurely pace in his country practice. His wife was busy with her Sunday school – one of the first to be founded – but she provided a relaxed Christian home which was the ideal setting for his investigations into medicine and nature study.

Jenner wrote up his findings:

17 June

'Saw a hedgesparrow's nest at Mr Bromedge's with two hedgesparrows in it just hatched, two eggs not hatched and a cuckoo just hatched.'

18 June

'In the morning early there were four hedgesparrows and the yound cuckoo in it. About noon it contained the cuckoo and one hedgesparrow only and at night the cuckoo was left alone in the nest.

'The nest was placed so near the extremity of the hedge that I could distinctly see what was going forward in it; to my astonishment saw the young cuckoo though so newly hatched in the act of turning out the young hedgesparrow.'

Jenner had observed that the cuckoo himself was the villain of the piece. But he was meticulous in checking his evidence. Only after repeated observations did he submit his paper to the Royal Society. The doctor who rid the world of smallpox also solved one of the tantalizing riddles of the bird world.

PRAYER
We thank you, Lord, for the wonders of the world you created. Give us eyes that recognize and appreciate all that you have made. Amen

See also 7 March

14 March

Mothering Sunday

Spring and Easter still seemed far off. Something special was
needed to help everyone through the remaining bleak days of
winter. On Mothering Sunday, the village churches stayed shut
while everyone walked to morning service at their nearest
'mother' church – the cathedral or large parish church.

Mothering Sunday became a special day for mothers of
families too. Girls and boys who were 'in service' or apprenticed
away from home were given the day off to visit their families.
They would arrive with some little gift for their mothers and join
the walk to church. Then the whole family would enjoy dinner
together.

Simnel Cake

Nowadays simnel cakes are eaten at Easter, but they used to be
baked and taken by girls to their mothers on Mothering Sunday.
No one know where simnel cakes originated, but they were being
made before 1066!

To make a simnel cake: Use a fruit cake recipe. Put half the
uncooked mixture in the cake tin then put a layer of marzipan
before adding the rest of the mixture. Decorate the cooked cake
with marzipan only. Put eleven marzipan balls round the edge to
represent the apostles – without Judas.

PRAYER
We thank you today, Lord, for our mothers. We are so close
to them that we often see their faults instead of remembering all their love and unselfishness. Help us to show by
gifts, words or helpful actions that we appreciate them.
Amen

15 March

Bible faith

'To have faith is to be sure of the things we hope for, to be certain of the things we cannot see. It was by their faith that people of ancient times won God's approval ... No one can please God without faith, for whoever comes to God must have faith that God exists and rewards those who seek him.'
From *Hebrews 11*

'It is by God's grace that you have been saved through faith. It is not the result of your own efforts, but God's gift, so that no one can boast about it.'
From *Ephesians 2*

'God puts people right through their faith in Jesus Christ. God does this to all who believe in Christ ... '
From *Romans 3*

'Now that we have been put right with God through faith, we have peace with God through our Lord Jesus Christ.'
From *Romans 5*

'Consider the experience of Abraham; as the scripture says, "He believed God, and because of his faith God accepted him as righteous." You should realize then, that the real descendants of Abraham are the people who have faith.'
From *Galatians 3*

See also 16 March

16 March

The Jews regard Abraham as the father of their nation. St Paul says that Abraham is also the spiritual 'father' of all Christians, because he showed the way to be right with God through faith and obedience.

Destination unknown

'Look up at the sky – can you count how many stars there are? Look down at the ground – can you count the specks of dust? The number of your descendants will be as numerous as that. I will give you a son and I will give you a country where the nation of his descendants shall live.'

Many years before he made these promises, God had first made himself known to Abraham, while he was living in the city of Ur, where the people were moon-worshippers. Abraham had learned to worship the One who *made* the moon, and to trust what he said to be true.

He was seventy-five years old when God first told him about the great future for him and his descendants. Although he and his wife Sarah were both so old and had never been able to have a child, Abraham got ready to do as God told him. He left the comfortable city home in Haran, where they were then living, and set off to travel as a desert nomad, not knowing where he was going or how his son would be born, but trusting God to keep his word.

The Bible puts it this way:

'It was faith that made Abraham obey when God called him to go out to a country which God had promised to give him. He left his own country without knowing where he was going . . . It was faith that made Abraham able to become a father, even though he was too old . . . He trusted God to keep his promise.'

From *Hebrews 11*

PRAYER
Help us, Lord, to trust you as firmly and patiently as Abraham did. Thank you that you keep every promise you make to us, through Jesus Christ. Amen

See also 15 March

17 March

In 1912 Captain Scott and his four companions reached the South Pole, only to find that the Norwegian explorer, Amundsen, had arrived there a month before them. Their journey home was dogged by bad weather and hampered by frostbite and shortages of food and fuel. Oates, particularly, was badly affected by frostbite in his feet. Scott's diary tells the story.

'The end is not far'
Friday 16 March or Saturday 17

'Lost track of dates but think the last correct. At lunch, the day before yesterday, poor Titus Oates said he couldn't go on; he proposed we should leave him in his sleeping-bag. That we could not do, and we induced him to come on, on the afternoon march. He struggled on and we made a few miles. At night he was worse and we knew the end had come. We can testify to his bravery. He has borne intense suffering for weeks without complaining. He did not – would not – give up hope till the very end. He slept through the night before last hoping not to wake; but he woke in the morning – yesterday. It was blowing a blizzard. He said, "I am just going outside and may be some time." He went out into the blizzard and we have not seen him since. It was the act of a brave man and an English gentleman. We all hope to meet the end with similar spirit, and assuredly the end is not far.'

POSTSCRIPT
The bodies of Scott and his two remaining companions were found eight months later inside their tent, pitched only eleven miles from the depot and certain relief. Under Scott's shoulders was the wallet containing his notebooks and charting the course of the disastrous expedition. Oates's body was never found.

PRAYER
We thank you, Lord Jesus, for all who by their brave actions and self-sacrifice have died that others may live. Thank you for giving us the supreme example by laying down your life for us all. Amen

18 March

William Tuke was born in March 1732.

William Tuke was a Quaker who lived in Yorkshire in the eighteenth century.

The Retreat

One of William Tuke's fellow Quakers had been admitted to the local lunatic asylum and her relatives asked Tuke to visit her. All Tuke's attempts to do so failed. The authorities would not let him near the place. Soon after, he learned that the patient had died.

But Tuke was not prepared to put the matter out of his mind. He had heard too much about the cruelty meted out to so-called 'mad' patients. He found a way of seeing inside the asylum. He and one or two other Quakers managed to become governors of the asylum. As a governor, he had every right to make a thorough examination. He was horrified at what he saw, and determined to set up a hospital where proper treatment would be given. Many years ahead of his time, Tuke recognized that mental disorder was an illness needing compassion and medical treatment, like any other sickness.

In 1792, he founded 'The Retreat', a hospital for the mentally sick, in York. His son and grandson followed in his footsteps and brought medical training and skill to the proper treatment of mental illness. As well as compassionate nursing, patients received – and still receive – medical care and the possibility of cure.

See also 1 October

19 March

Bishop Ken died on 19 March 1711.

Thomas Ken lived through the reigns of many different monarchs. Sometimes he suffered persecution for his beliefs. But he refused to trim his sails to the wind. He was a man who combined moral courage with mercy and kindness to others.

'Be sure to sing'

'Be sure to sing the Morning and Evening hymns in your chamber devoutly, remembering that the Psalmist assures you that it is a good thing to tell of the loving kindness of the Lord early in the morning and of his truth in the night season.'

So wrote Bishop Ken in a book of prayers specially compiled for the scholars of Winchester School. The tunes he sang – to the viol or spinet – are unknown, but the words of his hymns have been sung ever since. These are the opening verses of one of his best-known hymns:

An evening hymn, 1695
Glory to thee, my God, this night
For all the blessings of the light;
Keep me, O keep me, King of kings,
Under thy own almighty wings.

Forgive me, Lord, for thy dear Son,
The ill that I this day have done,
That with the world, myself, and thee,
I, e'er I sleep, at peace may be.

Teach me to live, that I may dread
The grave as little as my bed;
Teach me to die, that so I may
Triumphing rise at the last day.

20 March

David Livingstone, missionary, doctor and explorer, was
born in March 1813.

Call of the unknown

When David Livingstone went to Africa, he expected the life of a
missionary to be one of constant advance – leaving new converts
behind in their own communities and moving forward to break
fresh ground. He was horrified to find his fellow missionaries
settled in stations made as permanent as possible and like 'home'
in England. He had no intention of settling down with them. The
unknown called to him. Besides that, he seemed unsuccessful at
winning converts. He felt a failure as a missionary, and his
missionary society was inclined to agree.

But Livingstone had skills and vision that other missionaries
lacked. 'I shall open up a path into the interior or perish,' he
declared, and through his exploration he opened a whole
continent to the preaching of the gospel.

Livingstone took a keen delight in everything he saw on his
famous journeys into the interior of Africa. He noted birds,
insects and plant-life. When at last he saw the Zambezi river he
could only exclaim, 'How magnificent! How glorious! How
beautiful!' It reminded him so much of his native Scotland. 'The
long-lost scenes came back so vividly I might have cried,' he
wrote. But he added that he kept back the tears lest his African
guide thought they were caused by fear of the basking crocodiles!

Within ten years of his death, the region Livingstone had
explored was dotted with Christian missions, and a cathedral
stood on the site of the great slave-market in Zanzibar.

See also 21 March

21 March

'How I found Livingstone'

Livingstone was sick at heart and wretched. He was near the end of his journey – almost within reach of the lakes he hoped to find – when a terrible and barbarous massacre in the town where he was staying brought his dreams to an end. About 400 people died as a result of the killing deliberately stirred up by the slave-drivers. Livingstone sank into despair as he moved back to Ujiji. He was skeleton-thin, with no money or supplies.

'I felt as though I were the man going down from Jerusalem to Jericho but no Good Samaritan would come my way,' he wrote.

But he was wrong. Henry Stanley, American journalist, had been sent by his paper to look for Livingstone, who had lost contact with the outside world. He arrived at Ujiji on 10 November 1871, to the sound of gun salutes and beating drums. Livingstone came out of the house to see what the noise was about – then waited for Stanley under a large mango tree near the lake.

'Dr Livingstone, I presume,' Stanley said, as he alighted from his horse.

Livingstone gravely replied, 'Yes, that is my name.'

Then they talked endlessly. Livingstone was too polite to ask what had brought Stanley to Ujiji. 'It was not my business,' he said. He waited patiently to open the long-delayed mail that Stanley had delivered. When at last he opened the letters, he found that the government had voted £1,000 for his relief.

The two spent Christmas together, then Stanley returned with his story for the world. He was captivated by Livingstone's gentleness and sincerity. 'A Christian gentleman,' he pronounced, and wrote of his experiences in his best-seller, *How I Found Livingstone.*

See also 20 March

22 March

Bible wisdom – on enjoyment!

'Every good gift and every perfect present comes from heaven; it comes down from God the Creator.'

From *James 1*

'God . . . generously gives us everything for our enjoyment.'

From *1 Timothy 6*

'Everything that God has created is good; nothing is to be rejected, but everything is to be received with a prayer of thanks.'

From *1 Timothy 4*

'How precious, O God, is your constant love! We find protection under the shadow of your wings. We feast on the abundant food you provide; you let us drink from the river of your goodness. You are the source of all life, and because of your light we see the light.'

From *Psalm 36*

'You will show me the path that leads to life; your presence fills me with joy and brings me pleasure for ever.'

From *Psalm 16*

23 March

Anna Sewell was brought up a Quaker. She lived with her strong-minded mother, who wrote improving stories and verses. She was lame in one foot following an accident and spent her last seven years as an invalid, confined to a couch. When she was twenty-five, Anna heard a 'powerful sermon' which changed her life. 'As I listened, I truly felt Christ precious,' she wrote. 'I believed I was justified from all things. I do now trust in none but Jesus.'

Black Beauty

'I am writing the life of a horse,' Anna confided in her diary in November 1871.

Scenes and events came clearly into her mind as she lay on her couch. She sadly missed her own little pony which she had driven, like so many before him, with skill and kindness. When she could no longer go out, she had given the pony and chaise away. She still listened with pleasure for the clip-clop of her brother Philip's black mare, Bessie, when he came to visit.

Anna talked horses with Philip. She also learned from the passers-by beneath her window.

'I have for six years been confined to the house and my sofa and have been writing what I think will turn out a little book, its special aim being to induce kindness, sympathy and an understanding treatment of horses. Some weeks ago I had a conversation at my open window with a cabman who was waiting at our door, which has deeply impressed me.'

At last the book was finished and sent to a publisher. Anna received £20 payment. It was only after her death that *Black Beauty* became a best-seller, topping two million copies in two years in the United States – a record in publishing history.

PRAYER
We pray for all who because of illness or handicap are confined to bed or home. Help them to keep an interest in life around them and to find ways of helping others. Amen

See also 28 March

24 March

Malcolm Muggeridge was born on 24 March 1903.

In spite of frequent television appearances, Malcolm Muggeridge is a harsh critic of the medium for falsifying the truth. But he does recall some positive experiences from working with television (see also 26 March).

The light of love

'We had only five days' filming in Calcutta to make the forty-minute programme on Mother Teresa. The normal allowance for a film of that length would have been two to three months. At every point we had to take all sorts of chances, one of them being to film in the very poor light of her home for the dying, where derelicts from the streets of Calcutta are brought, mostly to die, sometimes to live. To everyone's amazement, including the cameraman, Ken MacMillan's, and mine, this particular footage came out very well, showing the home for the dying . . . bathed in a soft and very beautiful light. There has been some dispute about this. My own feeling was, and remains, that love carried to the point that Mother Teresa has carried it, has its own luminosity, and that the medieval painters, who showed saints with halos, were not so far wide of the mark as a twentieth-century mind might suppose.

'The moral would seem to be that what is required to make a successful Christian television programme is merely to find a true Christian, and put him or her on the screen. This, rather than any television skills or devices, would seem to be the key.'

From *Christ and the Media*, by Malcolm Muggeridge

See also 17 and 19 October

25 March

From early centuries, the church has celebrated 25 March –
nine months before Christmas Day – as the day when the
angel Gabriel announced to Mary the good news of Jesus'
coming birth. In the Middle Ages it was a holiday, and a
synod of 1240 in Worcester forbade 'servile' work to be
done. It is also a Quarter Day, when tenants' quarterly rents
were due and when farm or land tenancies could begin or
end.

The promise to Mary

'God sent the angel Gabriel to a town in Galilee named Nazareth.
He had a message for a girl promised to a man named
Joseph . . . The girl's name was Mary . . .

'The angel said to her, "Don't be afraid, Mary; God has been
gracious to you. You will become pregnant and give birth to a son,
and you will name him Jesus. He will be great and will be called
the Son of the Most High God. The Lord God will make him a
King . . . "

'Mary said to the angel, "I am a virgin. How, then, can this be?"

'The angel answered, "The Holy Spirit will come on you, and
God's power will rest upon you. For this reason the holy child will
be called the Son of God . . . There is nothing that God cannot
do."

'"I am the Lord's servant," said Mary; "may it happen to me as
you have said."'

From *Luke 1*

PRAYER
Thank you, Father, that Mary was willing to become the
mother of our Lord Jesus Christ. Help us to be willing
servants, whatever your plan for our lives. Amen

'Dear brother in Christ!'

'There is something . . . I owe to television that has brought me great comfort and joy . . . People quite often come up to me and, by one means or another, indicate that they, too, are Christians. Thus, when I'm leaving a restaurant, perhaps, a waiter comes padding after me and silently shakes my hand. Or, in of all crazy places, a make-up room, the girl who is attending to my ancient visage whispers in my ear, "I love the Lord". Or turning a corner, I come face to face with a West Indian, who, with an enormous grin of recognition, shouts out, "Dear brother in Christ!" . . . I could go on giving examples for ever.

'The experience is altogether delightful, but there is more in it than that. Notice that it never for a moment occurs to me to want to know whether these diverse people are educated or uneducated . . . Roman Catholics or Anglicans . . . or brown or white or yellow, what their IQ is, how much they earn, or what sort of accent they have. All the different categories we have devised just don't apply. There is but one category: our common fellowship in Christ. This, it seems to me, is a true image of Christian brotherhood. Work-a-day encounters, glorified by participation in a common lot, as children of the same God, redeemed by the same Saviour, destined for the same salvation. Marx saw . . . a victorious proletariat living happily ever after in a society in which government has withered away. Bunyan saw us as souls, for whom, when our pilgrimage is over, the trumpets will sound on the other side. I am for Bunyan.'

From *Christ and the Media*, by Malcolm Muggeridge

See also 24 March

27 March

Palm Sunday falls on the Sunday before Easter Day. You can read the story in Mark 11. G.K.Chesterton – essayist, writer and poet – tells the story from the donkey's point of view.

The Donkey

When fishes flew and forests walked
And figs grew upon thorn,
Some moment when the moon was blood
Then surely I was born.

With monstrous head and sickening cry
And ears like errant wings,
The devil's walking parody
On all four-footed things.

The tattered outlaw of the earth,
Of ancient crooked will;
Starve, scourge, deride me: I am dumb,
I keep my secret still.

Fools! For I also had my hour;
One far fierce hour and sweet:
There was a shout about my ears,
And palms before my feet.

28 March

Anna Sewell, whose birthday was in March 1820, was deeply concerned for animal welfare – she particularly wished to see an end to the cruel treatment of horses.

In 1924, a Texas cow-puncher was sentenced to prison for one month for ill-treating a pony – and ordered to read Anna Sewell's book, *Black Beauty*, at least three times! It was not until 1941 that the RSPCA finally persuaded undertakers in Britain to abolish the use of bearing-reins for funeral horses.

Anna would have been glad

'The worst of the almost innumerable cruelties practised on [the horse's] matchless frame.' That was how one writer in 1845 described the use of the bearing-rein on carriage horses. This rein was attached to bit and harness for the sole purpose of making the horse arch his neck and hold his head high – in other words, to *look* good.

Vets recognized that the bearing-rein caused intense suffering to the horse, making breathing difficult and causing great pain in neck and head. Correspondents wrote letters to *The Times* and vets spoke out, but it was Anna Sewell in *Black Beauty* who did most to stamp out its use.

When Anna died, her friends and relatives gathered in the upstairs drawing-room to await the arrival of the funeral cortège. When the horse-drawn hearse drew up outside, Anna's mother exclaimed, 'This will never do!' and hurried downstairs. She talked urgently to the undertaker, who listened quietly, then went from one horse to the next, removing the offending bearing-reins. Anna would have been glad.

See also 23 March

29 March

Charles Wesley died on 29 March 1788.

Think big!

Charles Wesley was the youngest son of Samuel and Susanna Wesley, their eighteenth child. Although he was a great preacher like his brother John, he is best known for the hymns he wrote – about 6,500 in all! They are some of the greatest hymns in the English language and many are still sung today.

These are just some of the happenings that inspired Charles to write a hymn: his conversion; his marriage; an earthquake panic; the defeat of Prince Charles Edward at Culloden; the Gordon riots; the festivals of the Christian church; the doctrines of the Christian faith; striking scenes in biblical history; the death of a friend.

This great hymn was written in May 1738, at the time when both John and Charles Wesley found peace with God through faith in Christ. So which of them wrote this hymn? Most hymn-books give Charles the credit.

> And can it be that I should gain
> An interest in the Saviour's blood?
> Died he for me, who caused his pain?
> For me, who him to death pursued?
> Amazing love! How can it be
> That thou, my God, shouldst die for me!
>
> Long my imprisoned spirit lay
> Fast bound in sin and nature's night;
> Thine eye diffused a quickening ray –
> I woke, the dungeon flamed with light;
> My chains fell off, my heart was free,
> I rose, went forth, and followed thee.

30 March

On 30 March 1945, Mother Maria, born Elizabeth Pilenko, died in Ravensbruck.

The greatest love

It was a spring day, a day of hope. But there was no hope on the faces of the prisoners who filed across to line up outside what the guards called the 'bath-house'. Every day at roll call, they would shout out the names of those who were to go there. Those who went never returned.

Life at Ravensbruck concentration camp was terrible. With only a bowl of thin soup and a crust each day for food, the prisoners were expected to work in the stone quarries outside the barbed-wire enclosure, or to chop wood in the forest. Some were forced to dig the trenches that would become their graves. They were there because they were Jews, and Hitler had determined to exterminate the whole Jewish nation.

On this particular day, one young girl did not wait quietly outside the bath-house. She knew that a horrible death lay within, and she began to scream with terror. The guards moved threateningly towards her, but someone else was first at her side. Mother Maria, born a wealthy Russian, but by choice a poor nun, was at Ravensbruck for defying German orders and helping Jews in distress. Now she put a comforting arm round the young girl's shoulder.

'Don't be frightened,' she whispered. 'I'll come with you.' So together they entered the deadly gas chamber. Some say that the girl went free and that Mother Maria took her place.

BIBLE VERSES
Jesus said: 'The greatest love a person can have for his friends is to give his life for them.'
From *John 15*

Paul said: 'God has shown us how much he loves us – it was while we were still sinners that Christ died for us! By his death we are now put right with God.'
From *Romans 5*

31 March

John Donne, poet and clergyman, died on 31 March 1631.

Death conquered

There is only one effigy in St Paul's Cathedral that remains from the previous building and survived the Great Fire of London. It is that of John Donne, Dean of St Paul's.

In an age without many of the modern entertainments we take for granted, people flocked to listen to famous preachers, and sermons often lasted several hours. Crowds, including the king himself, came to hear John Donne.

Plague, war and disease made death a common happening for young as well as old. Donne wrote and thought much about death, and though we may think that morbid, he would probably think us foolish or cowardly to ignore something we must all face.

But for Donne, death was not a final disaster. Christ had conquered death:

Death, be not proud, though some have called thee
Mighty and dreadful, for thou art not so;
For those whom thou thinkest thou dost overthrow
Die not, poor death; nor yet canst thou kill me.

One short sleep past, we wake eternally,
And death shall be no more. Death, thou shalt die!
John Donne

1 April

Practical jokes

The first of April, some do say,
Is set apart for All Fools' Day.
But why people call it so
Nor I nor they themselves do know.

That rhyme appeared in *Poor Robin's Almanack* of 1760. If they didn't know then the origin of April Fools' Day, there isn't much hope of our knowing now. But the first mention of the day for tricks and practical jokes goes back to 1698, so the custom must be at least 300 years old.

Poet Frederick Harvey thinks God showed a sense of humour when he created the animals – and us!

When God had finished the stars and whirl of coloured suns
He turned his mind from big things to fashion little ones,
Beautiful tiny things (like daisies) he made, and then
He made the comical ones in case the minds of men
    Should stiffen and become
    Dull, humourless and glum:
And so forgetful of their Maker be
As to take even themselves – *quite seriously*.
Caterpillars and cats are lively and excellent puns:
All God's jokes are good – even the practical ones!
And as for the duck, I think God must have smiled a bit
Seeing those bright eyes blink on the day he fashioned it.
And he's probably laughing still at the sound that came out
    of its bill!

2 April

On 2 April 1974, Anna Vasilievna Chertkova was given a
court hearing in the USSR.

A place to call home?

The concrete wall, three and a half metres high, is topped by a
metre of barbed wire. Beyond the wall is a wooden fence and
between the two a fence of barbed wire with a twelve-volt electric
current running through it. Between the fences, armed guards
patrol night and day. Behind the impenetrable walls of this
Tashkent 'hospital' are murderers and the criminally insane.
Anna Chertkova is also imprisoned there.

Anna's father died for his faith in a labour camp when Anna
was only ten. All her life she has suffered persecution as a
Christian. Although she worked as a government clerk, the
authorities refused to give her anywhere to live. Nothing
daunted, Anna began to build her own house but the militia
arrived and bulldozed it down. She put up a straw cabin and for
two bitter winters made that her home. Then a 'home' was found
for her. Anna was arrested and sentenced to indefinite detention
in the Tashkent Psychiatric Hospital – that grim fortress of
concrete and barbed wire where she still lives.

She is poorly fed but crammed full of drugs. If she talks about
her faith, she is dosed even more heavily. Her mail is censored
and guards are present when visitors come. Anna has no way to
protest her innocence or mental fitness. Her only crime – or
illness – is to be a Christian.

PRAYER
Lord, hear our prayer for all in prison or psychiatric hospital
because they have bravely confessed their faith in you. Help
us to find practical ways to help to bring about their release.
Amen

3 April

'When the sweet showers of April fall . . . then people long
to go on pilgrimages.'
From the Prologue to *The Canterbury Tales*, by Geoffrey Chaucer

Chaucer's parson

Geoffrey Chaucer was a busy civil servant looking after customs
and excise and the maintenance of walls, ditches and sewers for
the king of England in the fourteenth century. He also found time
to write poems – including *The Canterbury Tales*.

Pilgrimages were popular in the Middle Ages and 'package
tours' were arranged to faraway places. In England, the tomb of
the martyr Thomas à Becket was a favourite shrine. As Chaucer's
imaginary band of pilgrims rode to Canterbury together, they
took turns to tell stories to pass the time. First Chaucer describes
his pilgrims, bitterly satirizing the rogues and hypocrites among
the church dignitaries. But for the parson and his ploughman
brother, Chaucer has only kind words. Their goodness shines.

A holy-minded man of good renown
There was, and poor, the parson to a town,
Yet he was rich in holy thought and work . . .

He found sufficiency in little things.
Wide was his parish with houses far asunder
Yet he neglected not in rain or thunder,
In sickness or in grief, to pay a call
On the remotest, whether great or small,
Upon his feet, and in his hand a stave.
This noble example to his sheep he gave,
First following the word before he taught it
And it was from the gospel he had caught it . . .
His business was to show a fair behaviour
And draw men thus to Heaven and their Saviour.

From Nevill Coghill's translation of *The Canterbury Tales*, by Geoffrey Chaucer

See also 24 October, 29 December

4 April

On 4 April 1968, Martin Luther King, leader of the negro civil rights movement in the USA, was assassinated.

In August 1963, about 250,000 people, black and white, marched in Washington to demonstrate the need for legislation to integrate blacks with whites. Dr King made one of his most memorable speeches to the thousands packed in the capital. The last words, from the Negro spiritual 'Free at last!', form the inscription carved on his grave.

'I have a dream'

'I have a dream that one day on the red hills of Georgia the sons of former slaves and the sons of former slave-owners will be able to sit down together at the table of brotherhood . . .

'I have a dream that one day every valley shall be exalted and every hill and mountain shall be made low. The rough places will be made plain and the crooked places will be made straight . . . With this faith we will be able to hew out of the mountains of despair the stone of hope. With this faith we will be able to work together, to pray together, to struggle together, to go to jail together, to stand up for freedom together, knowing we will be free one day . . .

'When we allow freedom to ring from every town and every hamlet, from every state and every city, we will be able to speed up that day when all of God's children, black and white men, Jews and Gentiles, Protestants and Catholics, will be able to join hands and sing in the words of the old Negro spiritual, "Free at last! Free at last! Great God Almighty, we are free at last."'

From *My Life with Martin Luther King*, by Coretta King

See also 15 and 16 January

5 April

Robert Raikes, pioneer of Sunday schools, died on 5 April 1811.

Sooty Alley

It was Sunday – a day for the rich and respectable citizens of Gloucester to go to church. But as Robert Raikes, wealthy owner and editor of *The Gloucester Journal*, walked quietly through the city, he stopped in concern at the sight of a bunch of children shrieking and fighting together. He asked a bystander the reason. She explained that the children lived in the houses around and had nothing better to do on Sundays than fight and gamble. Every other day of the week they worked twelve hours or more in the local pin factory. On Sundays they ran wild.

Raikes was deeply concerned for these dirty, swearing scraps of humanity. He cared because he was a Christian, and he determined to try to give them some education as a first step towards reform.

He discussed his plans with others and a Sunday school was first opened in 1780 in Sooty Alley, where the chimney-sweeps lived. The Bible was taught and also used as a tool to teach reading.

Raikes used another tool. As the owner and editor of a newspaper, he was able to run a bold and long campaign on behalf of these children. His new school got wide publicity. People in other parts of the country began similar schemes. The Sunday school movement began in earnest.

6 April

On 6 April 1968, Eldridge Cleaver, the American Black Panther leader, miraculously avoided death in a police raid.

Later, when he met Jesus Christ, he recognized that God had a purpose in saving him from death on that memorable night. 'I'm just so glad to have found the Lord,' he said in a TV interview long afterwards. 'Jesus completely changed my life . . . If I had known this Jesus long ago, how different my life would have been! But it's beautiful! . . . It's better late than never!'

Pigs and Panthers

Police bullets whined and ricocheted around them as they lay still on the basement floor. 'It was like being the Indians in all the cowboy movies I had ever seen,' Cleaver said afterwards. A lull – and the two men scrambled to their feet and began to put up a barricade of boxes. A tear-gas canister lobbed in at the window stopped further efforts. The cellar filled with stinging, blinding gas, and another hail of bullets showered them. One exploded against Cleaver's leg, wounding him badly. They staggered out into the blackness of the night, illumined by the strong police searchlights. Then they fell exhausted.

'The pigs pointed to a squad car parked in the middle of the street and told us to run to it. I told them I couldn't run. Then they snatched little Bobby and shoved him forward. Bobby ran and was shot dead.' Cleaver believed it was a police plot and that, had he been able to run, they would have shot him too.

Black Panthers, like their namesakes, would not attack, but were ready to defend their cause to the death. Their cause was that of the black people and their target was communist power. They hated the white police, who in turn determined to break the power of the Panthers. The deadliest of those Black Panthers was Eldridge Cleaver.

Continued on 7 April

7 April

Eldridge Cleaver, leader of the anti-white, communist Black
Panthers, took refuge in the South of France from arrest in
his own country, USA.

Black Panther meets Christ

'One night, in this very depressed state of mind, I found myself
sitting on my twelfth-storey balcony under this clear Mediterranean sky with all the stars and a very full moon. The shadows on
the moon suddenly formed into a face. It was my face! I saw
myself in the moon. Then there was a succession of mostly
bearded men . . . Fidel Castro . . . Karl Marx . . . Mao Tse-
tung. Then there was one final face – Jesus Christ! It really upset
me because I had not gone around thinking of Jesus. I was afraid I
was coming unglued. I started crying then, uncontrollably. I fell
down on my knees and said parts of the Lord's Prayer and the
twenty-third psalm. I had the Bible we kept through my travels. I
found that Bible and began to read – the twenty-third psalm
again. After I don't know how long I got up and went inside. I
went to sleep. My sleep had always been so broken. But after that
experience I had the most peaceful sleep that I ever had.

'That was my real confrontation with Jesus Christ and the
beginning of my life turning round. It was a focus on Jesus –
because it was a rejection of the others . . . My life has turned
180 degrees. I would call it a conversion experience because I was
not the same after it as I was before.'

Excerpts from interviews given by Eldridge Cleaver in the USA

POSTSCRIPT
Cleaver had been travelling from one communist country to
another, unable to return to the USA for fear of arrest. After
his conversion, he gave himself up. He was freed on bail
given by a white American businessman he once would
have hated – now a brother in Christ.

See also 6 April

8 April

William Law died in April 1761.

William Law was a teacher and a cleric. He spent ten years as chaplain and tutor to the Gibbon household, whose grandson was to become author of *The Rise and Fall of the Roman Empire*. Many people came to visit and consult him, including John Wesley.

Be thankful!

'Would you know who is the greatest saint in the world? It is not he who prays most or fasts most; it is not he who gives most alms, but it is he who is always thankful to God, who receives everything as an instance of God's goodness and has a heart always ready to praise God for it.

'If anyone would tell you the shortest, surest way to all happiness and perfection, he must tell you to make a rule to thank and praise God for everything that happens to you. Whatever seeming calamity happens to you, if you thank and praise God for it, you turn it into a blessing. Could you therefore work miracles you could not do more for yourself than by this thankful spirit; it turns all that it touches into happiness.'

From William Law's *Serious Call to a Devout and Holy Life*, 1728

BIBLE VERSES
'Praise the Lord! Give thanks to the Lord, because he is good.'
From *Psalm 106*

'Be thankful in all circumstances. This is what God wants.'
From *1 Thessalonians 5*

See also 9 April

9 April

Since his death in April 1761, William Law's writings have
continued to influence many people.

In Law's day, larks and linnets were sold in cages. He would
buy them so that he could set them free. His character was
a blend of great gentleness and strict personal discipline.

'Slugabeds'

William Law believed in getting up early. He himself rose at five
for prayers, then went to milk the cows. After that, he cooked
gruel, or porridge, for the beggars who came to the Gibbon great
house for breakfast. But it was not till nine o'clock that he
indulgently woke the rest of the sleeping 'slugabeds'.

Early to rise

'I take it for granted that every Christian, that is in health, is up
early in the morning; for it is much more reasonable to suppose a
person up early because he is a Christian than because . . . he
has business that wants him. If he is to be blamed as a slothful
drone that chooses the lazy indulgence of sleep to worldly
business, how much more is he to be reproached that would
rather lie folded up in a bed than raising his heart to God in praise
and adoration! . . .

'Receive . . . every day as a resurrection from death, as a new
enjoyment of life; . . . meet every rising sun with such
sentiments of God's goodness as if you had seen all things new
created on your account; and under the sense of so great a
blessing, let your joyful heart praise and magnify so good and
glorious a Creator.'

From Law's *Serious Call to a Devout and Holy Life*

See also 8 April

10 April

William Booth, founder of the Salvation Army, was born on 10 April 1829.

In 1980, the Salvation Army in the United States celebrated its centenary. A sixteen-year-old Salvation Army girl had emigrated from England to America, and, with her parents, began evangelistic meetings in an old shed. In response, the Salvation Army sent a group to New York, arriving March 1880.

'Ash-barrel Jimmy'

New York did not know what to make of these newcomers. The little group of Salvation Army members from England would stand at street corners, singing their new-fangled hymns. The tunes were familiar – *My Old Kentucky Home* and *The Old Folks at Home* – but the words strange. The preaching was different too – not at all what they were used to in church. Most of the group were women, quite young ones, and uneducated.

So the Salvation Army tried a different tack. They appealed to the theatres in the city to give up their Sunday performance in favour of a Salvation Army meeting. None was willing, except Harry Hill, who ran what was known as a 'disreputable den' of a music-hall. But even he was not prepared to stand down for the visiting singers and preachers. He merely billed them as part of the performance, a gimmick that he hoped might draw the crowds. The crowds turned up all right, but the Salvation Army contribution went off like a damp squib. Most thought it good only for a laugh.

The little group left the theatre feeling that their attempts to preach the gospel had been in vain. But someone was waiting patiently for them in the damp fog at the stage door.

'It's Ash-barrel Jimmy,' they were informed.

As they chatted to the down-and-out tramp they learned how he had come by his nickname. He had once been discovered dead drunk, upside-down in a barrel. Every human being mattered to them and they invited Jimmy to the meeting they had arranged for the next night. Jimmy turned up, and the message of the gospel changed his whole life.

Ash-barrel Jimmy was the first Salvation Army convert in the United States of America.

See also 24 June, 2 and 20 July

11 April

In April 1769, John Newton's prayer meeting moved to larger premises.

Write a hymn – it's Tuesday!

Four prayer meetings a week – that was the general rule in the little village of Olney in Bedfordshire when the Reverend John Newton was in charge. The Tuesday evening prayer meeting became so popular that Newton wrote to a friend: 'We are going to remove our prayer meeting to the great room in the Great House. It is a noble place with a parlour behind it and holds one hundred and thirty people conveniently.'

The highlight of the Tuesday meeting was a brand-new hymn, composed each week by John Newton himself or by his friend William Cowper, the poet, who was living at Olney at the time. Many of their hymns, still sung, were written specially for the Tuesday prayer meetings. When the move to the Great House took place, *two* new hymns were written. Prayer meetings were fun!

> Glorious things of thee are spoken,
> Zion, city of our God;
> He whose word cannot be broken
> Formed thee for his own abode.
> On the Rock of Ages founded,
> What can shake thy sure repose?
> With salvation's walls surrounded,
> Thou may'st smile at all thy foes.
> Written by John Newton for a Tuesday prayer meeting at Olney

See also 6 March

12 April

Easter is one of the movable feasts in the Christian
calendar. Jesus was crucified at the time of the Jewish
Passover – and the date of that is fixed according to the
moon. It is often at about this time in April.

The road to the cross

CENTURION (*shouting*): Come on! Come on! What's the matter now?

3rd SOLDIER: Prisoner's down again, Centurion.

CENTURION: Well, don't stand staring. Get him on his legs again.

CROWD (*helpfully*): Chuck a bucket of water over him . . . Let him get his breath back. Give him a drink . . . He's only shamming . . . Take the whip to him.

CENTURION: Stand back there!

BRUTAL VOICE: Come on magician! Do your stuff! Take up your cross and walk!

(*Laughter*)

4th SOLDIER: Nothing doing, Centurion. He's all in.

CENTURION: Sure? Let's have a look at him . . . Now my man, it's no good trying it on . . . No, Publius, you're right . . . Let him be a moment.

3rd SOLDIER: I think we flogged him too hard . . .

4th SOLDIER: He's coming round.

CENTURION: That's a mercy. If he died on our hands we'd be for it. Law says they must be crucified alive – (*sotto voce*) – poor devils!

SIMON OF CYRENE (*shouting from the crowd*): And a wicked law it is! Roman law. Bloody and cruel . . .

CENTURION: That'll do my lad . . . Can he walk now? . . . Wait . . . Steady . . . give him a hand, he can't see where he's going.

3rd SOLDIER: What's he groping about for?

4th SOLDIER: He's stretching out his hands for the cross.

3rd SOLDIER: Well I'll be – (*The soldiers laugh, not unkindly*)

CENTURION: This is the most willing prisoner I ever saw. Goes like a lamb to the slaughter.

From *The Man Born to be King*, by Dorothy L. Sayers

See also 6 January, 14 and 16 December

13 April

George Frederick Handel was a German-born composer who settled in England in 1712. He wrote operas, orchestral works and oratorios, the most famous of which is *Messiah*.

'All heaven before me'

On 13 April 1742, a notice appeared in the Dublin papers about the first performance of Handel's oratorio, *Messiah*.

'The doors will open at eleven and the Oratorio will begin at twelve. The favour of the ladies is requested not to come with hoops this day to the Musick Hall in Fishamble Street. The gentlemen are desired to come without their swords.'

Crowds were expected to attend, and the fashionable hooped petticoats would have taken up valuable space. Swords could be dangerous in a crush. Sure enough, a capacity audience of 700 filled the hall, and hundreds more waited outside in the street.

Seven months earlier, Handel had sat alone in the little front room of a house in Brook Street, London. His health was broken and many people thought his career was ended. He looked at some words sent to him by a writer called Jennens. The words were not Jennens' own but taken from all parts of the Bible and all telling of Jesus, the Messiah. Handel began to compose the music to fit the words. For twenty-four days he did not leave the house. His servant brought him food, but he often left it untouched. One day, the servant came in to find Handel composing the 'Hallelujah Chorus'. He sat at the table with the tears streaming down his face.

'I did think I did see all heaven before me, and the great God himself,' he exclaimed.

14 April

One of the most telling facts about Jesus' resurrection is that his own disciples were more surprised than anyone to discover that he was alive.

Traveller in disguise

'Two of Jesus' followers were going to a village named Emmaus about eleven kilometres from Jerusalem, and they were talking to each other about all the things that had happened. As they talked and discussed, Jesus himself drew near and walked along with them; . . . somehow they did not recognize him. Jesus said to them, "What are you talking about . . . ?"

'They stood still, with sad faces. One of them, named Cleopas, asked him, "Are you the only visitor in Jerusalem who doesn't know the things that have been happening there these last few days?"

'"What things?" he asked.

'"The things that happened to Jesus of Nazareth," they answered. " . . . Our chief priests and rulers handed him over to be sentenced to death, and he was crucified. And we had hoped that he would be the one who was going to set Israel free! Besides all that, this is now the third day since it happened . . . "

'Then Jesus said to them, "How foolish you are, how slow you are to believe everything the prophets said! Was it not necessary for the Messiah to suffer these things and then to enter his glory?" And Jesus explained to them what was said about himself in all the Scriptures . . .

'As they came near to the village to which they were going, Jesus acted as if he were going farther; but they held him back, saying, "Stay with us; the day is almost over and it is getting dark." So he went in to stay with them. He sat down to eat with them, took the bread, and said the blessing; then he broke the bread and gave it to them. Then their eyes were opened and they recognized him, but he disappeared from their sight.'

From *Luke 24*

15 April

Medal for Malta
'Buckingham Palace, 15 April 1942

'The Governor, Malta
   'To honour her brave people I award the George Cross to the Island Fortress of Malta to bear witness to a heroism and devotion that will long be famous in history.
'George R'

The sirens wailed in Valletta, on the besieged island of Malta, but the governor-general, Sir William Dobbie, went on writing at his desk in the palace. Two young army officers approached him apologetically: 'There's a raid on, sir.'
   'Yes, I know,' the general replied and went on writing. Then he looked up and added, 'I must finish what I am doing but I think the roof over there will be the best place to watch from. I will be up there in a minute. I just want to finish this page.'
   It never occurred to General Dobbie to be frightened, and the people of the island took their cue from him. His courage and faith in God won their trust and affection. 'If we do as *he* tells us and trust in God, all will be well,' one of the islanders said.
   Dobbie determined that the beleaguered island would not only defend itself from attack by air or sea, but also use its prime position to take the offensive against the enemy who threatened the freedom of the world.
   In recognition of that contribution and courage, the whole island was awarded the George Cross. It is the only time that a community rather than an individual has been given this highest British civil award.

BIBLE VERSE
God said: 'Come back and quietly trust in me. Then you will be strong and secure.'
From *Isaiah 30*

16 April

Easter is an occasion for very special celebration in the
Russian Orthodox Church.

Christ is risen!

'This midnight service remained for ever after one of the happiest
and most vivid memories of Nekhlyudov's life.

'The service had already begun when he rode into the
churchyard out of the black night, relieved only here and there by
patches of white snow, his horse splashing through the water and
pricking its ears at the sight of the little lights round the church.

'Some peasants . . . led him to a dry place to dismount, tied up
his horse and conducted him into the church, which was full of
people.

'On the right stood the men: old men in home-spun
caftans; . . . the younger ones in new cloth tunics with bright-
coloured belts round their waists, and top-boots. On the left were
the women, with red silk kerchiefs on their heads, sleeveless
velveteen jackets, bright red blouses and gay-coloured
skirts . . . The men were crossing themselves and bowing,
shaking back their hair when they brought their heads up; the
women, especially the old women, riveting their faded eyes upon
one of the many ikons . . . and made the sign of the
cross . . . The children imitated their elders and prayed
earnestly whenever anyone was looking at them . . .

'Everything was festive, solemn, happy and beautiful: the
clergy in their silver cloth vestments with gold crosses; . . . the
choir singers in their best clothes, with their hair well oiled; the
gay dancing melodies of the Easter hymns; the continual blessing
of the people by the clergy with their triple flower-bedecked
candles; and the ever-repeated salutation: "Christ is risen! Christ
is risen!" It was all lovely, but best of all was Katusha in her white
dress and blue sash, with the little red bow on her dark head, and
her sparkling rapturous eyes.'

From *Resurrection*, by Leo Tolstoy

Continued 17 April; see also 7 and 8 November

17 April

The kiss of peace

'During the pause between the first and second service Nekhlyudov went out of the church . . . It was light enough to see but the sun had not yet risen. People were sitting on the graves in the churchyard. Katusha had remained in the church, and Nekhlyudov stopped, waiting for her.

'The congregation was still coming out and, clattering with their nailed boots on the flagstones, walked down the steps and scattered in the churchyard . . .

'A very old man with shaking head, his aunt's pastry-cook, stopped Nekhlyudov in order to give him the Easter kiss, and his wife, an old woman with a wrinkled Adam's apple showing under her silk neckerchief, took a saffron-yellow egg from her pocket-handkerchief and gave it to him. At the same time a smiling muscular young peasant in a new sleeveless coat and green belt came up.

'"Christ is risen!" he said . . . and coming close to Nekhlyudov enveloped him in his peculiar agreeable peasant odour, and, tickling him with his curly beard, kissed him three times squarely on the mouth with his firm fresh lips . . .

'[Katusha] had come out into the porch . . . and stopped, distributing alms to the beggars. A beggar with a red scar in place of a nose went up to Katusha. She took something from her pocket-handkerchief, gave it to him and then drew nearer to him and without showing the least disgust – on the contrary, her eyes shone with joy as brightly as ever – kissed him three times. And while she was exchanging kisses with the beggar her eyes met Nekhlyudov's with a look as if she were asking, "Am I doing right?"

'"Yes, yes, dear, everything is right, everything is just as it should be, and I love you."'

From *Resurrection*, by Leo Tolstoy

See also 16 April, 7 and 8 November

18 April

On 18 April 1521, Martin Luther made his defence at the
Diet of Worms.

'Here I stand'

Something had to be done about Martin Luther, the religious
authorities decided. His preaching was bad enough – but his
books were worse. And they were rolling off the newly-invented
printing presses and selling like hot cakes. So Luther was
summoned to appear before a court presided over by Charles V,
the Holy Roman Emperor.

A big, imposing man, Dr Ecken, solemnly asked Luther
whether he was ready to renounce his writings. Luther maintained that he would do so on one condition only. If anyone, even
a child, could prove him wrong *from Scripture*, then he would
retract. In vain, his accuser insisted that all heretics claimed to
base their beliefs on the Bible. Luther was too sure of his ground.
He stood for:

Faith alone – Men and women are freely forgiven by God not by
good works or penances, but by putting faith in Jesus Christ.

Grace alone – Salvation comes through God's undeserved love
and goodness.

The Bible alone – No church rules, decrees or traditions have
any weight if they contradict the teaching of the Bible.

Dr Ecken pleaded: 'For the last time I ask you, Martin. Do you
or do you not repudiate your books and the errors they contain?'

'I cannot and will not recant,' Luther replied, 'for to go against
conscience is neither right nor healthy. Here I stand, I cannot do
otherwise.'

See also 18 February, 31 October

19 April

On Easter Sunday, 19 April 1981, music from Adrian Snell's modern cantata, *The Passion,* was broadcast.

Adrian Snell graduated at Leeds College of Music. He plays piano, double-bass, cello, electric and acoustic guitar, organ, percussion and synthesizer. He composes and sings his own music, which reflects classical, jazz and rock influences.

Music with a message

Adrian Snell is a musician and he's also a Christian – a Christian who wants to sing about his faith. He's not concerned only with the easy bits of belief, but with the deeper problems – such as how to reconcile suffering with a loving God. He is one of the few artistes to record on a Christian label *and* reach a secular audience too. Music from *The Passion* and *The Virgin* have been broadcast. Adrian believes that what he sings is for everyone to hear – not just Christians, who know much of his message already. So he is glad of the success he has achieved. He does not believe that success should lead to an inflated ego. It's how you handle success that counts.

From an interview in *New Music*

PRAYER THOUGHT
Have you prayed for your favourite Christian 'superstar' lately? Why not today?

20 April

On 20 April 1653, Oliver Cromwell expelled the Long Parliament by force.

'Take away this bauble!'

There was not a moment to lose. Oliver Cromwell did not even wait to change his grey worsted stockings for something more suitable for parliament. Even now the vital bill was being debated and only an urgent summons from a friend had brought him to the House in time.

Cromwell posted a guard within call, then entered and waited for the Speaker of the House to put the motion that 'this bill do now pass'. Then he intervened. He reminded the House of the abuses that they had fought in battle to abolish. Now they wanted to maintain parliament in their own hands as a permanent body, with no freely elected members.

Cromwell paced up and down. 'The Lord has done with you,' he concluded and, calling the guard, ordered the Speaker to step down. Finally, the Speaker and all the members filed out of the chamber, leaving Cromwell and his soldiers in possession.

'Take away this bauble!' Cromwell shouted, snatching up the mace from the table. He was determined that a new rule of justice should begin.

CROMWELL'S LAST PRAYER
Lord, I come to thee for thy people. Thou hast made me, though very unworthy, a mean instrument to do them some good. Lord, however thou do dispose of me, continue and go on to do good for them. Give them consistency of judgement, one heart and mutual love: go on to deliver them and make the name of Christ glorious in the world.
Amen

Continued on 21 April

21 April

The tolerant Protector

When the new parliament assembled, Cromwell told them, 'You are called with a high call and why should we be afraid to think that this may be the door to usher in the things that God has promised?'

But in spite of his cocksureness that God was on his side, he was determined that others who thought differently should be left in peace. He refused to punish Roman Catholics in England who did not observe the state form of worship. He dealt kindly with the new, enthusiastic Quaker sect, and showed sympathy for the Jews, who had been bitterly persecuted by Christians for centuries. After a 300-year ban, they were again allowed into the country and given freedom of worship.

Cromwell's sympathies were with ordinary people who had no power or influence. He immediately pardoned some of the small-time criminals who had been sentenced to death. He hated the practice of hanging for petty crimes. 'To hang a man for six and eightpence and I know not what, to hang for a trifle and acquit for murder – to see men lose their lives for petty matters, this is a thing God will reckon for.'

PRAYER
Lord, help me to stand up for the rights of the underdog and the weak today. Amen

See also 20 April

22 April

Schoolgirl star

A-levels loomed ahead and Dana – or plain Rosemary Brown as
she was at school – had in any case decided against a career in
music. But in the Christmas holidays, the phone rang. She was
asked to take part in the contest to find Ireland's representative
for the Eurovision Song Contest. A check with the headmistress
of her convent school – who agreed – and Dana was off to sing *All
Kinds of Everything*. She won – and that meant asking for more
time off school to sing for Ireland in Amsterdam in April.

The rest of the story is musical history. Dana became the
youngest singer ever to win the trophy. No wonder that reporters
soon besieged the Browns' home in Bogside Derry!

Dana had been brought up in a warm, loving Roman Catholic
family. Her faith went back as far as she could remember, and,
even when she did go through a bad patch, a sympathetic priest
had helped her. After her success, she began to meet Christians
from many different backgrounds whose experience widened
and strengthened her own. She went on singing and telling others
of her faith.

See also 23 April

23 April

Singer without a voice

Dana sat up in bed and for the first time since her operation felt well enough to look at the paper. A headline caught her eye: ONLY 50/50 CHANCE OF REGAINING VOICE SAYS DANA'S DOCTOR.

'What rubbish!' Dana thought; typical of the press to blow things up out of all proportion. It was true that the first operation had been unsuccessful and that she had needed a second urgent one for a growth on her throat. But the seriousness of it had not struck her.

Now she questioned her doctor and he admitted that the papers were right. Though tests showed that the growth had not been malignant, Dana's voice did not come back. A year later she still could not sing – a singer without a voice.

One day, she sat at her kitchen table, deeply depressed, and prayed, 'Lord, you've got to help me. I don't know where to turn. I don't know what to do.'

Already two teachers had been unsuccessful, but Dana was sure that God was telling her to ask her doctor about a singing teacher. She phoned him – to find that he had been meaning to ring her for a couple of weeks to tell her of someone who might be able to help. Through *that* singing teacher Dana learned to sing again.

See also 22 April

24 April

Anthony Trollope, novelist, was born on 24 April 1815.

Trollope's *Chronicles of Barsetshire* centre on life in the cathedral close. Both good and bad religious people are convincingly portrayed. In this extract, Mr Harding, once warden of a charity hospital for old men, has been wrongly accused and sacked, then later tricked out of reappointment. With typical Christian generosity, he decides to introduce the new warden to the inmates.

'All for the best'

'It was a bright clear morning, though in November, that Mr Harding and Mr Quiverful, arm in arm, walked through the hospital gate . . . Now that he re-entered . . . with another warden under his wing he did so with . . . quiet step and calm demeanour . . . one might have said that he was merely returning with a friend . . . '

'Arm in arm they walked into the inner quadrangle of the building and there the five old men met them . . .

'"I am very glad to know that at last you have a new warden," said Mr Harding in a very cheery voice.

'"We be very old for any change," said one of them, "but we do suppose it be all for the best."

'"Certainly – certainly it is for the best . . . It is a great satisfaction to me to know that so good a man is coming to take care of you and that it is no stranger but a friend of my own . . . "

'"What I can do to fill the void which [Mr Harding] left here, I will do," [Mr Quiverful said]. "But to you who have known him I can never be the same well-loved friend and father that he has been."

'"No sir, no", said old Bunce . . . "no one can be that. Not if the new bishop sent a hangel to us out of heaven."'

From *Barchester Towers*, by Anthony Trollope

PRAYER
Father, make us large-hearted and forgiving and help us to show our generosity in our words and actions. For Jesus' sake. Amen

25 April

John Keble was born on 25 April 1792.

Red Letter Days

Saints' days meant holy days and holy days were holidays! People in the Middle Ages looked forward to them eagerly, as they were the only time off work, and fairs and processions as well as all kinds of celebrations took place. When *The Book of Common Prayer* was published in 1662, it was decided that the number of official saints' days should be whittled down to thirty-two. These were marked in red in the prayer-book and became known as 'red letter days', while every other day was printed in black.

The Puritans under Cromwell's rule went much further. No day was to be observed as holy except Sunday – the Lord's Day.

It was John Keble who helped to bring the events of the Christian calendar to everyone's notice again. He wrote a volume of poems, called *The Christian Year*, with a poem to celebrate every saint and commemorate every special festival.

BIBLE VERSE
Paul said: 'One person thinks that a certain day is more important than other days, while someone else thinks that all days are the same. Each one should firmly make up his own mind.'
From *Romans 14*

See also 28 May

26 April

Norman Rotherham is a Christian and a senior industrial relations officer with ACAS. His birthday is in April and he joined the Civil Service during this month too.

'Help! – Fire!'

A favourite quiz question: What do the initials ACAS stand for? Answer: Advisory Conciliation and Arbitration Service.

ACAS doesn't only function in British national strikes. It handles individual and industrial problems all over the country. It has three different ways of dealing with what Norman Rotherham sees as a kind of 'fire' hazard of smouldering troubles.

'Fire prevention'

Any firm with tricky pay or staffing problems can call in ACAS advisers to suggest what should be done. It often stops trouble breaking out.

'Fire-fighting'

If the advice isn't asked for – or doesn't work – arguments and trouble can flare up. Workers may already be on strike. That's when someone like Norman is called for to conciliate, or bring the two sides together. Sometimes, he says, the atmosphere is friendly and everyone sits round the table anxious to find a way out, with no bitterness. At other times, threats and insults fly across the table. 'I have to rule with a rod of iron,' he admits, 'and lay down the law.' A good conciliator helps each side to see the other's point of view and moderate his claims.

'Fire damage'

Even the best conciliator sometimes fails. If real trouble breaks out, ACAS can send an arbitrator or judge. Both sides are expected to accept his ruling. But Norman aims to see that it doesn't come to that. He hopes to put the fire out before it's really ablaze.

BIBLE VERSE
Jesus said: 'Happy are those who work for peace!'
From *Matthew 5*

See also 27 April

27 April

God's Conciliation and Arbitration Service
Conciliation
Paul said: 'God . . . through Christ changed us from enemies into his friends and gave us the task of making others his friends also. Our message is that God was making all mankind his friends through Christ . . .

'Here we are, then, speaking for Christ, as though God himself were making his appeal through us. We plead on Christ's behalf: let God change you from enemies into his friends!'
From *2 Corinthians 5*

'There is one God, and there is one who brings God and mankind together, the man Christ Jesus, who gave himself to redeem all mankind.'
From *1 Timothy 2*

Arbitration
'God . . . has fixed a day in which he will judge the whole world with justice by means of a man he has chosen. He has given proof of this to everyone by raising that man from death!'
From *Acts 17*

PRAYER
Thank you, Lord Jesus, for coming as a Conciliator, to make us God's friends. May we accept the offer of peace made possible through your death and resurrection, so that we need not fear when you come as Arbitrator and Judge.
Amen

See also 26 April

28 April

Anthony Ashley Cooper, seventh Earl of Shaftesbury, was born on 28 April 1801.

'The cause of the poor and friendless'

Anthony Ashley Cooper was about fourteen at the time and a pupil at Harrow.

'Walking one day down Harrow Hill, he heard from a side street the sound of a low song. He watched in fascinated horror as a party of drunken men came staggering round the corner carrying a rough coffin. Suddenly they let the coffin fall to the ground and broke into a flood of oaths and curses.'

The boy was horrified. There and then, according to his first biographer, 'Before the sound of the drunken song had died away, he had determined that with the help of God he would devote his life to pleading the cause of the poor and friendless.'

Ashley Cooper was born into a wealthy family, but he knew what it was to be desperately unhappy. His parents were uncaring and his early school-life pure misery. Only one person loved and cared for him – a servant girl who had become housekeeper in their London home. She gave little Ashley all the love he needed, and taught him to share her faith in a loving, caring God. Ashley was only seven when she died, but he never forgot her teaching and example. He did not picture God as a stern disciplinarian, like many in his time, but as a loving Father. His own unhappiness, his compassion and his deep commitment to Christ, led him to do more to lessen misery for others than any other person in England.

See also 1 and 8 October

29 April

Utchunu, a Hixkaryana Indian Christian living on the banks of the Amazon, died at the end of April 1971.

From fear to faith

Desmond and Grace Derbyshire, members of the Wycliffe Bible Translators' team, had visited Utchunu's tribe and it was Utchunu, with his quick-wittedness, who had helped them learn the language of the Hixkaryana and advised them as they translated the New Testament into a language which had never before been written down.

Utchunu, still busy hunting and fishing, collecting brazil nuts in the rainy season and clearing a new little bit of the forest every year for planting with crops, took time to think about this new religion.

It was some time before he decided to commit himself to Jesus Christ, but when he did, his life was transformed. No longer did he go to the shamans or witch-doctors for healing, nor did he fear the evil spirits that were said to haunt everything around and bring illness or bad luck.

Before his death from cancer, he wrote a journal, describing his experiences. His life had changed, not because he had given up the culture of his own people to adopt Western values, but because, as he said, 'When we belong to Jesus, we have to be different.' Love and trust displaced the old hates and fears.

See also 30 April

30 April

'Go good – I am with you'

Utchunu lay desperately ill in the hospital at Belem in Brazil. But he was not afraid.

Although he had lived all his life in a remote village – two hours' canoe-trip from the next village upstream – he had decided, when he became ill, to hitch-hike by boat the 700 miles to Belem, the big city at the mouth of the Amazon. Once he had arrived for the first time in the city with all its bewildering bustle and buildings, Utchunu had prayed: 'Father, I am going to this important man because I want to get into the hospital. Send your Spirit ahead of us.' God had answered him: 'Don't worry. Go good. You are with me and I am with you. I have brought you here because you are one of my people.'

Now, on top of the illness that had brought him to Belem, Utchunu caught smallpox. For forty-five days he was so ill that he was 'completely unable to eat meals, unable to see or talk, in a state of paralysis, not able to move at all,' as he described it later.

But he was able to tell the doctor, 'God will help me get better if it is his will.'

The doctor said, 'Forget about God. He can't help you.'

So Utchunu said to him, 'God has let me be sick so that he can show you his power. He will make me well again so that you can see his power.'

And Utchunu was healed of his smallpox.

Dialogue taken from *Utchunu's Journal*, as yet unpublished

See also 29 April

1 May

On 1 May 1851, Queen Victoria opened the Great Exhibition in Hyde Park, London.

The Great Exhibition was a show-case for Britain's engineering and manufacturing achievements. It was housed in the Crystal Palace, which was designed by Sir Joseph Paxton and made of glass on a framework of iron. In 1854, the Palace was taken down and re-erected in south London, where it was an exhibition and entertainment centre until it burned down in 1936.

For time – or for eternity?

'Dear Friend,

'It is there! The Crystal Palace is before you in all its glory; its banners are waving in the breeze and the light of heaven is shining through its walls.'

These were words that a visitor to the Great Exhibition, strolling through Hyde Park, might have idly read from a leaflet politely pressed into his hand by a young man.

George Williams and his friends in the newly-formed YMCA found in the Great Exhibition a superb opportunity to spread the gospel to the many thousands of people in London. They set about the campaign in a business-like way. London was divided into thirty-six districts, each in the charge of two young men, who were provided with a printed plan.

Every Sunday, 16,000 Christian tracts were to be distributed to the crowds converging on Hyde Park. The tracts were carefully written to capture attention and suit the interests and experience of those who took them. In some, the writer contrasted the splendour of the Crystal Palace – which would pass – with the far greater splendours of God's kingdom, which would never end. Then came the challenge:

'Are *you* safe for eternity?'

See also 11 October

2 May

Leonardo da Vinci, born in 1452, was the illegitimate son of a young Florentine noble and a country girl. He is perhaps the most versatile genius who has ever lived. He studied music, painting and poetry, then at fifty-four, began a career as an engineer. Centuries ahead of his time, he suggested the parachute, man-powered flight, the centrifugal pump and hydraulic press. He wrote pop songs and musicals. And he painted the famous *Mona Lisa* portrait and the mural of *The Last Supper.*

Tested by experiment

The guests were enjoying themselves hugely. Leonardo was official Master of Revels at the court of Milan and always provided brilliant entertainment. They gazed up in wonder at this latest party-trick of his. Charming little figures were actually floating around the room above the table where they sat.

For Leonardo it was perhaps less of a party-trick and more of a scientific experiment. He had filled hollow wax figures with hot air to make them float and hit upon the principle that would launch the hot-air balloons of the future.

Leonardo was no fanciful or unrealistic inventor. His anatomical as well as his engineering drawings are models of accuracy. His advice to all scientists and engineers was, 'Before you make a result a general rule, test it by experiment two or three times to see if you get the same result each time.' Many times in his writings the comment beneath reads, 'Tested by experiment'.

PRAYER
We thank you, Lord, for all men of genius who have given so much to bring us pleasure and understanding. We acknowledge that all their gifts come from you, the Giver of all. Amen

See also 3 May

3 May

Leonardo da Vinci's, *The Last Supper*, has been restored
and repainted so often that no touch of the original
hand remains, though his great genius does. His
error lay in experimenting with oils that flaked. The
monks, too, neglected their treasure and it was
vandalized by invading soldiers.

Unfinished portrait

The Dominican prior in Milan was growing impatient. He complained to the duke, who was Leonardo's patron, that the artist was taking far too long to complete the mural in his monastery. The duke made soothing noises.

'Men of genius are sometimes producing most when they seem to be labouring least,' he reassured him.

The subject of the painting was the Last Supper, at the moment when Christ said, 'One of you shall betray me.' Two faces presented a challenge that even Leonardo found hard to meet – the treacherous face of Judas and the face of Christ, for which there could be no model.

He suggested to the duke that he could always use the head of 'that troublesome and impertinent prior' as model for Judas. He did complete that figure, but the head of Christ was never completed. Even the genius of Leonardo was baffled by the mystery of God made man.

PRAYER
Lord Jesus, not even the greatest artists and poets can
describe or express you. You are God's own Son and
we humbly worship you. Amen

See also 2 May

4 May

The Council of Constance, meeting on 4 May 1415, decreed
that the remains of John Wyclif, the Bible translator,
should be dug up and burned.

Burned with a Bible round their necks

No one could understand a word of it – any more than they could
follow the services in church. For a start, the Bible was in Latin –
fair enough for scholars and rich men, but totally incomprehen-
sible to peasants and ordinary people. The priests mumbled so
that even their Latin was not audible.

John Wyclif, himself a priest and scholar, determined to make
the Bible understood by everyone. First, he sent out his followers
two by two, to teach and preach the gospel round the countryside.
Their enemies dubbed the poor preachers Lollards, or 'mum-
blers'. The Lollards took with them the New Testament in
English that Wyclif had translated, often with their help. Since
there was no printing, each copy had to be written out laboriously
by hand. It took about ten months and cost £40 to produce.
Amazingly, some 170 copies still survive.

It was dangerous to possess or even be found reading this
English New Testament. The church vented its bitter hatred on
Wyclif and his followers. Many Lollards were arrested and their
Bibles burned. Some were themselves burned, with their Bibles
round their necks. Wyclif was declared a heretic and though he
died naturally, his body was dug up and burned. But his Bible
survived.

Luke 11:2-4 in the Wyclif Bible (about 1384)

Fadir, halewid be thi name. Thi kingdom come to. Give to us to
day oure eche dayes breed. And forgyve to us oure synnes, as and
we forgyven to ech owynge to us. And leed not us in to
temptacioun.

See also 6 October

5 May

Søren Kierkegaard, Danish philosopher and Christian, was born on 5 May 1815.

From suffering to glory

'Kierkegaard was the seventh child of elderly parents . . . He was undersized, vulnerable, highly intelligent, combative, often malign and always somehow forlorn . . . he became increasingly an oddity, with one trouser-leg shorter than the other, given to high spirits and sharp talk in public and to melancholia in private. After some early disorderly behaviour he turned to the study of theology, but never became a minister . . .

'A curious episode arose out of his friendship with Meir Goldschmidt, editor of *Corsair* – a satirical and sometimes scurrilous weekly, a Copenhagen *Private Eye* . . . Kierkegaard occasionally helped Goldschmidt with a piece of information, and in consequence enjoyed immunity in the pages of his magazine. Then one day he asked Goldschmidt to spare him no longer, and for a whole year *Corsair* went for him regularly, making cruel fun of all his peculiarities, including his misshapen body. The campaign was so successful that the children in the streets cried out after him . . .

'"Only when a man has become so unhappy, or has grasped the misery of this existence so profoundly that he can truly say, 'For me life is worthless'," Kierkegaard wrote, "only then can life have worth in the highest degree." As he continually points out, all that is most mediocre and contemptible in human beings derives from the pursuit of earthly happiness. It is the glory of Christianity to have denounced and defied this pursuit . . .

'Such is his message, assiduously and skilfully proclaimed during his short life (he died when he was 42) and echoing on ever more loudly after his death . . . To a bruised twentieth-century mind . . . he brings the balm of reconciliation with the true, terrible and sublime circumstances of human life . . . he turns us away from the frantic noise of history and all its hopes and desires in search of other, fairer and more enduring vistas.'

From *Jesus Rediscovered*, by Malcolm Muggeridge

6 May

On 6 May 1843, George Borrow wrote to the Bible Society, for whom he had worked for many years, 'I can't forget that I spent the happiest years of my life in its service. Long may it flourish in spite of enemies and evil times.'

George Borrow had an amazing ability with languages. His autobiography is called *Lavengro*, which is Romany for 'word master'. He also loved walking. The story goes that when he was summoned to the Bible Society interview described, he walked the 112 miles from Norwich to London in twenty-seven hours, spending only 5½d (old pence) on a pint of ale, half a pint of milk, a roll and two apples.

The word master

'Go home and learn Manchu,' the Bible Society committee told George Borrow.

This candidate had successfully passed the examination in Arabic, and they were told that he could read the Bible in thirteen languages. He certainly seemed the best they had interviewed for the daunting new assignment.

Someone was needed to superintend the printing of a New Testament in Manchu – the Chinese language spoken at court. It was not possible to send anyone direct to China, for Russia was the only country represented at the Chinese court. So to Russia their man must go.

Borrow was equal to the task. Twenty-nine years old, six feet three inches tall, with hair already white, he was an unusual person in every way. He went back from London to the country, armed with the few books available in Manchu. He could not even get a grammar and the books promised him were delayed in coming. But he wrote, 'I was determined not to be discouraged.'

George Borrow tackled the task of learning Manchu at full gallop. Not many weeks after his interview, he wrote to the Bible Society to say that he had mastered the difficult language. He was ready to leave for Russia.

Continued on 7 May; see also 5 and 26 July

7 May

Russian assignment

Having learned the Manchu language, George Borrow set off for St Petersburg where Czar Nicholas lived in splendour.

First, Borrow had to contact the Russian who had made a preliminary translation of the New Testament into Manchu. This man could speak no other European language, so Borrow had to discuss the work in Russian.

The next problem was to find the special type needed to print Chinese characters. When Borrow found the cellar where the type had been stored, he found that it had burst out of its original case, and the tiny bits of metal had been trampled under mud and filth from a flood some years before. Retrieving it all, cleaning and sorting it for use was a painstaking task.

Then he had to bargain for paper at the nearby mill – *and* teach printers how to use this unfamiliar type. It's not surprising that he wrote rather tartly to the Bible Society when they complained that his letters home were not very frequent!

It took two years to complete the task. He had edited the text, and superintended the whole printing process. All that remained was to take the Testaments to the Chinese court. Then, to Borrow's great disappointment, the Czar refused to issue him with a visa. Someone else must go.

Borrow returned dutifully to London, but was soon off on another expedition for the Bible Society – taking the Bible to Spain.

PRAYER
Help us, Lord, to come to terms with disappointment,
especially when it follows months or years of hard work.
Give us courage to start afresh. Amen

See also 6 May, 5 and 26 July

8 May

Henry Dunant was born in Geneva on 8 May 1828.

The man in white

Henry Dunant was a man with a conscience about the poor and underprivileged of his day. He travelled to Italy to meet the emperor, Napoleon III, suitably dressed in a white suit, to enlist his sympathies. Napoleon was leading his army against the Austrian rulers of Italy and invited Dunant to come and watch the battle. He agreed, but was horrified by what he saw at Solferino.

Worse was to come. After twelve hours of fighting, over 40,000 men lay dead or wounded. The wounded were carried on carts or strapped to the pack-saddles of mules and taken – should they survive – to the town of Castiglione. Once there, little was done for them. There were too few trained helpers and not enough organization to ensure that all received even the food and water that *was* available.

Still in his white suit, Dunant busied himself to improve conditions. He set up headquarters in a church and began to wash and bandage the wounded himself. He sent the boys in the town to fetch fresh water and clean straw for bedding and even roped in any tourists to lend a hand. Eventually he had 300 helpers.

At first, the women of the town would only care for the French wounded – their allies. But they saw that Dunant cared nothing about 'them' and 'us'. He treated French and Austrian wounded alike – and soon his helpers did the same.

POSTSCRIPT
Dunant's horrifying experiences at Solferino led in time to the founding of the Red Cross – the international society which recognizes, as its founder did, the rights of all who are needy and wounded to receive help and medical care.

See also 18 May

9 May

The British and Foreign Bible Society was founded in 1804.
On 9 May 1979, the Bible Society celebrated its 175th
anniversary.

Hunger for Bibles

Thomas Charles decided he *must* make the journey to London.
Bibles were still desperately needed in Wales. He had ordered
and distributed a first edition of 10,000 Welsh Bibles and they
had gone like hot cakes. A second 10,000 went just as quickly.
Still more were needed. In London he talked about some of the
people who wanted Bibles – people like Mary Jones.

Mary was a young country girl who had determined to learn to
read and then buy a Bible. When a school was opened, she was
able to attend and learn to read. So she began to save up for a
Bible and when at last she had enough, set off to walk twenty-five
miles across the hills to find Mr Charles. But his supply had run
out. He was so touched by her story that he let her have one
promised to someone else so she was able to return home with
her ambition fulfilled.

The story of Mary Jones and her Bible was not written down
until some sixty years after the event, but she talked about her
experience when she was an old lady. It is certain that many
Welsh people were as determined as she was to get a Bible in their
own tongue. As a result of their efforts and Thomas Charles's
visit to London, a meeting was held that led to the formation of
the British and Foreign Bible Society. Today it meets the hunger
for Bibles all over the world.

10 May

10 May 1970 was the scheduled date for the Far East Broadcasting Association (FEBA) to 'go on the air'.

FEBA, the only British Christian radio station, is based on the Seychelles Islands, in the Indian Ocean. Its radio beams penetrate 36 million square miles and can reach 1,140 million listeners.

Oil change

There were only four weeks to go before broadcasting should begin and tests were going well. Then came the shock. The chemical content of the oil used to cool the transformers had gone bad. How could they possibly hope to change hundreds of gallons of oil by 10 May? Where would they get replacement oil?

The FEBA team prayed and also worked. They built a crane from scrap parts – and did it in four days. A brave volunteer climbed inside the drained 300-gallon tank and scrubbed off the thick deposit left by the bad oil.

Finding new oil required another miracle. Thirteen drums were needed and Shell provided seven – a ship being providentially near to transport it. Then, out of the blue, the contractors from the newly-constructed Mahé Airport on the island phoned to say they had discovered six drums of oil covered with tarpaulin – unused and unwanted. It was just the right oil for the job. The right quantity and quality of oil had been provided. FEBA went on the air on schedule.

PRAYER
Thank you, Lord, for radio and the pleasure it brings. Please use Christian radio to bring the good news of Jesus to people all over the world. Amen

See also 9 and 10 September

11 May

A naturalist writes in May 1776.

The Reverend Gilbert White was interested in pets as well as wild life, and kept a tortoise.

Cats and hares

'My friend had a little helpless leveret brought to him, which the servants fed with milk in a spoon, and about the same time his cat kittened and the young were despatched and buried. The hare was soon lost and supposed to be gone the way of most fondlings, to be killed by some dog or cat. However, in about a fortnight, as the master was sitting in his garden in the dusk of the evening, he observed his cat, with tail erect, trotting towards him, and calling with little short inward notes of complacency, such as they use towards their kittens, and something gamboling after, which proved to be the leveret that the cat had supported with her milk and continued to support with great affection.

'Why . . . a cat should be affected with any tenderness towards an animal which is its natural prey, is not so easy to determine. This strange affection was probably occasioned by . . . maternal feelings which the loss of her kittens had awakened . . . till she became as much delighted with this foundling as if it had been her real offspring.'

From Gilbert White's *Natural History of Selborne*

PRAYER
We thank you, Father, for the happiness pets bring and for their individual ways. We thank you for the companionship they give to the lonely, the elderly, the handicapped, the prisoners as well as to families. They are part of your wise creation, and we thank you for them. Amen

See also 9 March

12 May

Florence Nightingale was born on 12 May 1820.

Waiting

Florence Nightingale knew now exactly what she wanted to do. She would be a nurse. That seems an ordinary enough career ambition today, but in 1842 it was quite extraordinary, especially for someone of Miss Nightingale's class and position.

Seven years earlier she had received God's call. She never forgot that occasion, and kept the anniversary to her dying day. She had waited, wondering what God would call her to do. But even when she knew, she kept quiet.

She had two very good reasons for doing so.

The first was her family. Florence came from a wealthy, well-connected family, where daughters were expected to help their mother in the social round and then marry. Florence fell ill with the frustration of the trivial programme. Yet she dreaded the rows and scenes that attended any attempt to break free. So she waited.

But she did not waste the years of waiting. She got up early to study mathematics and organize the store cupboards of the large household. At Lord Shaftesbury's suggestion, she also studied public health records and hospital reports. Long before entering a hospital she knew all about the running of it.

The second great obstacle for Florence was the image that nursing had. Hospitals were places of unimagined filth; nurses were almost always drunk and often immoral. They had to sleep and eat in the hospital corridors. Training was unheard of.

What is incredible is not that Florence waited so long before embarking on her God-given vocation, but that she ever did so at all.

See also 21 and 25 October

13 May

Bible wisdom – about listening

'Good people think before they answer. Evil people have a quick reply but it causes trouble.'

'Listen before you answer. If you don't, you are being stupid and insulting.'

'If you listen to advice and are willing to learn, one day you will be wise.'

From the *Book of Proverbs*

'I am listening to what the Lord God is saying.'
From *Psalm 85*

'The Lord came and stood there, and called ... "Samuel! Samuel!"

'Samuel answered, "Speak; your servant is listening."'
From *1 Samuel 3*

'Remember this, my dear brothers! Everyone must be quick to listen, but slow to speak.'
From *James 1*

Jesus said: 'Every man who has ears should use them!'
From *Mark 4 (J.B.Phillips)*

14 May

Mary Seacole died in England on 14 May 1881.

All have heard of Florence Nightingale, but few know about Mary Seacole, a Jamaican woman with the same resolve and compassion. Her experience of 'doctoring' and her warm affection for the British led her to travel at her own expense and on her own initiative to the Crimea, to nurse and care for British troops.

Daughter of the 'doctress'

There could be no doubt about it – the patient was suffering from cholera. Mary Seacole had seen too much of the disease at home in Jamaica not to recognize the symptoms now. She had arrived on a visit to her brother in Panama, but in no time at all she was back at her familiar task of nursing the sick. When cholera had broken out in Jamaica in 1850, Mary had developed a medicine which produced remarkable results. She used this now in Panama, and brought relief to many who at first had been reluctant to receive medical help from a foreigner – and a *woman*.

Mary had years of experience behind her. Her mother, who had kept a house for army officers and their wives, was known locally as the 'doctress'. She had great skill in dealing with the sick and not surprisingly Mary learned from her, and also from the army doctors and surgeons whom she watched. She even conducted a post-mortem examination on a baby in Panama who died of cholera, in order to learn more about the disease.

Afterwards, the Americans honoured her work at a 4 July banquet. They drank a toast to her, but added their regrets that she wasn't white. Mary was a match for them. In her reply, she drank to them and to 'the general reformation of American manners'!

PRAYER
Thank you, Father, for all those to whom you have given the gift of healing. May they have your strength and compassion as well as your skill today. Amen

See also 14 November

15 May

On 15 May 1919, Eglantyne Jebb appeared in court.

Publicity from Eglantyne Jebb's trial – at which she was convicted and fined £5 – brought money flooding in, and the Save the Children Fund was set up. Before she died at fifty-two, worn out with hard work, she told her sister: 'I can trust God with the future of the Save the Children Fund. How very odd, how ridiculous it would be if I could not.'

Save the children

They stare at us from newspapers and hoardings: wistful faces and thin, emaciated bodies – the starving children of our world. The very first such photographs were distributed on a handbill in 1919 by a beautiful and determined woman called Eglantyne Jebb. She had heard, through the reports of the Red Cross and overseas newspapers, that thousands of children were dying of hunger as a direct result of the blockade imposed by the victorious Allies on the defeated nations after the First World War. She had only £10, so she invested it in printed handbills which would tell the tragic story to the people of Britain.

As a result, she was charged in court with distributing her handbills without the permission of the censors. Many branded her a traitor to the Allies, because she wanted to help the children of the 'enemy'.

The prosecutor read out the charge against her, and in the interval Eglantyne walked across to him. There was a whispered conversation, then, back in her place, the prisoner announced to the court triumphantly, 'He has promised to contribute to my fund for the children once the trial is over!'

16 May

On 16 May 1763, James Boswell met Dr Johnson for the
first time. He became his ardent admirer and wrote the
famous *Life of Johnson*.

Putting on airs – Journey in a stage-coach

'On the day of our departure, in the twilight of the morning, I
ascended the vehicle with three men and two women. We sat
silent for a long time, collecting importance into our faces.'
(Arrived at an inn, they sat round the table, and conversation
began.)

'"I remember," says the gentleman in the red surtout, "it was on
just such a morning as this that I and my Lord Mumble and the
Duke of Tenterden were out upon a ramble."

'Then one of the ladies began to remark the inconvenience of
travelling which they who never sat at home without a great
number of attendants found. One of the men who had hitherto
said nothing, called for the latest newspaper and having perused
it for a while with deep pensiveness, "It is impossible," says he,
"for any man to guess how to act with regard to the stocks: last
week I sold out twenty thousand pounds." A young man upon this
closed his snuff-box and told us he had "a hundred times talked
with the Chancellor and the Judges on the subject of these
stocks". Thus we travelled on four days without any endeavour
but to outvie each other.

'At length the journey was at an end and time and chance, that
strip off all disguises, discovered that the intimate of lords and
dukes is a nobleman's butler, the man who deals so largely in the
funds is a clerk of a broker; the lady keeps a cook-shop and the
young man who is so happy in the friendship of Judges works in a
garret in the Temple.'

Adapted from *The Adventurer*, by Samuel Johnson

PRAYER
Help us, Lord, not to try to impress others with our own
cleverness or importance. Teach us to be sincere and to be
ourselves whoever we are with. Amen

See also 13 December

17 May

On 17 May 1881, the Revised Version of the New
Testament was first published.

The same – but different

No one wanted change. The King James Version of the Bible
(often known as the 'Authorized Version', because it was
undertaken at the king's command) was dearly loved, treasured
and memorized.

But the English language had changed a good deal in over
250 years. Some words had acquired new meaning. The
word 'prevent' which meant 'go ahead or before' in Queen
Elizabeth I's reign, meant 'stop or obstruct' when Victoria
was queen.

There had been discoveries too. Ancient manuscripts had
come to light that far predated those on which the King James's
translation of the Bible had been based.

So it was decided to revise the old version in the light of these
changes and discoveries. But the new version was to be based on
the old one wherever possible. That way it was hoped that
everyone would be kept happy.

1 Thessalonians 4:15

'For this we say unto you by the word of the Lord, that we which
are alive and remain unto the coming of the Lord shall not
prevent them which are asleep.'

King James Version (1611)

'For this we say unto you by the word of the Lord, that we that are
alive, that are left unto the coming of the Lord, shall in no wise
precede them that are fallen asleep.'

Revised Version (1881)

18 May

The Red Cross story

Henry Dunant could not forget the horrors he had witnessed at the Battle of Solferino and the sufferings of the wounded. A few years later, he wrote a book – *A Memory of Solferino* – and paid to have it printed. Dunant realized that war itself was the real evil. But he did not see how that could be prevented. At least, as a Christian, he could try to alleviate the worst of the sufferings it brought. In his book he put forward an entirely new idea. In peace-time people should be trained, so that when war came they could treat the wounded of both sides. The helpers would be recognized and allowed anywhere on the field to do their work of mercy.

As a result of Dunant's book and the determination of others who felt the same way, the people of sixteen countries met in Geneva and, in 1864, drew up the Geneva Convention, which gave protection to all those who care for the wounded in any war. In order to be recognized, these helpers would carry a special sign – the red cross.

Today, the International Red Cross works in peace as well as war – bringing relief to victims of every kind of disaster all over the world.

See also 8 May

19 May

The Football Association Cup Final usually takes place in England on the second or third Saturday in May.

Alan West is a mid-field player with Millwall Football Club. As a Christian, he often speaks to audiences about his faith and his football on behalf of the Christians in Sport organization.

A Christian – in football

The buffet supper was held in Torquay, and Alan West was guest speaker. At the meal he chatted to the guest sitting next to him, who turned out to be a referee of league football, present because of his interest in sport.

A few months later, when Alan's team was playing at Newport, he recognized the referee as his dinner companion at Torquay. The game began. About half-way through, Alan tackled and the referee's whistle blew shrilly. He came running across to Alan, who had committed an unintentional foul. The referee asked his name in official tones, with no hint of recognition. Then, as he produced the yellow card, he challenged, 'What was all that about *Christians* in sport?'

Alan could only reply that he had never claimed to be perfect. As a Christian, he is only too conscious of his failings and the forgiveness Christ gives. But he is very much aware that being a Christian in sport, as in every job, means that people are watching how he acts. The onlooker expects a high standard. What he does must back up what he says.

PRAYER
Lord, we pray for Christians who are in the public eye. Thank you for their courage in confessing their faith. Help them to withstand criticism and live for you in their chosen work. May we too serve you in what we say and what we do. Amen

20 May

In May 1980, *Dayspring II* set out on her last voyage, and in May 1981, *Dayspring III* set out on her first.

Ron Russell and his wife live in New Zealand, the base for their island mission. On *Dayspring III*, they visit the inhabitants of the thousands of remote islands in the South Pacific, taking Bibles and Christian literature.

Wreck of the 'Dayspring II'

Ron Russell lay wedged between the deep freeze and the galley. Huge waves pounded the boat. It was dark except for the tiny dot of the compass light. Ron's mind went back to the time seventeen years before when a freak wave had swamped and sunk his twenty-one-foot sloop in the Caribbean. Then he had been desperately scared – unable to pray to a God he did not believe in. How different now! A great sense of peace filled him in spite of the noise of the storm and the imminent danger.

He heard the other two men calling in the darkness. Soon all three were able to locate each other and huddle together for warmth, wrapped in the heavy canvas of the storm jib to protect them from the surf that drove over the rail. *Dayspring II* was helpless, shuddering on a remote coral reef among the islands of Fiji.

The three men prayed confidently, committing themselves completely to God's care. Life-raft and dinghy had been swept away, but Ron saw that the radio batteries were still dry and radioed a Mayday call to Radio Suva in Fiji. They waited silently, then called again, knowing that in minutes the batteries would be submerged and the radio out of use. The peace of God was real, whether life or death should be the outcome.

They were off the most distant island of Fiji, where no regular boat service operates, and the airstrip was incomplete. But two government vessels were in the vicinity that night. Next day, Ron and his crew were rescued and taken to safety.

21 May

Elizabeth Fry, Quaker reformer, was born on 21 May 1780.

The gate to hell

'Of all the seats of woe on this side Hell, few, I suppose, exceed or equal Newgate.'

From a letter to *The London Chronicle*

Elizabeth argued patiently with the turnkeys of Newgate prison. They refused to let her into the women's yard. The screams of the women almost drowned their conversation. One woman rushed from a doorway and snatched the caps off the other prisoners with shrill, furious laughter.

'They'll do the same to you, ma'am,' the turnkeys warned.

'I am going in to them,' Mrs Fry insisted. 'Here is my letter of authorization from the governor.'

'At least take off your watch,' they begged. But Elizabeth refused, saying that it went everywhere with her.

Reluctantly the men opened the gate against the press of women, and Elizabeth Fry, in her sober Quaker dress, went through. The gate clanged behind her. There was a moment's hush, then the whole crowd of prisoners surged towards her and nothing could be seen except the tip of her white cap. But no one bit or scratched or tore at her clothes. Her quiet, gentle firmness had its effect.

She stooped and picked up a tiny child. Then she talked to the women as mothers, like herself, and began to make plans for their children. She told them a story about Jesus Christ, then promised to come again. When she went out through the gates, the wretched women inside had begun to hope.

Continued on 22 May

Patchwork in prison

Elizabeth Fry hated delay. She began at once to plan a school for prisoners' children and young prisoners. It did not need much money or an act of parliament to set about a practical matter like that. But the London authorities and the governor of Newgate thought otherwise. They believed that it was useless to try to help such wicked women. Anyway, there was no space.

The prisoners themselves suggested a small room that could be used and proposed that one of the prisoners, well qualified to teach, should take on the job. The mothers tidied up their children and got them ready for school.

When the thirty children, mostly under seven, had squeezed into the narrow room, a crowd of older prisoners stood outside and begged to be allowed to learn to read and write too. Elizabeth determined to help them and also to find work for the prisoners who had nothing to do all day but drink and cause trouble. Permission was at last given to use a large laundry-room, but no money was allowed for materials. In response to Elizabeth's plea, Quaker merchants provided thousands of scraps of material – just right for patchwork.

So, supervised by helpers, the prisoners of Newgate made patchwork quilts and Elizabeth found a market for them. English settlers in New South Wales, Australia, bought them gladly – perhaps they were a welcome reminder of 'home'. In exchange, the prisoners received small payments and were able to buy soap, tea and sugar. Their self-respect began to return.

See also 21 May

23 May

Ascension Day is always on a Thursday and comes forty days after Easter.

Jesus returns to his Father

For about six weeks after his resurrection, Jesus went on appearing from time to time to his disciples, teaching them about himself. Then he finally left earth to go back to the realm of heaven. Luke gives us two accounts of the happening.

'Then he [Jesus] led them out of the city as far as Bethany, where he raised his hands and blessed them. As he was blessing them, he departed from them and was taken up into heaven. They worshipped him and went back into Jerusalem, filled with great joy.'
From *Luke 24*

'Jesus said to them . . . "When the Holy Spirit comes upon you, you will be filled with power, and you will be witnesses for me . . . to the ends of the earth." After saying this, he was taken up to heaven as they watched him, and a cloud hid him from their sight. They still had their eyes fixed on the sky as he went away, when two men dressed in white suddenly stood beside them and said, "Galileans, why are you standing there looking up at the sky? This Jesus, who was taken from you into heaven, will come back in the same way that you saw him go to heaven."'
From *Acts 1*

24 May

Canada celebrates Victoria Day on 24 May each year.

Joseph Scriven was an Irishman. In 1845, he emigrated to Canada, where he died in 1886.

'The Lord and I did it between us!'

Joseph Scriven lay dying. His friend and neighbour who was sitting with him picked up a sheet of manuscript lying among his papers and read the words of a hymn he had never seen before. The sick man shyly admitted that he had written it many years before. 'The Lord and I did it between us,' he added. He said that he had written it to comfort his mother when she had been going through a time of special sorrow. Scriven's understanding and sympathy sprang from his own experience of tragedy. His bride-to-be had been drowned as the result of an accident the very day before they were to be married.

Scriven's hymn has become a great favourite over the years:

What a Friend we have in Jesus
All our sins and griefs to bear;
What a privilege to carry
Everything to God in prayer!
O what peace we often forfeit,
O what needless pain we bear;
All because we do not carry
Everything to God in prayer.

25 May

Nicholaus Copernicus died in May 1543.

Copernicus was born in Poland in 1473. He studied law and medicine in Italy and was a distinguished churchman. He advised his government on currency reform and was asked by the pope to help revise the calendar.

Centre of the universe

Copernicus was sure that nature was simple. Why then were the paths of the planets so very complicated? Ptolemy had first stated the system, and in 1350 de Dondi in Padua had made a splendid clockwork machine of the heavens. It had seven faces, each representing the path of a planet as it revolved round the earth. The sun was included as one of those revolving planets. At the centre of everything was the earth, immovable.

Copernicus decided that the planets' path looked complicated because of the viewpoint from which they were observed – our earth. If it were possible to look at the sky from a different place . . . why not put the sun at the centre? It was a revolutionary idea in every sense of the word, and it had far-reaching effects. It was Galileo who bore the full brunt of the church's wrath at this displacement of earth from the centre of the universe.

Copernicus wrote a book explaining his theory. The first printed copy was rushed to his bed as he was dying and placed in his hands. Copernicus never knew that someone had inserted a preface saying that his brilliant new findings were 'only theory'.

See also 11 February

26 May

Bob Dylan was born in May 1941.

Bob Dylan was one of the great pop phenomena of the sixties, along with the Beatles and the Rolling Stones. He studied English at the University of Minnesota. A folk poet, his early songs were songs of protest – against nuclear bomb testing, against pollution and against the war in Vietnam.

The way home

'How does it feel, how does it feel
To be on your own
With no direction home?'

Those were words in Bob Dylan's lyric, *Like a Rolling Stone*. Life meant being lost – no God, no friend in the whole universe.

Bob Dylan remains a private person – he has never given many interviews or had much to do with the press. After a motor-cycle accident, he retired into his shell almost completely. His songs became more personal and he began to search for his own Jewish roots. He visited the Western ('Wailing') Wall in Jerusalem, and supported Jewish organizations. Always he was looking for direction – for a way home.

Now, through conversion to Christ, he has found it. In the past, Dylan spoke out against the ills of society. Now he sings too about the urgency and importance of following Jesus. Many critics disapprove of his new songs, but none can doubt that Bob Dylan has stopped being a rolling stone – he has found the way home.

27 May

27 May is the Feast Day of the Venerable Bede.

The tomb of the Venerable Bede is in Durham Cathedral.
His book – the *Ecclesiastical History of the English Nation* –
tells many wonderful stories of the early saints and
preachers in Britain.

Finished!

It was Ascension Day in the year AD 735 in the monastery at Jarrow in Northumberland. An old man's voice droned on, so feebly and quietly now that the young scribe, busily scratching with his quill across the vellum, had to turn his head to catch each syllable. He wrote hurriedly, anxiously, aware of the urgency to finish.

They had reached the last chapter of John's Gospel, which the learned monk was translating from Latin into English. The Venerable Bede was dying.

'Write quickly,' he ordered, and the dictation continued until the chapter was almost finished. Then Bede stopped and sent for the other monks. He received each in turn and gave each some small gift – a few peppers and some napkins – and said goodbye. They left the room and the scribe wondered if his master could finish the task.

'There is still one sentence to be written,' he said. With a final supreme effort, Bede dictated the closing words of the Gospel.

'It is done,' he said. His work and his life were finished.

See also 28 May

28 May

The Venerable Bede is thought to have been the first person to draw up a calendar of the Christian year in England.

Special days

The year is full of special days – birthdays or anniversaries – that remind us of friends or relatives. The early Christians wanted to keep certain days special to remind them of outstanding martyrs and saints whose example they should follow. They used the Roman calendar – based on the sun – for these days, so they come at fixed dates each year.

But the church also wanted to commemorate the great historic events of Christianity: when Jesus died, rose again, ascended to heaven, and when the Holy Spirit was given. These happenings are linked to the Jewish calendar, which is calculated by the moon. For example, the Jewish Feast of Passover, which was the time at which Jesus was crucified, varies from year to year according to when the full moon occurs in the month.

The Christian calendar is therefore a mixture of fixed feasts and so-called movable feasts – those that can fall on different dates in different years.

BIBLE VERSE
'*This* is the day which the Lord has made; let us rejoice and be glad in it.'
From *Psalm 118 (Revised Standard Version)*

See also 25 April

29 May

G.K. Chesterton was born on 29 May 1874.

Gilbert Keith Chesterton was a poet, artist and popular
defender of the Christian faith. Perhaps he is best known
today for his Father Brown detective stories.

A celibate simpleton?

Valentin, head of Paris police, was in England, tracking down
the notorious criminal, Flambeau. He caught his first glimpse of
Father Brown, arriving by train with other clerics to attend a
Eucharistic Congress:

'He had a face as round and dull as a Norfolk dumpling; he
had eyes as empty as the North Sea; he had several brown paper
parcels which he was quite incapable of collecting . . . He had a
large, shabby umbrella, which constantly fell to the floor. He did
not seem to know which was the right end of his return ticket.
He explained with a moon-calf simplicity to everybody in the
carriage that he had to be careful, because he had something
made of real silver "with blue stones" in one of his brown-paper
parcels.'

Naturally, Flambeau, disguised as a cleric, set about stealing
the valuable blue and silver cross, but the apparent simplicity of
Father Brown proved more than a match for him. After
following the trail carefully laid by Father Brown, Valentin came
upon the two, walking and talking in the twilight on Hampstead
Heath – the tall, towering form of Flambeau and the short
dumpy figure of Father Brown.

When Flambeau revealed his identity and demanded the
cross, he was horrified to discover that the little priest had both
penetrated his disguise and despatched the cross to safety.
Flambeau asked him how he knew all the tricks of the thief's
trade.

'"Oh, by being a celibate simpleton, I suppose," he said. "Has
it never struck you that a man who does next to nothing but hear
men's real sins is not likely to be wholly unaware of human evil?
But, as a matter of fact, another part of my trade, too, made me
sure you weren't a priest."'

'"What?" asked the thief, almost gaping.

'"You attacked reason," said Father Brown. "It's bad
theology."'

From *The Blue Cross*, by G. K. Chesterton

30 May

Whitsun coincides with the Jewish festival of Pentecost and comes seven weeks after Easter. It celebrates the giving of the Holy Spirit to the disciples, just as Jesus had promised. This is how Luke describes the event:

Wind of the Spirit

'When the day of Pentecost came, all the believers were gathered together in one place. Suddenly there was a noise from the sky which sounded like a strong wind blowing, and it filled the whole house where they were sitting. Then they saw what looked like tongues of fire which spread out and touched each person there. They were all filled with the Holy Spirit and began to talk in other languages as the Spirit enabled them to speak . . .

There were Jews living in Jerusalem, religious men who had come from every country in the world. When they heard this noise, a large crowd gathered. They were all excited, because each one of them heard the believers speaking in his own language.

'Amazed and confused, they kept asking each other, "What does this mean"?

'But others made fun of the believers, saying, "These people are drunk!"

'Then Peter stood up with the other eleven apostles and in a loud voice began to speak to the crowd: "Fellow-Jews and all of you who live in Jerusalem, listen to me and let me tell you what this means . . . this is what the prophet Joel spoke about:

'This is what I will do in the last days, God says:

I will pour out my Spirit on everyone."'

From *Acts 2*

31 May

On 31 May 1899, two American businessmen launched the scheme which led to the formation of Gideons International.

Gideons International place Bibles in hotel rooms, hospital wards and schools. The crew of the *Apollo 8* spacecraft – Frank Borman, James Lovell and William Anders – were presented with copies of Gideon New Testaments, and a special Gideon Bible was carried on the moon-flight.

Message from space

Television audiences worldwide watched the first manned flight around the moon. As *Apollo 8* reappeared from the further side of the moon, they heard the crew say, 'We are now approaching lunar sunrise and for all the people back on earth the crew of *Apollo 8* has a message: "In the beginning God created the heaven and the earth. And the earth was without form, and void; and darkness was upon the face of the deep. And the Spirit of God moved upon the face of the waters. And God said, Let there be light: and there was light. And God saw the light, that it was good: and God divided the light from the darkness."'

Minutes later, a Japanese newsman telephoned NASA's newsroom in Houston, Texas, and asked if someone could read him the transcript of the crew's message.

The NASA public affairs officer asked, 'Where are you?'

'In my hotel room.'

'Look in the drawer of your bureau and read the first page of the book you find there.'

The Japanese newsman did as he was told. There in the drawer lay a Gideon-placed Bible. He was amazed at the efficiency of the NASA public affairs office in supplying a transcript in his own hotel room!

1 June

Henry Francis Lyte was born on 1 June 1793.

Henry Lyte, author of the hymn, 'Praise my soul the King of heaven', had hoped to become a doctor but was not strong enough. He was ordained and appointed to the quiet Devon living of Brixham. He died at fifty-four after years of ill-health.

Abide with me

Those who haven't sung it in church have probably heard it at the FA Cup Final. Henry Lyte's best-known hymn is usually to be found in the 'Evening' section of the hymn-books, but when Lyte wrote 'Abide with me' he was not thinking about the close of day. He had been deeply concerned, since the death of a fellow clergyman, about the ending of life and he guessed that he himself hadn't long to live.

One late afternoon, he took a walk by the sea and saw a dramatically beautiful sunset. He had only a few more days left in England – his health was so poor that a winter abroad had been prescribed. Lyte went home and wrote his famous hymn. Then he announced that he wanted to preach that evening. His family protested, as he had been very unwell, but he insisted and, as his daughter reported, 'he did preach, amid the breathless attention of his hearers'.

Before he went to bed, Lyte gave the copy of that afternoon's hymn to a close relative. He died a month or two later in Nice.

Abide with me; fast falls the eventide;
The darkness deepens; Lord, with me abide!
When other helpers fail, and comforts flee,
Help of the helpless, O abide with me.

Swift to its close ebbs out life's little day;
Earth's joys grow dim, its glories pass away;
Change and decay in all around I see;
O thou who changest not, abide with me.

2 June

Bible stories – about ingratitude

'There was a little town without many people in it. A powerful king attacked it. He surrounded it and prepared to break through the walls. A man lived there who was poor, but so clever that he saved the town. But later no one remembered him.'

From *Ecclesiastes 9*

'He [Jesus] was going into a village when he was met by ten men suffering from a dreaded skin-disease. They stood at a distance and shouted, "Jesus! Master! Take pity on us!"

'Jesus saw them and said to them, "Go and let the priests examine you."

'On the way they were made clean. When one of them saw that he was healed, he came back, praising God in a loud voice. He threw himself to the ground at Jesus' feet and thanked him. The man was a Samaritan. Jesus said, "There were ten men who were healed; where are the other nine? Why is this foreigner the only one who came back to give thanks to God?"'

From *Luke 17*

PRAYER
Dear Lord, keep us from the sin of ingratitude. Thank you for all your kindness and love to us. Thank you, too, for other people who have helped us in our individual lives, as well as those who work hard for the good of our nation. May we not be ungrateful or forgetful once our need is past. Help us to put thanks into words and actions so that others feel the warmth of our appreciation. Amen

3 June

Pope John XXIII died on 3 June 1963.

Pope John was the eldest son of poor tenant farmers in northern Italy. In his short term as pope, he aimed to unite all Christians and to 'fend off all that divides'. He was deeply loved for his goodness, humour and charity to all. Archbishop Bruno Heim could say, 'In the five years I spent working with him I never saw him angry, impatient or upset. On the contrary, he accepted everything with contentment.'

Love and contentment

The newly-elected pope strolled through the Vatican gardens, stopping to chat with a group of gardeners. He looked at what they were doing with interest, then asked about their families and how much they earned. The pope thought the wages too low and saw to it himself that they got a rise.

Inside the palace, Pope John was a splendid host to his many visitors. He always insisted that the guest should have the best bedroom – which was his own. So he would often turn out and sleep in a little room adjoining his study.

Pope John woke one night with a problem on his mind. 'I must take this up with the pope,' was his first waking thought. 'But I *am* the pope! Then I must take it up with God!'

4 June

In June 1969, Brian Greenaway received his first prison sentence.

H-a-t-e to L-o-v-e

Hospital isn't everyone's favourite place. But after the rigours of Dartmoor Prison, three weeks in Grendon Underwood prison hospital seemed like a holiday to Brian Greenaway. Brian's life had been changed since reading in his cell the yellow-backed *Living Bible*, which made the words of Jesus come alive for him. Now he wanted to get rid of the hate in his life – and that was why he was in hospital.

Across the four fingers of his left hand were tattooed the letters 'H-A-T-E'. Hate had summed up most of Brian's life before his meeting with Jesus Christ. He had grown up knowing no love, knocked about by mother, father and stepfather.

Life in a residential home wasn't much better, and he found little love when he ran away and tried to fend for himself, nor when he came up against the law. When he became president of a Hell's Angel chapter, he had to be in the forefront of vendettas against rival gangs. He had given as well as received plenty of hate.

Now he wanted to lead a life where hate had no place, as he explained to the surgeons who removed the tattoo. Back in Dartmoor, other prisoners came to him with their problems and unhappiness, and Brian was able to put love into practice instead, and give them help from his yellow-backed Bible.

POSTSCRIPT
Brian Greenaway, once president of a Hell's Angel chapter, almost destroyed by violence and drugs, now works for the London City Mission, visiting and helping prisoners in London's gaols.

5 June

Tony Jasper's birthday is on 5 June.

Tony Jasper writes regularly about music in *Music Week*, the *Manchester Evening News* and *The Methodist Recorder*. He writes material for BBC Schools broadcasts, as well as presenting and taking part in radio and television programmes. His book, *Cliff* (about Cliff Richard) was among the national top ten best-sellers.

Let's celebrate!

About 120 singles records arrive at Tony Jasper's flat every week, plus albums – and he listens to them all. Then he writes his comments in *Music Week*, the leading trade journal of the music world, consulted by music companies and record shops.

'Music is one splendid way of celebrating,' Tony explains, 'celebrating God, Jesus, ourselves and all the good things in life.'

Some critics argue that Christians can have little in common with pop songs that advocate mindless violence, turn women into sex objects and men into mere hunters. But Tony insists that pop music is neutral in itself. It can be good or bad – like a film or a play. Many of the lyrics are asking important questions about self, about life, love and death. Once such questions have been asked and faced, there is the opportunity for the church to do its part by offering answers. Christians can't stand aside from their own society and culture – unless they want to be spectators on the touch-line instead of players who take risks, but get involved in the game.

Pop music matters and the best pop music needs to be listened to because it's for and about young people. It's asking questions and Christians believe there are answers to be found. And . . . there's the sheer enjoyment of it too.

So let's celebrate!

6 June

Lord Gordon began the trouble with a Protestant march against the House of Commons to have the Catholic Relief Act repealed. It was a hot summer and feelings ran high. Mob violence spread – Roman Catholic churches and homes were burned down. When some rioters were imprisoned in Newgate, the mob set fire to the gaol, and broke open prisons. No police force existed so troops were called to restore order. At least 450 people died in the riots.

Grim reality

This is part of the poet George Crabbe's description of the scene:

'Never saw anything so dreadful. The prison was a remarkably strong building; but determined to force it, they broke the gates with crows and other instruments and climbed up the outside. They broke the roof, tore away the rafters and having got ladders they descended, flames all around them. The prisoners escaped – they were conducted through the streets in their chains. Three of them were to be hanged on Friday. You have no conception of the frenzy of the multitude.'

William Blake was another spectator. The trouble started near to his home and perhaps 'the terrible flames and prisons, smoke and chains that appear in Blake's pictures and in his poetry owe some of their grim reality to this time of violence'.

PRAYERS
Lord, we pray for those whose job is to keep law and order.
Give them fairness and compassion as well as strength and wisdom to do their duty. Amen

We pray for those places where religious faith causes war, violence and murder instead of brotherhood and peace.
Help us to love one another as Jesus Christ taught. Amen

7 June

Sir James Simpson was born on 7 June 1811.

James Simpson was the seventh son of a baker in Bathgate near Edinburgh. He trained as a doctor and specialized in midwifery. Although he became a fashionable doctor, attending royal and titled people, he made no distinction between rich and poor patients, seeking only to relieve pain and save life.

Miss Anaesthesia!

It was supper-time in the Simpson household and Dr Simpson and two colleagues were waiting for their meal after a late night at work. As Simpson searched among his papers for something he wanted, he came across a sample of chloroform that the local chemist had given him to test. Impressed by early trials of ether to anaesthetize patients during operations, Simpson was always on the look-out for some improved substance, suitable for mothers, to relieve the pain of childbirth. The only way to test a new substance was to try it himself.

Simpson poured the liquid into a tumbler and the three doctors took a good sniff at it. When Mrs Simpson came to call them to supper, she found all three under the mahogany table! Simpson came to first, delighted to have found something so effective. Five days later, he used chloroform in a midwifery case. He later kept a photograph on his desk of the little girl born so painlessly. He nicknamed her 'Miss Anaesthesia'.

PRAYER
We thank you, Lord, for all who work to relieve pain. Guide and help those engaged in research to find safe ways to combat disease and lessen suffering. For Jesus' sake. Amen

Continued on 8 June; see also 18 October

8 June

Dr James Simpson's desire to relieve pain and suffering came from his Christian faith. When he was dying, he said to his nephew: 'From extreme pain, I have not been able to read or even to think much today, but when I think, it is of the words, "Jesus only", and really that is all that is needed, is it not?'

A necessary evil?

We take it for granted today that pain is to be relieved whenever possible. In Simpson's day, many thought differently – especially about pain in childbirth. They quoted the words in Genesis 3 where God told Eve: 'In sorrow shalt thou bring forth children.' They interpreted 'sorrow' as 'pain', and insisted that pain was divinely intended in childbirth. No doubt those that held the view were men!

Simpson refused to be quelled by such 'theologians', although they thundered against him from the pulpit and in the press, as well as writing him abusive letters. He wrote pamphlets to counteract their arguments, explaining that the word 'sorrow' meant 'toil', not pain. If, he argued, drugs were used to ease pain in ordinary illness, how could it be wrong to relieve the pain of mothers too?

Most, but not all, doubters were convinced by Simpson's humane attitude. However, when Queen Victoria herself accepted chloroform at the birth of her ninth child, Simpson's cause knew certain triumph.

See also 7 June, 18 October

9 June

Elizabeth Garrett Anderson was born on 9 June 1836.

Elizabeth Garrett was the first woman to qualify in Britain as a doctor and surgeon. It took years of endurance and determined effort against deep-rooted prejudice. She married Skelton Anderson and had children of her own as well as continuing her pioneering medical work. She believed strongly in the God who had given knowledge to women as well as to men and above everything cherished charity, which she defined as 'that genuine care for others which makes us postpone our own interests'.

Practice makes perfect

'Good speed to the Women's hospital is the earnest prayer of – Florence Nightingale.'

So ended the letter written to her by the famous heroine, which would prove splendid ammunition in Elizabeth Garrett Anderson's new fund-raising campaign. She envisaged a hospital staffed entirely by women, that would provide for patients who particularly wished to be treated by doctors of their own sex. But there was another reason for building such a hospital. Although, through Elizabeth's pioneering efforts, women were now beginning to qualify in medicine and surgery, there was nowhere for them to gain experience. Prejudice against them was so strong that even in hospitals dealing exclusively with women's diseases, women doctors were refused jobs.

One group of newly qualified women doctors specially needed practical experience. They planned to go to India, where women were forbidden to consult a male doctor. Even Queen Victoria, not usually in favour of women forsaking their traditional roles in the home, was touched by the need of women in that part of her Empire and encouraged medical women to go out to help them.

By tact, enthusiasm, shrewdness and hard work, Elizabeth overcame both opposition and lack of funds. In May 1889 the Princess of Wales laid the foundation stone of the New Hospital for Women in Euston Road. After the death of its founder it was renamed the Elizabeth Garrett Anderson Hospital, in honour of the person who did so much for women – patients and doctors alike.

10 June

Abbé Michel Quoist was born in June 1918 at Le Havre, France.

Michel Quoist lived for four years in one of the poorest parts of the city. As a parish priest, he worked as chaplain to various youth clubs in and around Le Havre. Although he has received many academic honours, his real care is still for the poor and the young. Many of his published prayers tell God exactly how he is feeling and help to work out – for him and for his readers – attitudes and reactions to some of life's big problems.

Green blackboards

The school is up-to-date.

Proudly, the Principal tells of all the improvements.

The finest discovery, Lord, is the green blackboard.

The scientists have studied long, they have made experiments;

We know now that green is the ideal colour, that it doesn't tire the eyes, that it is quiet and relaxing.

It has occurred to me, Lord, that you didn't wait so long to paint the trees and the meadows green.

Your research laboratories were efficient, and in order not to tire us, you perfected a number of shades of green for your modern meadows.

And so the 'finds' of men consist in discovering what you have known from time immemorial.

Thank you, Lord, for being the good Father who gives his children the joy of discovering by themselves the treasures of his intelligence and love,

But keep us from believing that – by ourselves – we have invented anything at all.

From *Prayers of Life*, by Michel Quoist

11 June

'Barnabas' was the nickname given to Joseph, a Christian Jew from Cyprus. It means 'one who encourages'. Barnabas was the one who persuaded the doubting Christians in Jerusalem to accept Paul after his dramatic conversion, and who went with Paul on his first overseas mission.

The 'one who encouraged'

Barnabas rarely quarrelled – and certainly not with his great friend and colleague Paul. He usually made the peace when others seemed ready to come to blows. But this time he stood firm, and the whole episode ended in sharp argument.

It began when Paul suggested that they should set sail to revisit the little groups of Christians who had been converted on their first overseas trip. Barnabas readily agreed.

'We'll take John Mark again.'

'No, we most certainly won't,' Paul retorted. 'Not after the way he let us down last time – turning back home when we needed him.'

'He'll be different this time,' Barnabas pleaded. 'He's learned his lesson and he needs to feel we trust him again.'

But Paul would not budge. Every member of such a dangerous and demanding expedition had to be hand-picked. They could not afford to risk someone who might be a liability. But for Barnabas, John Mark's needs came before streamlined efficiency.

The disagreement ended with the two friends parting company. Paul went without Mark *or* Barnabas, choosing a new companion, Silas. Barnabas took the dejected John Mark with him on his own missionary trip to his beautiful home island of Cyprus.

Adapted from *Acts 15*

PRAYER
Help us, Lord, like Barnabas, to encourage those who lack confidence or are depressed and afraid. Teach us when to stand firm and when to give way to others. Amen

12 June

Charles Kingsley was born on 12 June 1819.

Charles Kingsley, a country vicar, felt strongly about the harsh and insanitary conditions in Victorian England. He joined a group called Christian Socialists, who worked to encourage fair dealing and justice between employers and employees. He also wrote books exposing the terrible conditions that existed. *The Water Babies* is a moral tale for children, but it also highlights the way in which even small children were employed to sweep the rambling chimneys that no larger person could reach.

The little chimney sweep

'Once upon a time there was a little chimney sweep, and his name was Tom . . . He lived in a great town in the North country where there were plenty of chimneys to sweep and plenty of money for Tom to earn and his master to spend. He could not read nor write, and did not care to do either; and he never washed himself, for there was no water up the court where he lived. He had never been taught to say his prayers. He never had heard of God or of Christ . . . He cried half his time and laughed the other. He cried when he had to climb the dark flues, rubbing his poor knees and elbows raw; and when the soot got into his eyes, which it did every day of the week; and when his master beat him, which he did every day in the week; and when he had not enough to eat, which happened every day in the week likewise. And he laughed the other half of the day, when he was tossing halfpennies with the boys, or playing leap-frog over the posts, or bowling stones at the horses' legs as they trotted by, which last was excellent fun, when there was a wall at hand behind which to hide. As for chimney-sweeping, and being hungry, and being beaten, he took all that for the way of the world, like the rain and snow and thunder, and stood manfully with his back to it till it was over, as his old donkey did to a hail-storm; and then shook his ears and was as jolly as ever; and thought of the fine times coming, when he would be a man, and a master sweep.'

From *The Water Babies*, by Charles Kingsley

See also 13 June

13 June

Rains and drains

'Pray for a dry summer,' begged his parishioners, but the Reverend Charles Kingsley refused.

'Shall I presume, because I think it is raining too long here, to ask God to alter the tides of the ocean, the form of the continents, the pace at which the earth spins round, the force, the light and speed of sun and moon? For all this, and no less I shall ask, if I ask him to alter the skies, even for a single day.'

But Mr Kingsley had another reason for not praying for a dry summer. He explained in his sermons the value of rain. It cleared the drains, sewers and wells, and kept drinking water pure, so that if cholera struck, it stood less chance of spreading. Cholera took many lives and Kingsley believed it could be checked if drains and sewers were improved. He had been horrified to see the filthy sewers in Bermondsey in south London, from which, unbelievably, people drew drinking water.

Christians should be practical people, so he begged money from friends in order to provide a water-cart. Christians then took it round the area providing clean water until long-term action was taken. He lectured and wrote articles on sanitary reform, and had a staunch ally in Prince Albert, husband of Queen Victoria. When their son, the Prince of Wales, fell ill with fever, Kingsley moved near Sandringham to receive daily bulletins which he telegraphed home to be posted on the church door.

When the prince recovered, Kingsley preached a sermon in which he told the congregation that within a few years, 2,000 people had died of fever that could have been prevented. Kingsley hoped that the publicity given to the prince's illness might awaken people to the need for clean water, fresh air, and good drains.

See also 12 June

14 June

Harriet Beecher Stowe was born on 14 June 1811.

Harriet Beecher, daughter of a well-known Christian minister, married Calvin Stowe, a college lecturer, and lived for eighteen years just across the river from a state where slavery was legal. She hid runaway slaves on their way to Canada. She determined to awaken consciences by her writing. *Uncle Tom's Cabin* came out first as a magazine serial. The published book was an overnight success, translated into many European languages. It was a main factor in abolishing slavery in the southern States. And the Fugitive Slave Act – which made it illegal for anyone to hide a runaway slave – is said never again to have been enforced.

Theory and practice

Mr Bird, returned from his duties as senator, was discussing with his wife the new Fugitive Slave Act which he had voted for. Mrs Bird was horrified and tried to convince her husband – unsuccessfully – that it would be un-Christian and inhumane to hand over a poor, suffering, exhausted human being to a ruthless and revengeful master.

At that very moment, there was a commotion in the kitchen. A distraught, injured black girl, clutching her little son, had staggered into their house, after crossing from the slave state on the other side of the river. Mr Bird was as concerned as his wife. The runaway was fed, clothed, cared for and taken across difficult terrain to a house of safety by Mr Bird himself!

In this kind of way, *Uncle Tom's Cabin* enlisted the compassion and loyalty of readers. High drama and personal involvement speak more clearly than reasoned arguments. The book was a huge success because it is a first-rate story, moving and exciting in its own right.

Not every one approved. Some blacks sensed a patronizing air even among enlightened whites. They despised the meek Uncle Tom, who from Christian convictions refused to stand up to his white bosses, or to run away. But the book transformed attitudes to slavery – not only in the USA, but all over Europe.

See also 15 June

15 June

In this extract from *Uncle Tom's Cabin*, Eliza is running
away from her master because her little son has been sold
to a ruthless trader and will be separated from her. She
arrives at the river dividing her from a non-slave state, only
to find that broken pack-ice prevents the ferry crossing.
While she waits at the tavern, she sees the pursuing slaver
arrive.

On the other side

'A thousand lives seemed to be concentrated in that one moment
to Eliza. Her room opened by a side door to the river. She caught
her child and sprang down the steps towards it. The trader caught
a full glimpse of her just as she was disappearing down the bank;
and throwing himself from his horse . . . he was after her like a
hound after a deer. In that dizzy moment her feet to her scarce
seemed to touch the ground, and a moment brought her to the
water's edge. Right on behind they came; and, nerved with
strength such as God gives only to the desperate, with one wild
cry and flying leap she vaulted sheer over the turbid current by
the shore on to the raft of ice beyond. It was a desperate leap –
impossible to anything but madness and despair . . .

'The huge green fragment of ice on which she alighted pitched
and creaked as her weight came on it, but she stayed there not for
a moment. With wild cries and desperate energy she leaped to
another and still another cake; stumbling; leaping; slipping;
springing upward again! Her shoes were gone – her stockings cut
from her feet – while blood marked every step; but she saw
nothing, felt nothing, till dimly, as in a dream, she saw the Ohio
side, and a man helping her up the bank.'

See also 14 June

16 June

The universal vice

'There is one vice of which no man in the world is free; which everyone in the world simply loathes when he sees it in someone else; and of which hardly any people except Christians, ever imagine that they are guilty themselves ... There is no fault which makes a man more unpopular, and no fault which we are more unconscious of in ourselves. And the more we have it ourselves, the more we dislike it in others.

'The vice I am talking of is Pride ... Pride leads to every other vice; it is the complete anti-God state of mind ... If you want to find out how proud you are the easiest way is to ask yourself, "How much do I dislike it when other people snub me, or refuse to take any notice of me, or patronise me or show off?" The point is that each person's pride is in competition with everyone else's pride. It is because I wanted to be the big noise at the party that I am so annoyed at someone else being the big noise ... Pride is essentially competitive ... The Christians are right: it is Pride which has been the chief cause of misery in every nation and every family since the world began ... Pride always means enmity – it *is* enmity. And not only enmity between man and man but enmity to God ... Pride is spiritual cancer: it eats up the very possibility of love, or contentment, or even commonsense.'

From *Mere Christianity*, by C.S.Lewis

See also 17 June, 8 July, 6 August

17 June

Nixon's 'hatchet man'

'NIXON HATCHET MAN – CHUCK COLSON – HANDLES PRESIDENT'S DIRTY
WORK'

So ran a telling *Wall Street Journal* headline in 1971.

There was no one closer to the president and no one keener to
have him re-elected for another term of office. But there were
problems. Serious leaks of secret information were harming the
Nixon administration. 'I want the traitor exposed, Chuck,' Nixon
told his chief trouble-shooter. 'I don't care how you do it, but get
it done.'

One step led to another – including burglary of the Democratic
offices at Watergate. And Nixon won the election. But the past
has a habit of catching up on people. Colson himself knew
nothing of the Watergate affair or the secret taping of conversations at the White House, but he did admit that what had begun as
legitimate political tactics had degenerated into dirty tricks and
downright immoral actions. When Colson discovered the full
extent of the damage, he was up to his neck in it – guilty or not.
Yet it had all begun in such small ways.

After his conversion to Christ and his imprisonment, Chuck
Colson realized increasingly how easily small ways of 'bending'
the rules can lead to a downhill moral slide. He needed Christ's
forgiveness for the past and Christ's power to help him go straight
in the future.

PRAYER
Lord, keep us today from small dishonesties, tiny lies, and
insincerities which may not seem to matter. Lead us not
into temptation but deliver us from evil. For yours is the
power. Amen

See also 8 July

18 June

The Battle of Waterloo was fought on 18 June 1815.

Fifty years on

'Called on Esther Rogers, and found her at home after three times finding the garden gate padlocked. I gave her a copy of Uncle Francis Bathwick's Sermons. She told me that her brother was a heavy dragoon and was killed at Waterloo. His horse had been killed under him or disabled. Going to fetch a fresh horse, as he was walking in a lane with two other English soldiers, they came upon a troop of French cavalry, probably lancers. The three English soldiers lay down and pretended to be dead, but her brother was thrust through as he lay on his face on the ground. She just remembered her brother as a fine tall man and has a vivid recollection of a picture of him in a scarlet uniform mounted on a black horse with white hoofs. It was curious to hear the old Waterloo story told more than half a century after by a quiet fireside in Wales.'

From *Kilvert's Diary*

PRAYER
We pray today for all the victims of war – sailors, soldiers, airmen and civilians. We pray that national pride and greed may give place to discussion, arbitration and a genuine seeking for peace. Hasten the day when Jesus Christ, the Prince of Peace, will reign and all wars cease. Amen

See also 23 and 24 September

19 June

Blaise Pascal, French philosopher and mathematician, was born on 19 June 1623.

Pascal loved mathematics – perhaps because he never went to school. His father, a mathematician, encouraged him. At eighteen, he invented a calculator, working on cogged wheels, which could add and subtract. He was often ill and lived only until he was thirty-nine, yet he wrote on geometry and physics, and discovered the physical law that 'the pressure acting on a point in a fluid is the same in all directions' (Pascal's Law).

Surrender - to Jesus Christ

During the night of 23 November 1654, Pascal had a strange and wonderful vision of God. He was told to renounce the world and surrender to Jesus Christ. That night changed him, and for the rest of his life he wore round his neck a scrap of parchment bearing the date of his conversion. Over 300 years later, he is known best not for his scientific or mathematical work but for his *Pensées* ('Thoughts'), the scattered sentences about his faith which he jotted down but did not live to revise or set in order.

'The God of Christians is not a God who is simply the author of geometrical truths, or of the order of the elements . . . the God of Christians is a God of love and comfort, a God who fills the soul and heart of those whom he possesses.'

'We can have an excellent knowledge of God without that of our own wretchedness, and of our own wretchedness without that of God. But we cannot know Jesus Christ without knowing at the same time both God and our own misery.'

'All men seek happiness. This is without exception. Whatever means they employ, everyone tends to this end. Some go to war, others do not; but all have the same desire in view . . . Yet without faith no one ever reaches the goal of happiness to which we all aspire, even after years of trying.'

20 June

Extracts from John Wesley's entry in his *Journal* for 20
June 1774 reveal the hazards of eighteenth-century travel,
and Wesley's courage – he was seventy-one.

Guardian angels

'About nine I set out from Sunderland. I took Mrs Smith and her
two little girls in the chaise with me. About two miles from the
town, on a sudden both horses set out, without any visible cause
and flew down the hill like an arrow out of a bow. In a minute John
fell off the coach-box. The horses went on full speed. A narrow
bridge was at the foot of the hill. They went directly over the
middle of it. They ran up the next hill with the same speed, many
persons getting out of the way. Near the top of the hill was a gate
which led into a farmer's yard. It stood open. They turned and
ran through it, without touching the gate on one side or the post
on the other. I thought, "the gate on the other side of the yard will
stop them"; but they rushed through it as if it had been a cobweb
and galloped on through the cornfield. The little girls cried out; I
told them, "Nothing will hurt you; do not be afraid"; feeling no
more fear than if I had been sitting in my study. The horses ran on
till they came to the edge of a steep precipice. Just then, Mr
Smith, who could not overtake us before, galloped in between.
They stopped in a moment. Had they gone on ever so little, he
and we must have gone down together!

'I am persuaded both evil and good angels had a large share in
this transaction; how large we do not know, but we shall know
hereafter.'

See also 2 March, 28 June, 24 July

21June

Isaiah was a Jewish prophet who lived in the eighth century BC. God chose him to bring his message to the people of Judah. Somehow Isaiah had to make them listen. At the annual grape harvest there was always a mood of holiday, and singers probably entertained the crowds. Isaiah may have sung this song, with its unexpected sting in the tail, to the people who had come to enjoy themselves. They listened to his song – and heard God's message.

Bible story – about disappointing results

'Listen while I sing this song,
   a song of my friend and his vineyard.
My friend had a vineyard
   on a very fertile hill.
He dug the soil and cleared it of stones;
   he planted the finest vines.
He built a tower to guard them,
   dug a pit for treading the grapes.
He waited for the grapes to ripen,
   but every grape was sour.'

From *Isaiah 5*

PRAYER
Thank you, Father, for all the loving care you lavish on us. Thank you for the advantages of freedom, security, education, family and church. Help us to respond, in lives that bring pleasure to you and benefit to others. Amen

22 June

In June 1965, the Corrymeela site at Ballycastle, County Antrim, was bought.

The Pollen of Peace is one of the songs specially written for the Corrymeela Singers. (See 23 October for the story of the Irish Peace Movement.)

Words and music by Roger Courtney. Reprinted by permission of the Corrymeela Community. © 1980 The Corrymeela Community.

23 June

The annual Lawn Tennis Championships at Wimbledon take place each year at the end of June and beginning of July.

Gerald Williams is Tennis Correspondent for the BBC Radio Sports Department. He also hosts all-round sports programmes and commentates on football. He spends six months of each year travelling with the tennis teams on their world circuit.

New brother – new sister

What's the best part about being a Christian in his job? Gerald Williams answers without hesitation: 'Knowing that down there – out in the scrum of the field or the high tension of the court, far removed from the peaceful oasis of the commentary-box, is a brother or sister – another Christian.'

One day, Gerald was covering the American Tennis Championships at Flushing Meadow. 'It had been a gruelling day and it was nearly midnight when we were packed tight in the coach taking us back to our hotels. There were players, sports-writers, the press – all jammed together. No one felt much like smiling. Then I noticed a bright-eyed girl, with a racket, sitting not far from where I was squeezed in. I leant across.

'"Are you Wendy White?"

'"Yes – Hi!" she replied, with a friendly grin.

'"Then you and I are brother and sister," I said.

'"Isn't that great? That makes the third new Christian brother or sister I've met today," Wendy responded.

'Suddenly the tiredness, the crush, the disappointments of the day didn't seem to matter any more.'

BIBLE VERSE
'Now that you have faith in Christ Jesus you are all sons of God. You are all one in Christ Jesus.'
From *Galatians 3 (J.B.Phillips)*

24 June

On 24 June 1965, a special centenary meeting of the
Salvation Army was held in the Albert Hall in London.

A brass band!

'Mr Booth! A brass band!' exclaimed a young Salvation Army officer, who was used to singing her solos to the accompaniment of a chapel organ. 'I don't think I should like it in connection with religious services.'

But William Booth and other enthusiastic officers thought otherwise. A father and his three sons, who all played brass instruments, first decided that a bit of cornet- and trombone-playing might quell the noise of hecklers at open-air meetings. The band not only drowned interruptions, it also drew a crowd. By Christmas 1879, a band had been formed in Consett, County Durham, in time to play carols for local residents. Salvation Army bands still do this countrywide.

'Bring out your cornets and harps and organs and flutes and violins and pianos and drums and everything else that can make a melody,' General Booth ordered in the magazine *War Cry*. 'Offer them to God and use them to make all the hearts about you merry before the Lord.'

'I don't think I've ever seen a gloomy member of the Salvation Army,' the Archbishop of Canterbury declared at the centenary celebrations in 1965.

PRAISE
'Praise him with trumpets.
   Praise him with harps and lyres.
Praise him with drums and dancing.
   Praise him with harps and flutes.
Praise him with cymbals.
   Praise him with loud cymbals.
Praise the Lord, all living creatures!
Praise the Lord!'
From *Psalm 150*

See also 10 April, 2 and 20 July

25 June

Sydney Smith could not afford to read for the bar, so entered the church as one of the professions open to the sons of gentlemen. But he did much to help his parishioners. He was a brilliant and witty writer, whose forthright views sometimes made him unpopular.
Many Christians today have a conscience about over-eating. Cookery books are written to suggest ways in which we can be more resourceful and less extravagant in our food consumption, so that the half of the world that is hungry may have enough to eat. This kind of thinking is not new to our age, it seems. Sydney Smith felt the same way and put his ideas humorously to a friend who obviously ate far too much.

Enough is enough

Part of a letter from Sydney Smith to Lord Murray:

'If you wish for anything like health and happiness in the fifth act of life, eat and drink about one half what you *could* eat and drink. Did I ever tell you my calculation about eating and drinking? Having ascertained the weight of what I could live upon, so as to preserve health and strength, and what I did live upon, I found that, between ten and seventy years of age, I had eaten and drunk forty four-horse wagon-loads of meat and drink more than would have preserved me in life and health! The value of this mass of nourishment I considered to be worth seven thousand pounds sterling. It occurred to me that I must, by my voracity, have starved to death fully a hundred persons. This is a frightful calculation, but irresistibly true; and I think, dear Murray, your wagons would require an additional horse each!'

PRAYER
We thank you, Lord, for food and drink and for the enjoyment they give. Help us not to misuse the plenty we have. May we never be wasteful, self-indulgent or greedy. Teach us to live simply so that others may simply live. For Jesus' sake. Amen

26 June

The United Nations was founded on 26 June 1945.

Dag Hammarskjöld had a brilliant career. He was a member of the Swedish Cabinet before becoming Secretary General of the United Nations. He worked relentlessly at being an 'international civil servant'. He believed his task was to serve others and never spared himself. He was killed in 1961 in an air crash, while on a UN peace mission.

The only true profile

'Dear Leif

'Perhaps you may remember I once told you that . . . I kept a diary which I wanted you to take charge of someday. Here it is. It was begun without a thought of anybody else reading it. But what with my later history and all that has been said and written about me, the situation has changed. These entries provide the only true "profile" that can be drawn. If you find them worth publishing you have my permission to do so.

'Dag'

Dag Hammarskjöld's diary is not a day-to-day record of events but contains his innermost thoughts about life, death and God. He called them 'signposts, pointing a path of which the traveller did not wish to speak while he was alive'. They have helped to point the way to many other people.

PRAYER OF DAG HAMMARSKJÖLD
Give me a pure heart – that I may see thee,
A humble heart – that I may hear thee,
A heart of love – that I may serve thee,
A heart of faith – that I may abide in thee.

See also 27 June

27 June

Signposts – to humility

'He came with his little girl. She wore her best frock. You noticed what good care she took of it. Others noticed too – idly noticed that last year it had been the best frock on another little girl. In the morning sunshine it had been festive. Now most people had gone home. The balloon-sellers were counting the day's takings. Even the sun had followed their example and retired to rest behind a cloud. So the place looked rather bleak and deserted when he came with his little girl to taste the joy of Spring and warm himself in the freshly polished Easter sun.

'But she was happy. They both were. They had learned a humility of which you still have no conception. A humility which never makes comparisons, never rejects what there is for the sake of something "else" or "more" . . . '

'To be humble is *not to make comparisons*. Secure in its reality, the self is neither better nor worse, bigger nor smaller than anything else in the universe . . . '

'There is nobody from whom you cannot learn. Before God, who speaks through all men, you are always in the bottom class of the nursery school.'

PRAYER
Hallowed be thy name,
  Not mine.
Thy kingdom come,
  Not mine.
Thy will be done,
  Not mine.
Give us peace with thee,
Peace with men,
Peace with ourselves,
And free us from all fear.
Extracts from *Markings*, by Dag Hammarskjöld

See also 26 June

28 June

John Wesley was born on 28 June 1703.

John Wesley declared that the world was his parish. He did not stay inside church preaching to wealthy congregations but went out and about among ordinary people in the tradition of preaching friars of bygone times. He never forgot how his own heart had been 'strangely warmed' when he trusted in Christ alone for salvation. It was this gospel message which changed lives and changed England in the eighteenth century. Elderly people are sometimes interviewed on radio or television and asked how they account for their long life and health. Wesley lived at a time when the average life expectancy for a man was only forty years. In his *Journal* he gives his rather unusual reasons for feeling fitter than ever at seventy-one.

Secrets of a healthy old age!

'This being my birthday, the first day of my seventy-second year, I was considering how is it that I find just the same strength as I did thirty years ago? That my sight is considerably better now and my nerves firmer than they were then? That I have none of the infirmities of old age and have lost several I had in my youth? The grand cause is the good pleasure of God who doeth whatsoever pleaseth him. The chief means are:

'1) My constantly rising at four for about fifty years; 2) My generally preaching at five in the morning, one of the most healthy exercises in the world; 3) My never travelling less, by sea or land, than four thousand five hundred miles in a year.'

From John Wesley's *Journal*

See also 2 March, 20 June, 24 July

29 June

29 June is St Peter's Feast Day.

Never mind him!

They strolled across the firm sand beside the lake. Peter felt warm and comfortably full after the good breakfast Jesus had cooked for him and the other disciples. The cold and frustration of the night's fruitless fishing expedition were forgotten. But the deep sense of his denial and failure was still in Peter's mind.

'Peter, do you love me?' Jesus asked him.

'You know I do, Lord!' Peter answered warmly.

'Then take care of my sheep,' Jesus said. 'Following me won't be easy,' he went on. 'When you are old, you will be taken by others – where you don't want to go!'

Peter didn't flinch. He wanted the chance to show that he *was* prepared to face arrest or death for the Master. But he couldn't help wondering what the future held for the rest of the group. There was John, now, walking a bit behind them.

'What about him?' he asked Jesus, with a jerk of the head in John's direction.

'Never mind about him,' Jesus replied. 'It's not your business what happens to John. What matters is that *you* follow me.'

Peter spent the rest of his life, before his own martyrdom, doing what Jesus had asked: following in Jesus' steps and caring for his sheep – all the men and women who made up the 'flock', or church of Jesus, the Good Shepherd.

Adapted from *John 21*

See also 30 June

30 June

Peter wrote his first letter to Christians throughout the
Roman Empire in about AD 63. The storm was brewing.
Christianity was becoming a forbidden religion and
Christians unpopular. In the year 64, Rome was burned
down and Emperor Nero, looking for a scapegoat, blamed
the Christians. Peter warns his readers of coming
persecution and tells them how to face present suffering.

Suffering for Christ

'My dear friends, do not be surprised at the painful test you are
suffering, as though something unusual were happening to you.
Rather be glad that you are sharing Christ's sufferings, so that
you may be full of joy when his glory is revealed. Happy are you if
you are insulted because you are Christ's followers; this means
that the glorious Spirit, the Spirit of God, is resting on you. If any
of you suffers, it must not be because he is a murderer or a thief or
a criminal or meddles in other people's affairs. However, if you
suffer because you are a Christian, don't be ashamed of it, but
thank God that you bear Christ's name. . . . So then, those who
suffer because it is God's will for them, should by their good
actions trust themselves completely to their Creator, who always
keeps his promise.'

From *1 Peter 4*

'If you endure suffering even when you have done right, God
will bless you for it. It was to this that God called you, for Christ
himself suffered for you and left you an example, so that you
would follow in his steps. He committted no sin, and no one
ever heard a lie come from his lips. When he was insulted, he
did not answer back with an insult; when he suffered, he did not
threaten but placed his hopes in God, the righteous Judge.
Christ himself carried our sins in his body to the cross, so that
we might die to sin and live for righteousness. It is by his
wounds that you have been healed. You were like sheep that had
lost their way, but now you have been brought back to follow the
Shepherd and Keeper of your souls.'

From *1 Peter 2*

See also 29 June

1 July

Sir Thomas More was tried for treason on 1 July 1535.

Thomas More, born in 1478, was a great scholar and close friend of Henry VIII. Because he refused to countenance Henry's divorce of Catherine of Aragon and marriage to Anne Boleyn, he was accused of treason and executed. Forty years later, Thomas Stapleton wrote his biography. He learned many details of More's life from Dorothy Harris who was maid to More's much-loved daughter, Margaret Roper. He also had access to More's letters. He wrote his book in Latin and it was first translated into English only about sixty years ago.

The faithful servant of God and the King

'After receiving sentence of death and being led back to the Tower on July 1, 1535, Thomas More prepared himself for approaching death. He was in no way cast down or anxious in mind: he was not only quite resigned, but even cheerful and merry. During those last days, within the narrow limits of his prison, he would walk up and down clad in a linen sheet, like a corpse about to be buried, and severely discipline himself.

'When the day arrived which was to bring More death, or rather life, he was led out of his prison. His beard was long and disordered, his face was pale and thin from the rigours of his confinement. He held in his hand a red cross and raised his eyes to heaven. His robe was of the very poorest and coarsest. He had decided to make his last journey in a better garment and to put on a gown of camlet, which Bonvisi had given him in prison, both to please his friend and to be able to give it to the executioner. But through the avarice or wickedness of his gaoler, he who had held such high office, went out clad in his servant's gown made of the basest material that we call frieze.'

From Thomas Stapleton's *Life of Sir Thomas More*

See also 6 July, 3 September

2 July

On 2 July 1865, William Booth preached in London's East
End and a newspaper reported that 'Four professed to find
peace in believing and two backsliders were restored'.

Soldiers in the King's army

'In three Colts Lane in an old wool shed,
We frighten the living and raise the dead,
  Sing glory, hallelujah!
And while the rats were running round,
The boys and girls salvation found.'

The children sang their song lustily as they went with their
leader, William Booth, on a never-to-be-forgotten outing to
Epping Forest. Booth had seen enough of the effects of poverty
when he worked in a pawnbroker's shop, and determined to meet
the needs of the Londoners he came to help, not just attempt to
save their souls. 'What is the use of preaching the gospel to men
whose whole attention is concentrated upon a desperate struggle
to keep alive?' he asked. 'He cannot hear you any more than a man
whose head is under water can listen to a sermon.'

As well as a rat-ridden wool-shed, Booth used a dancing
academy, a skittle alley, hay-loft, public house and music-hall as
premises for preaching. He declared war on 'pinching poverty,
rags and misery'. A war was on, and the Salvation Army was there
to fight it. Under Booth's generalship, the meetings in the wool
shed grew into an international army combating poverty, suffering and sin.

See also 10 April, 24 June, 20 July

3 July

What Jesus said – about happiness

'Happy are those who know they are spiritually poor . . .
Happy are those who mourn . . .
Happy are those who are humble . . .
Happy are those whose greatest desire
  is to do what God requires . . .
Happy are those who are merciful to others . . .
Happy are the pure in heart . . .
Happy are those who work for peace . . .
Happy are those who are persecuted
  because they do what God requires.'

From *Matthew 5*

'There is more happiness in giving than in receiving.'

From *Acts 20*

PRAYER
Lord Jesus, we try to find happiness by pleasing ourselves,
by being aggressive and self-important and by closing our
minds to the unhappiness of others. Thank you for showing
us the way to true happiness. Help us to believe you and
make your teaching our guide for life, through your
strength. Amen

4 July

On 4 July 1776, America declared independence from Great Britain. 4 July is a national holiday in the USA.

George Washington had only six years of schooling before becoming a frontiersman. He fought in the war for independence. He was happiest at home on his farm at Mount Vernon, yet he served his country at great personal cost with complete integrity.

'His High Mightiness'

The first President of America stood, acknowledging the cheers of his people, dressed in a plain brown suit. He made his promises and kissed the Bible as he took the oath.

No foreign country had thought it an important enough occasion to warrant sending a minister to attend the celebrations and inauguration ceremony. But George Washington was not concerned with pomp and ceremony. His aim was to make a sound foundation for the new state of America.

But what was the correct way to address him? George Washington was the only chief of state in the world who was not a crowned monarch. Congress continued to discuss what to call him. 'His High Mightiness' was suggested, but some wit objected that the next president might not reach Washington's six feet two. With the emphasis on simplicity, it was decided that he should be simply 'Mr President'.

Washington kept his promises. He cared for the state but he also cared for individuals. In his will, he freed all his slaves, providing for those too old or young to care for themselves. After his death a member of Congress described him as 'First in war, first in peace and first in the hearts of his countrymen'.

5 July

George Borrow was born on 5 July 1803.

George Borrow translated Luke's Gospel into Romany, the language of the gypsies. His autobiography is called *Lavengro* ('word master' in Romany).

Two philosophies of life

1 The preacher

'One day, whilst I bent my way to the heath, I came to a place where a wagon was standing. There was a crowd about it which extended half way up the hill. A man in the wagon began to address the people; the subject of his address was faith. "It is the only thing we want, brethren, in this world; if we have that we are indeed rich; I would recommend you to seek faith; faith in our Lord Jesus Christ. Faith will teach us to love life when life is becoming bitter. It will teach us to face death with resignation."'

2 The gypsy

'I wandered along the heath till I came to a place where beside a thick furze sat a man, his eyes fixed intently on the red ball of the setting sun. "What is your opinion of death, Mr Petulengro?" said I as I sat down beside him. "My opinion of death, brother, is much the same as that in the old song which I have heard my grandam sing: – 'When a man dies he is cast into the earth, and his wife and child sorrow over him'." "And do you think that is the end of the man?" "There's an end of him, brother, more's the pity." "Why do you say so?" "Life is sweet, brother." "Do you think so?" "Think so! There's night and day, brother, both sweet things; sun and moon and stars, brother, all sweet things; there's likewise the wind on the heath. Life is very sweet, brother. Who would wish to die?"'

Extracts from *Lavengro*, by George Borrow

PRAYER
Thank you, Lord Jesus, for all the joy and pleasure of this life. But thank you for your promise of a richer, fuller life beyond death. May we have eternal life through knowing and trusting you. Amen

See also 6 and 7 May, 26 July

6 July

Thomas More was beheaded on 6 July 1535.

Kindness – to the executioner

'When he arrived at the place of execution and was about to mount the scaffold, he stretched out his hand for assistance, saying, "I pray you see me safe up, and for my coming down let me shift for myself." On the scaffold he wished to speak to the people, but was forbidden to do so by the Sheriff. He contented himself therefore with saying: "I call you to witness, brothers, that I die the faithful servant of God and the King and in the faith of the Catholic Church." After that, kneeling down, he recited aloud the fiftieth psalm: "Have mercy on me, O God."

'After saying the psalm and finishing his prayers he rose briskly and when, according to custom, the executioner begged his pardon, he kissed him with great love, gave him a golden angel-noble and said to him: "Thou wilt give me this day a greater benefit than any mortal man can be able to give me. Pluck up thy spirits, man, and be not afraid to do thine office."

'Even before, he had asked his daughter and other friends to do whatever acts of kindness they could to his executioner. Then the executioner wished to bind his eyes, but he said, "I will cover them myself." He covered his face with a linen cloth he had brought with him and joyfully and calmly laid his head on the block. It was at once struck off, and his soul sped to heaven.'

From Thomas Stapleton's *Life of Sir Thomas More*

See also 1 July, 3 September

7 July

Nearly 40 million Europeans were killed in the twentieth century's two terrible wars. After the Second World War, there was determination that that should never happen again. The bitter fight for national dominance between near-neighbours in a continent with a Christian culture was intolerable. So the European Economic Community (EEC) was founded in 1958.

Reaching agreement – in seven languages

'The idea of the European Community is to settle arguments democratically, by reason and compromise. It is not easy, but our democratic institutions work well.

'I represent a constituency of about 500,000 and in the parliament, was also elected the chairman of its Foreign Trade Committee. I have to get agreement in a committee of thirty-eight, with eight nationalities, seven languages and nine different political groups. No country or political group has anything like a majority, yet because we know that we have to work with each other to get anything done, it is always possible to get compromise and agreement.

'It is easy for the rich countries of the world to close their eyes to the poverty and disease elsewhere. I find the work I've been doing in trying to form the policy of this very rich group of countries towards others has been well worthwhile. But even though the parliament can get agreement, this may still be vetoed by any one of the Council of Ministers representing the member states. We still do not trust each other enough to accept a simple majority vote, and there is a long way to go to build up confidence in each other.

'I believe that each Christian has to take his duties as a citizen seriously. All adults have a vote, so we ought to use that power wisely and not selfishly. And if we have a chance to serve as a representative in parliament, then I believe we ought to take it.'
Sir Fred Catherwood

8 July

On 8 July 1974, Charles Colson began a prison sentence for his part in the Watergate affair.

Less than a week after his release from prison, Chuck Colson was back visiting those who had been his fellow-prisoners. He now works to help prisoners everywhere, not only by preaching the gospel, but by organizing training courses and encouraging prison reform.

People matter!

The Chuck Colson who had swept everyone out of the way in the interests of state and party had gone for ever. Now he was kneeling, alongside an old coal-miner, an ex-con man, a dope-peddler – praying for a sick fellow-prisoner. The White House 'hatchet man' who boasted that he would 'walk over his own grandmother' if necessary, was caring for the sick, illiterate, downtrodden in mind and body, in a rat-ridden gaol.

The change had come before his trial when he had first faced up to God through reading C.S.Lewis's book, *Mere Christianity*. If Christianity is true, he realized, every individual matters. Each has a life that will go on for ever, far longer than any state or political party. Chuck Colson accepted that belief. His pride broke down – he came as a sinner to Christ and a new way of life began.

PRAYER
Thank you, Lord, that every one of us matters supremely to you. Help us today to treat everyone we meet with that same importance, however unattractive or unpopular they may be. Help us to put people before causes. For Jesus' sake. Amen

See also 16 and 17 June

9 July

On 9 July 1643, George Fox set out from home and family to find a faith to live by.

George Fox was born in July 1624. The exact day is not known, nor are the details about his sisters and brothers, because a sexton's wife at the church of Fenny Drayton, Warwickshire, cut out the pages of the baptismal records at some time during the eighteenth century – to make covers for her preserves!

'Strike again!'

George Fox, founder of the Quakers, often faced imprisonment and abuse. One day he was dragged out of church, whipped by constables, then turned over to the crowd, who were armed with clubs and sticks. They beat him till he lay unconscious. Fox described the scene:

'I lay a little still, and the power of the Lord sprang through me, that I stood up again and stretched out my arms amongst them all and said with a loud voice, "Strike again!" There was a mason, a rude fellow, gave me a blow with all his might just atop of my hand with his walking-rule staff. And my hand and my arm was so numbed and bruised that I could not draw it unto me again. Then the people cried out, "He hath spoiled his hand for ever having any use of it more." The skin was struck off my hand and a little blood came, and I looked at it in the love of God, and I was in the love of God to them all that had persecuted me.

'And after a while the Lord's power sprang through me again, that in a minute I recovered my hand and arm and it was as well as it was before, and I had never another blow afterwards.'

PRAYER
Teach us to love our enemies and to do good to those who treat us badly. For Jesus' sake. Amen

See also 13 January

10 July

Dr Toyohiko Kagawa was born on 10 July 1888.

Toyohiko Kagawa, brought up a Buddhist, was captivated by the Christ he read about in the Gospels. He prayed: 'O God, make me like Christ.' He preached the gospel, lived and worked in the unimaginable squalor of the slums in Shinkawa. He knew that the slums would remain as long as Japanese labourers were paid such low wages and forbidden to negotiate with employers. So he organized trades unions among the dockworkers. 'Unions are necessary,' he said, 'but labour problems can only be solved by a change in the heart of the labourer himself.'

'Let there be peace!'

Every second counted. Kagawa ran as fast as he could. He *must* reach the bridge that led to the shipyard before the mob of workers got there. He was weak from tuberculosis and repeated bouts of pneumonia, and each step seemed to be tearing him apart. His heart was pounding, but still he ran – panting, heaving, gasping for breath. He reached the bridge and heard the oncoming hum of angry marchers increasing to a roar.

Kagawa had agreed to lead the workers in a peaceful demonstration, and as a result had been arrested and put in prison for two weeks. Meanwhile, communist hotheads had roused the workers to march on the shipyard to break up machinery and damage cargoes. Kagawa had heard of the march only just in time.

He leaned on the bridge for support, knowing he had neither strength nor authority to command the workers. He prayed, 'O God, let there be peace!' The first angry men grew near and Kagawa held up his hand. They stopped and he began to speak, urging them to go peacefully home so that negotiations could begin.

Moved by the entreaty of the man they loved and honoured, the rioters left their communist leaders and turned quietly back. As a result, talks began with the employers and the trades unions were recognized and accepted by management.

See also 15 August

11 July

Eric Liddell became a missionary to China. As a young man, he was chosen to represent Britain in the 100-metre sprint, but refused to enter because the heats were to be run on a Sunday. At the last moment, he began to train for the 400 metres. Because of his stand on Christian principles, the eyes of the world were on him. The film about Liddell and Harold Abrahams – *Chariots of Fire* – won four Oscars and Best Film of the Year Award for 1981.

'Chock full of fight'

'It was Liddell who first caught the eye as they came round the first bend. The Scot set up a terrific pace. He ran as if he were wild with inspiration, like some demon. As he flew along to the accompaniments of a roar, the experts wondered whether Liddell would crack, such was the pace he set . . .

'"Liddell!" was shrieked; "Imbach!" was thundered by the Swiss; "Taylor!" was shouted; "Butler!" "Fitch!" in turn were yelled.

'Liddell, yards ahead, came round the bend for the straight and as he did so, pulled the harder at himself for Fitch was getting nearer . . . It was the last fifty metres that meant the making or breaking of Liddell. Just for a second it was feared that he would kill himself by the terrible speed he had got up, but to the joy of the British camp, he remained chock full of fight. Imbach, perhaps some fifty yards from the tape, fell. It was then Liddell or Fitch. The Scotsman had so surely got all his teeth into the race that the American could not hold, and Liddell got home first . . . by a remarkable finish.'

From the *Edinburgh Evening News*, July 1924

See also 21 February

12 July

One fine and memorable 12 July, Dr Stanley Browne lunched with Queen Elizabeth II.

Stanley Browne went to the Belgian Congo (now Zaire) as a Baptist medical missionary in 1936. He became a pioneer in the treatment of leprosy and is now a leading specialist and world adviser on the disease.

'Mother of the bad leprosy'

Dr Browne persevered methodically with his survey of the villages in the Congo. His object was to discover how many people w˙re suffering from leprosy in one form or another. He had two African ex-cannibals to help him – one a witch-doctor and one a village chief. For all his medical training, he found that they were quicker than he to detect the early symptoms.

'Look,' they would say, pointing to a hardly noticeable patch of shiny skin, 'here is the beginning of the mother of the bad leprosy.'

Dr Browne knew only too well the deadly form of leprosy that they were describing. Lepromatous leprosy led to ulceration, disfigurement, deformity and eventual banishment from the tribe to live with others of their kind far from other human settlements. Stanley Browne could never forget the day that he had accidentally encountered a pitiful group of such sufferers during a journey through the forest.

Dr Browne collected his evidence, but at first no one would believe the results. They showed that exactly half the population in one district had diagnosable leprosy. He had encountered the highest leprosy rate in the whole world.

Continued on 13 July

13 July

Dr Stanley Browne never refers to his patients as 'lepers'
because of all the terrible associations the word has
acquired from Bible times to the present day. They are
sufferers from leprosy.

The package that answered prayer

Stanley Browne felt heavy at heart. All his attempts to help those
suffering from leprosy had failed. He had set up a self-contained
community where care and some relief could be given. There
was, of course, no cure. But while he was on home leave, the
inmates had abandoned it and returned to their villages, once
more to spread the dreaded bacillus. Then came a further blow.
His brightest African medical helper, Dickie, had contracted 'the
mother of the bad leprosy' – that worst form of the disease.

When he was invited to address a church leaders' conference
on the subject of leprosy, Dr Browne told them just how he felt,
and reasoned that as a foreign doctor he now needed the
co-operation of African Christians to show love and care for the
patients. Then all those present at the conference prayed in a
special way for the leprosy sufferers.

As they were praying, a small package was being delivered at
the nearest post office for Dr Browne. It was from the American
Mission to Lepers, and contained a sample of a new drug,
claimed to cure leprosy. There could be side-effects – the
American mission wanted Dr Browne to try it out. He refused to
test it on unsuspecting 'guinea-pigs', but asked for volunteers,
warning of possible drawbacks. Dickie was the first to come
forward: the first to volunteer – the first to be cured.

See also 12 July

14 July

What Jesus said – about prayer

'When you pray, go to your room, close the door, and pray to your Father, who is unseen. And your Father, who sees what you do in private, will reward you.

'When you pray, do not use a lot of meaningless words . . . Your Father already knows what you need before you ask him.'

From *Matthew 6*

'When you stand and pray, forgive anything you may have against anyone, so that your Father in heaven will forgive the wrongs you have done. When you pray and ask for something, believe that you have received it, and you will be given whatever you ask for.'

From *Mark 11*

'The Father will give you whatever you ask of him in my name.'

From *John 15*

Jesus' prayer before his death: 'Father . . . my Father! All things are possible for you. Take this cup of suffering away from me. Yet not what I want, but what you want.'

From *Mark 14*

15 July

Rain is forecast?

St Swithun's Day, if thou dost rain,
For forty days it will remain;
St Swithun's Day, if thou be fair,
For forty days 'twill rain na'mair.

No one knows the origin of the rhyme or if its weather forecast can be trusted.

St Swithun was Bishop of Winchester in the ninth century. He cared for his flock, built and repaired churches, and even built a bridge across the river. Because of his love for the countryside and for ordinary people, he requested that when he died he should be buried outside the church. He wanted sun and rain to fall on his grave and worshippers to walk across it.

His wishes were respected and in the next 100 years, weather and worshippers made all signs of Swithun's grave disappear. Then his remains were accidentally found, and the shocked monks hurried to bring his body inside the church and bury it with due honour. Legend says that the saint disapproved and that is why rain that falls on his day continues to fall for forty days and nights in his memory.

PRAYER
Father, we offer praise to you, the giver of rain and sun. We thank you for rain that makes crops and flowers grow and provides water to drink. We pray for those who are thirsty and whose fields are affected by drought. Forgive our grumbling about the weather. Amen

16 July

On 16 July 1969, an American spacecraft was launched to make the first manned moon landing.

Colonel James Irwin was born in Pennsylvania in 1930. He joined the US Air Force and later applied to NASA to become an astronaut. He took part in the *Apollo 15* mission of July 1971 and rode in the first moon buggy.

Since then, Irwin has founded the High Flight Foundation – a small mission staffed by astronauts who want to tell others about Jesus Christ. They tell both of their adventures as astronauts and their experiences as Christians.

High flight

What are the main impressions of someone who has had the unforgettable experience of travelling in space? Here are some of Jim Irwin's comments:

'It made me feel like an angel – weightless and free.'

'God became real – my faith in him came alive – I felt as though I had become a new person.'

'Earth looked like a beautiful marble.'

'Everything became crystal clear – our thinking, our understanding of each other. We found that we knew what each other was thinking before we spoke!'

'I've had my high flight. I want other people to have a high flight – not in that sense but in another. A high flight to God through Jesus Christ.'

17 July

Thomas Barnardo was born in July 1845.

Thomas Barnardo was a medical student in London, training in order to go as a missionary to China. He somehow found time to work among children, teaching in one of the so-called 'ragged schools'. Here he met Jim Jarvis. Barnardo told the story of that eventful meeting many times, but the first account appeared in a magazine, entitled 'How it all Happened'. What 'happened' was – the setting up of Dr Barnardo's Homes, which still care for children who have no parents or home of their own.

How it all happened

It was half past nine and time for the children to go home. One small straggler lingered.

'Come on, my lad,' Tom Barnardo encouraged. 'Time you were off. Your mother will be worrying.'

'I haven't got a mother – please let me stay here.'

'Where do you live?'

'Don't live nowhere.'

'Well, where did you sleep last night?'

'Down in Whitechapel, sir, in one of them carts that's filled with hay. A chap there told me to come to your school and perhaps you'd let me sleep by your fire tonight.' It was a cold night, the wind penetrating and the boy looked ill.

'Are there any more like you?' Barnardo asked.

'O yes, sir, heaps of them. More than I could count.'

Dr Barnardo took Jim back to his lodgings, gave him coffee and heard his story. An orphan, he had run away from a lighterman he called Swearing Dick, who ill-treated him. Barnardo in turn told him the story of Jesus. When he came to the crucifixion, Jim could only exclaim, 'O sir, that was worse than Swearing Dick give me.'

Continued on 18 July; see also 18 September

18 July

Goodbye China

Thomas Barnardo had one driving ambition – to take the gospel to China. This was why he had come as an almost penniless medical student to London. The goal was still crystal-clear on the night of his meeting with Jim Jarvis. But he wasn't going to wait to reach China before beginning missionary work. At midnight, he set out with Jim to find the 'heaps more' boys sleeping rough that Jim had talked of.

They reached a turning off Petticoat Lane where Jim suddenly shinned up the grooves of an iron shed and so onto the roof. He handed Dr Barnardo a stick to help him up too. This is what he saw:

'The roof was dome-shaped and adjoining was a large hay-loft used by dealers in china for packing their wares. The loft was closed but a good deal of straw had dropped from it into the gutter and was put into use by the lads whom we saw lying there asleep. With their heads upon the higher part of the roof and their feet in the gutter, in a great variety of postures, lay eleven boys, huddled together for warmth – no roof or covering of any kind was over them and the clothes they had were rags. That awful night of discovery was not forgotten. Again and again the faces of those boys entered like iron into my soul, until leaving my future in the hands of him who ruleth all hearts, I was enabled to renounce a life of usefulness in a distant land.'

Barnardo had discovered what his life's work was really going to be.

See also 17 July, 18 September

19 July

What Jesus said – about worry

'Can any of you live a bit longer by worrying about it? And why worry about clothes? Look how the wild flowers grow: they do not work or make clothes for themselves. But I tell you that not even King Solomon with all his wealth had clothes as beautiful as one of these flowers . . .

'So do not start worrying: "Where will my food come from? or my drink? or my clothes?" Your Father in heaven knows that you need all these things. Instead, be concerned above everything else with the Kingdom of God and with what he requires of you, and he will provide you with all these other things. So do not worry about tomorrow; it will have enough worries of its own. There is no need to add to the troubles each day brings.'

From *Matthew 6*

'Do not be worried and upset . . . Believe in God and believe also in me.'

From *John 14*

PRAYER
Lord Jesus, help me to put you first in my life today. Help me to trust you instead of worrying. Thank you for Christians in every age who have trusted you and found that you have taken care of them. Help me to follow their example. Amen

20 July

Catherine Bramwell Booth, daughter of the founder of the
Salvation Army, was born on 20 July 1883.

Lights in darkest England

In vain trades unions and individuals protested; in vain the
government passed regulations to protect the workers – the
match-makers still suffered. The pitifully low wages were bad
enough, but their work meant that they were also continually
handling deadly phosphorus. When they ate, the poison was
readily carried to their mouths and began by attacking their gums.
They called it 'phossy jaw', a painful and disfiguring disease
caused directly by phosphorus. The irony was that non-
poisonous, safety matches had already been invented, yet scarcely
any were being manufactured.

William Booth decided to do more than protest. In 1891, he
opened his own match factory in London's East End, producing
non-poisonous matches *only*. He employed about 100 people,
paid them well over the odds and provided comfortable work
space with facilities for washing and making tea.

Next, he organized a campaign to ensure that these matches
and not the guilty phosphorus ones were sold. His matches went
on sale as 'Lights in Darkest England', and advertisements were
displayed listing all stockists. Other Christians joined the
campaign. The public was encouraged to buy them – even from
the pulpit of Westminster Abbey. The British Match
Consumers' League was formed, whose members promised to
buy and use only safety matches. Matches became safe both for
users and for the factory workers who made them.

See also 10 April, 24 June, 2 July

21 July

Daniel lived centuries before Christ, but 21 July is set aside
in his honour in the Christian calendar.

Dare to be different

'You're in Babylon now, so forget you're Jews. We'll change your
names anyway. I picked you lot for your good looks and brains –
and because you're young and healthy. You won't be prisoners or
slaves. You'll live here at court, get a university education, then
join the king's advisers. The king – may he live for ever – says that
you're to have the best of everything. Food from the royal menu
and plenty of wine to wash it down. Any questions?'

Ashpenaz, the king's chief official, looked indulgently at the
four Jewish prisoners.

Their ringleader, Daniel, glanced quickly at his companions
then said, 'We have a request. Even though we're exiles, under
Babylonian orders, we *are* still Jews, and worshippers of the one
true God. We still want to serve him even though we're far from
our homes and from his temple. We don't want a life of luxury.
Please let us eat simple food – vegetables and pulses, with water
to drink. We don't mind being different.'

'I'd like to oblige you,' Ashpenaz replied, not unkindly, 'but it's
more than my life's worth. If his majesty noticed you were a bit
pale or off-colour it would be *my* head that would roll.' He turned
and left the room.

Daniel appealed to the guard in charge of students, who had
been standing nearby.

'Will *you* agree to our plain diet for just ten days? You can see
then if we're thriving on it or not.'

'All right,' the guard agreed dubiously, 'ten days on vegetables
and water.'

Adapted from *Daniel 1*

POSTSCRIPT
At the end of the trial period, Daniel and his friends were
healthier and stronger than the rest of the students. So their
vegetarian diet was continued and when they 'graduated' all
four became the king's favourite advisers. But even in front
of the king, all stood for God and what they believed to be
right, at the risk of their necks. You can read the stories about
them in the Old Testament book of Daniel.

PRAYER
Lord, give us courage, when to obey you means being
different from the crowd. Amen

22 July

22 July is the Feast Day of Mary Magdalene. She was the first person to see the risen Lord Jesus.

It wasn't the gardener!

Tears ran down her cheeks, blinding her. Then she made out the figure of a man standing close to her in the garden. Perhaps he could tell her what she longed to know. As if in answer to her thoughts, he spoke to her.

'Why are you crying?' he asked gently. 'You seem to be looking for someone.'

'Yes, I am,' she burst out. 'I'm looking for the body of my dearest Friend and Master. We buried him here in this rock tomb on Friday, and now his body is gone. Perhaps you're the gardener here and it's you who moved his body?'

For a moment she thought he wasn't going to answer. Then he said a single word – 'Mary!' In that instant she recognized the voice of Jesus.

'My Master!' she cried, rushing forward to grasp him.

Of course he wasn't dead – she should have known that he must conquer the power of death and rise again. She knew now that Jesus was alive for ever.

Adapted from *John 21*

23 July

Mary O'Hara married the American poet, Richard Selig, on 23 July 1956.

Mary O'Hara was known all over the world as a singer and harpist. Her husband died after only fifteen months of happy marriage and, grief-stricken, she entered an enclosed order of nuns, where she remained for twelve years. After a breakdown in her health, she left the convent and has resumed her singing and playing career. She tells her own story in her book, *The Scent of Roses.*

The music of silence

'One day last summer, after I'd been working on some songs, I left the harp before the open window. Suddenly I heard the sound of distant and very lovely music. It lasted only a few seconds and left me very puzzled. When it happened again I noticed that the sound came from the instrument and was caused by the gentle breeze from the open window playing on the harp strings.

'At times of prayer we can be like that harp, by allowing sufficient calm to gather round us so that the Holy Spirit, the Breath of God, may play his music on us. But remember, it was a very gentle breeze and the music could be heard only because of the surrounding stillness.'

Mary O'Hara

24 July

Letter written on 24 July 1732 by Susanna Wesley to her son, John, containing some of her rules on bringing up children.

Susanna, wife of the Reverend Samuel Wesley, had nineteen children, of whom the best known are the preachers and hymn-writers, John and Charles.

Cry softly!

'Dear Son,

'According to your desire, I have collected the principal rules I observed in educating my family; which I now send you.

1. When turned a year old (and some before), they were taught to fear the rod and to cry softly; by which means they escaped abundance of correction; and that most odious noise of the crying of children was rarely heard in the house.

2. It had been observed that cowardice and fear of punishment often led children into lying till they get a custom of it which they cannot leave. To prevent this, a law was made that whoever was charged with a fault of which they were guilty, if they would confess it and promise to amend, should not be beaten.

3. No child should ever be chid or beaten twice for the same fault; and that if they amended, they should never be upbraided with it afterwards.'

From Wesley's *Journal*

See also 2 March, 20 and 28 June

25 July

25 July is St Christopher's Day.

Christopher, first called Reprobus, is the patron saint of travellers. He died in about AD 250. The story is told that he determined to serve only the greatest and most powerful prince in the world. He found his Master in Jesus Christ and was told to serve him by carrying travellers across a strong-flowing river that had neither bridge nor ford.

The world on his shoulders

One night, so legend says, Christopher was awakened by a child calling from the river-bank. When he went there, he could see no one. The call came twice more and only on his third search did he find the child.

'Please carry me across the river,' the child asked, and Christopher tossed him on to his shoulders and prepared to stride across with ease, bearing such a light burden.

But the waters of the river swirled and rose higher and higher. The child on his shoulders grew heavier and heavier, until he was afraid that he would never make the far side. He struggled on, weighed down by his burden and tugged by the currents. At last he reached the shore and set the child thankfully down.

'I felt as though I had the whole world on my shoulders,' he confessed to him.

'Don't be surprised,' the child said. 'You have not only carried the world on your shoulders, but you have carried the one who made the world. I am Jesus Christ – the King you serve.'

So Reprobus was renamed Christopher – or 'the Christ-bearer'.

BIBLE VERSE
'Help to carry one another's burdens, and in this way you will obey the law of Christ.'
From *Galatians 6*

PRAYER
We pray today for all travellers, by land, sea or air. Keep them safe and give them peace of mind. Help them to be considerate for others as well as concerned for themselves, so may they safely reach their destinations. Amen

26 July

George Borrow died on 26 July 1881.

When George Borrow visited Wales, he asked for a walking
companion who spoke only Welsh so that he could improve
his skill in the language. He was introduced to Mr Jones.
He had once been a shepherd, but was now a weaver,
because he reckoned being able to attend chapel on Sunday
and join with other Christians, more important than
collecting three times the amount of money in his weekly pay
packet!

Another Jones!

'We set out; my guide conducted me along the bank of the
Camlas in the direction of Rhiwabon. I asked if he had been
anything but a weaver. He told me that when a boy he had kept
sheep on the mountain.

'"Why did you not go on keeping sheep?" said I. "I would
rather keep sheep than weave."

'"My parents wanted me at home, sir, and I was not sorry to
go."

'"A shepherd can earn more."

'"Sir, I would rather be a weaver with five shillings a week in
Llangollen than a shepherd with fifteen on the mountain. The
life of a shepherd, sir, is perhaps not exactly what you and some
other gentlefolks think. The shepherd bears much cold and wet
and he is very lonely; no society but his sheep and dog. Then, sir,
he has no privileges. I mean gospel privileges. The shepherd has
no chapel like the weaver."

'"Do you mean to say that you live with your family on five
shillings a week?"

'"No, sir, I do little commissions by which I earn something.
Then I have friends, very good friends. A good lady of our
congregation sent me this morning half a pound of butter. The
people of our congregation are very kind to each other, sir."

'"What was your wife's name before she was married?"

'"Her name was Jones, sir."

'"What, before she was married?"

'"Yes, sir, before she was married. You need not be surprised,
sir; there are plenty of the name of Jones in Wales. The name of
my brother's wife before she married was also Jones."'

Adapted from *Journey Through Wales*, by George Borrow

See also 6 and 7 May, 5 July

27 July

On 27 July 1943, Dietrich Bonhoeffer wrote to his parents
from prison:

If only . . .

'To think you came here yesterday in all that heat to bring me the
parcel! I hope it hasn't exhausted you too much. Many thanks for
coming and for all the things you brought for me. The summer
produce is particularly welcome, of course. Fancy the tomatoes
being ripe already! I am feeling the warmth for the first time just
now. But it is not too unpleasant in the cell, especially as I keep
pretty still most of the time. The only trouble is that I long more
and more for fresh air. If only I could spend an evening in the
garden again . . .

'Each time I hope this will be my last letter from prison. If only
we could have a few of these lovely summer days together!'

PRAYER
Father, we thank you that we are free to come and go and
enjoy liberty. We remember all who long for freedom. Give
courage and comfort to all who are in prison or labour
camp because of their Christian faith. For Jesus' sake.
Amen

See also 4 and 5 February

28 July

Dr Spooner was an excellent lecturer in spite of his slips of the tongue. His subjects were divinity, ancient history and philosophy. He knew all his students personally, and he and his wife always made them welcome at their house. He was best on social occasions and was known for his witty speeches. He was described as a good man 'undisturbed by outside storms' as he went quietly and calmly about his work of teaching and befriending generations of Oxford undergraduates.

Spoonerisms

The Warden of New College, Oxford, announced the hymn in morning chapel and a ripple of suppressed laughter ran round the congregation. 'Kinquering Congs their titles take,' he had solemnly pronounced.

This was not the first time that the much-loved gentle doctor had made the same kind of mistake. Talking gravely to a lazy student who was being sent down, he had said, 'You have deliberately tasted two worms and you can leave Oxford by the town drain.'

At least, that is what he is *supposed* to have said. It's hard to tell where true stories end and legend begins. But Dr Spooner's mistakes did give a new word to the English language – 'spoonerisms'.

29 July

William Wilberforce died on 29 July 1833.

Wilberforce is best known for his long campaign as a
Christian Member of Parliament, to abolish the slave-trade.
He also campaigned against cruelty to animals. In 1824 he
was a founder member of the society which has since
become the Royal Society for the Prevention of Cruelty to
Animals (RSPCA).

'Stop beating that animal!'

A short, bent, elderly gentleman trudged laboriously up the hill.
In the road alongside him, two tired horses struggled and strained
to drag their heavy load of coals up the steep street. Suddenly one
of the horses fell and lay still in the road, too exhausted to get up,
worn out with years of overwork. Its owner, a large, strong man,
was furious. He swore loudly at the horse, kicked it savagely, then
began beating it again and again to make it get up.

In an instant, the little old man had rushed across.

'Stop beating that animal!' he ordered. 'How dare you ill-use
your horse! He is too ill and too old to get up. He needs your care
not curses.'

The carter looked up astonished, face like a thunder-cloud,
glaring at the man who had dared to interfere. His whip was still
raised, and he looked as though he might use it on the stranger
instead of the horse. Then the other carter nudged him fiercely
and whispered, 'Look who it is – it's Mr Wilberforce!'

The mention of that well-known and respected name had
immediate effect. The angry carter dropped his arm and his look
changed from fury to wonder and admiration.

30 July

Pavel Timofeyevich Rytikov was born on 30 July 1930.

Pavel Rytikov became a youth evangelist in the Baptist Church in the USSR. He was arrested with his eighteen-year-old son, Vladimir, because they had been leading a camp for the children of Baptists in prison for their faith. Both are now in prison, sharing their Christian faith with their fellow-prisoners.

Would they have horns?

Life had been tough for Pavel Rytikov. An orphan by the age of twelve, he started work as a miner at thirteen. By the time he was twenty-two, he was experienced as a metal-worker – and also as a thief and gambler.

One night, when he and his pals had been out drinking, Pavel suggested visiting one of those places of prayer – just for a laugh. Christians did some pretty horrible things, according to the press, including offering human sacrifices. Pavel felt a shiver of excitement at what he might see. These Christians might even have horns!

They broke into the little meeting, noisy and half-drunk. To their amazement, the believers – some as young as they were – *looked* just like anyone else. But they weren't like everyone else, Pavel soon decided. They were so gentle and kind, their singing was so happy and joyful, their love for one another shone through for all to see. Pavel went back, and back again. One night, he too put his faith in the Lord and Saviour they worshipped, and a new way of life began.

31 July

Ignatius of Loyola died on 31 July 1556.

Before he died, the Society of Jesus, founded by St Ignatius, had grown from ten to 1,000 members.

Saint with a limp

The boys tittered when Ignatius made yet another mistake with his Latin translation. He was old enough to be their father, but he smiled too. In the playground, the boys took little notice when Ignatius limped past. Yet his wound had been gained fighting for Spain as a soldier.

It was while he was recovering at home in Loyola that his life had changed. Bored, he asked for the latest novel to read, but the castle contained only religious books. Ignatius began reading a life of Christ and idle curiosity soon changed to intense interest. He realized that he was faced with the choice of continuing his old life or serving a new Master, Jesus Christ. He chose to follow Christ and began to tell others about him.

Because he was not a trained priest, he was imprisoned and threatened with flogging for daring to preach. So he set about studying, first in a boys' school in Barcelona. Once qualified, he gathered a small band of followers and together they took vows of poverty, chastity and obedience to God and the pope. They formed themselves into a society to serve Jesus Christ.

PRAYER OF ST IGNATIUS OF LOYOLA
Receive, Lord, all my liberty, my memory, my understanding and my whole will. You have given me all that I have, all that I am, and I surrender all to your divine will, that you dispose of me. Give me only your love and your grace. With this I am rich enough and I have no more to ask.

1 August

Bread – to live by

The church in England was keeping Lammas as long ago as the time of King Alfred the Great.

Lammas probably comes from two Old English words – *hlaf* (loaf) and *mas* (feast). On 1 August, a special loaf of bread, made from the very first corn ripe that year, was brought to church. It was a time to thank God in anticipation of the harvest to come. The first promise of the ripening crops to follow could be seen in this new loaf.

In Old Testament times, there was also a custom of bringing to God the 'first-fruits' that ripened, and a sample loaf was made from the corn. It was a reminder that what God had already given was a guarantee of what was still to come when the full harvest was gathered.

BIBLE VERSE
Paul said: 'Christ has been raised from death, as the guarantee [first-fruits] that those who sleep in death will also be raised.'
From *1 Corinthians 15*

PRAYER
Thank you, Father, for Jesus Christ, the true Bread of Life. We believe that because you raised him from death, we who trust in him shall have everlasting life. Amen

2 August

John and Audrey Coleman, missionaries in Iran, were
arrested in August 1980, and, though innocent of any
charges, were held separately in prison for six months.

Lord of the rough and the smooth

It was December, and Chris was busy laying a garden path. His
thoughts slipped naturally to his parents in prison. He felt a
certain conviction that he should pray for their release. He
contacted another brother, Andrew, and found he had the same
compulsion. Strangely, up to that time, the four brothers had met
together to pray, but had not felt that the time was right to pray for
Dr and Mrs Coleman to be set free. But they found that, as
Christians, they could discover God in every situation.

'As a family we had had it pretty smooth until this happened,'
Chris admits. 'Finding ourselves in this rough situation, we
found God in it.'

Chris became chief spokesman for the family in the frequent
interviews on radio and television which followed the Colemans'
much-publicized arrest. Chris is glad that they had the
opportunity to let everyone know of their trust in God and their
freedom from bitterness against those who had unjustly
imprisoned their parents.

The last two weeks of waiting were the worst. Rumours kept
flying around that the Colemans would be released any day – yet
nothing happened. Their sons just turned back to God and hung
on to their belief that he was in control. As for John and Audrey
Coleman – they left Iran with love in their hearts for their captors,
and a longing to return. Dr Coleman made good use of his time in
prison – he read his Bible through five and a half times!

See also 21 August

3 August

On 3 August 1666, M. Beaufort, Grand Vicar, first met Brother Laurence and heard his story.

Later, he wrote down the conversations he had with Brother Laurence, together with letters Brother Laurence had written. The little book is called *The Practice of the Presence of God* and has been a source of help and inspiration to Christians ever since.

Parable of a tree

A young man of eighteen, Nicholas Herman, was out walking in midwinter. Snow was on the ground. He stopped, his eyes caught by the sight of a great tree, rising bare and gaunt, its branches standing cold and hopeless against the bleak horizon.

Suddenly, there flowed into his mind a picture of that same tree as it would be when spring came. Fresh green leaves and new growth would transform the bare trunk, and instead of apparent death there would be luxuriant life.

With that flash of his imagination came a deep and glowing realization of the power and purpose of God. His whole life was born anew. He no longer cared to continue with his job as a footman and soldier. He wanted to give himself wholly to the God of love and power who had made himself known to him in that instant of thought and time. He joined the barefooted Carmelite Order of monks in Paris, and because he was no scholar, he spent the rest of his long life as a lay brother, in the service of others.

PRAYER
Lord, open our eyes to your greatness and power. Bring life and beauty into our lives. Amen

Continued on 4 August

4 August

God among the pots and barrels

Nicholas Herman was renamed Brother Laurence and set to work in the monastery kitchen. The work was not the kind he naturally enjoyed, but he found a way to make it pleasurable. His love for God was so great that every task was done out of love. Love for God could make a pleasure out of picking up a straw from the kitchen floor. He learned to talk to God and recognize his presence all day long. The heat, the banging of pots and pans, the steam and the greasy dishes never ruffled him.

One day, he was ordered to Burgundy to buy the monastery's wine supply. Brother Laurence's heart failed – he had no head for business and besides, being lame, it would be hard for him to move around on the boat, unless he rolled his way over the wine-barrels. He told God his problem: 'I can't do this, Lord,' he prayed, 'unless you help me.'

The help that God gave was enough for the unexpected task, and the mission to Burgundy was successfully accomplished.

When he failed, Brother Laurence did not spend time bewailing the fact, but admitted that failure on his own was no more than he could expect. 'Lord, I keep failing,' he would say, 'I can't stop myself, but you can stop me and hold me up.'

God's love, God's power and God's presence made Brother Laurence's kitchen a place like heaven.

PRAYER
'To him who is able to keep you from falling, and to bring you faultless and joyful before his glorious presence – to the only God our Saviour, through Jesus Christ our Lord, be glory, majesty, might and authority, from all ages past, and now, and for ever and ever! Amen.'
From *Jude's letter*

See also 3 August

5 August

On 5 August 642, Oswald, 'most Christian king' of Northumbria, died in battle.

Oswald became king in AD 634, after a battle fought against the pagans. Before the battle, Oswald set up a cross and prayed for God's help against the heathen force. Heavenfield, the place where he prayed, can be visited in Northumberland. The Venerable Bede tells many stories about Oswald in his *Ecclesiastical History*. After his death, according to Bede, so many pious people came to take earth from the spot where he fell, so that the 'holy' dust might cure their ills, that they left a hole six feet deep!

Beggars' delight

One day, Oswald was sitting at supper, his dearly-loved Bishop Aidan, who lived on the nearby island of Lindisfarne, beside him. They were at Bamburgh Castle, home of the kings of Northumbria, looking down on the broad, golden sands and out over the wild North Sea. A large silver dish, set out with tempting meats prepared in the royal kitchen, had just been set before the king and his guests.

As the king was about to help himself from the loaded dish, a servant hurried into the room, bowing low to the king. Oswald recognized him as the official he had put in charge of caring for the poor.

'Your majesty,' the servant said, 'the street outside is full of poor and hungry people begging help from the king.'

Without a moment's hesitation, the king lifted the huge dish towards his servant.

'Take this,' he ordered. 'First share out the food, then have the dish cut into pieces so that all those in need may have a piece of silver.'

6 August

Bible wisdom – about pride

'The Lord has no use for conceited people but shows favour to those who are humble.'

'The Lord hates everyone who is arrogant; he will never let them escape punishment.'

'People who are proud will soon be disgraced. It is wiser to be modest.'

'Pride leads to destruction and arrogance to downfall.'

'Conceited people do not like to be corrected; they never ask for advice from those who are wiser.'

'Arrogance causes nothing but trouble. It is wiser to ask for advice.'

'If you brag all the time you are asking for trouble.'

From the *Book of Proverbs*

'Do not be proud, but accept humble duties. Do not think of yourselves as wise.'

From *Romans 12*

'All of you serve each other with humble spirits, for God gives special blessings to those who are humble, but sets himself against those who are proud. If you will humble yourselves under the mighty hand of God, in his good time he will lift you up.'

From *1 Peter 5 (The Living Bible)*

See also 16 June

7 August

August is the height of the cricket season in Britain. One of Brian Booth's daughters was born in August.

Brian Booth, Australian cricketer, played in his first Test Match in 1961, and scored his first Test century in Brisbane the following year. He first captained the Australian side in the 1965 Test series between Australia and England. He is married with four daughters, and lives in Sydney.

A member of the team

'One morning, I saw my name in the newspaper. I had been chosen for my first Test Match. I was invited to play in the Australian touring side against England.

'As I walked on to the field to bat at Old Trafford, an ambition was achieved. My batting partner greeted me with the words, "We're in trouble. We need a good partnership." I replied nervously, "Yes, the captain's depending on us." To do the job we needed each other, we couldn't bat alone. But to have purpose and direction, we needed our captain's guidance.

'As a schoolboy and as a college student, cricket had been my god. One evening, I was asked if I knew Jesus in a personal way. I didn't then – but I discovered soon afterwards that I could be a life-member of God's family, not through my own efforts or ability, but by taking God at his word, which says that Jesus is the Way to him.

'It's a tremendous experience to walk on to a cricket-field knowing you are a member of a Test team and have a fine captain to guide you. In life, however, there is only one captain who matters – the Lord Jesus Christ. As I follow him, I realize how much I need other people of like mind and how much they need me, but true fellowship depends on having Christ at the centre.

'Being a member of Christ's team gives considerable joy, happiness and responsibility. He is my captain, he has the book of rules and says, "If you love me, do what I tell you."'

Brian Booth

8 August

Izaak Walton was born on 8 August 1593.

Izaak Walton wrote biographies of such well-known clergymen of his time as John Donne and George Herbert, but he is best known for his book about fishing – *The Compleat Angler*. Even in his lifetime it ran into five editions. It is full of good advice about every aspect of fishing, but above all it sings the praises of fishing as the best of all recreations.

The Compleat Angler

'He that hopes to be a good angler, must not only bring an inquiring, searching, observing wit, but he must bring a large measure of hope and patience, and a love and propensity to the art itself; but having once got and practised it, then doubt not but angling will prove to be so pleasant, that it will prove to be, like virtue, a reward to itself.

'We may say of angling, as Dr Boteler said of strawberries, "Doubtless God could have made a better berry, but doubtless God never did"; and so, if I might be judge, God never did make a more calm, innocent recreation than angling . . .

'When I would beget content . . . I will walk the meadows, by some gliding stream, and there contemplate . . . the various little living creatures that are not only created, but fed, man knows not how, by the goodness of the God of nature, and therefore trust in him. That is my purpose; and so, let everything that hath breath praise the Lord: and let the blessing of St Peter's Master be with mine. And upon all that are lovers of virtue; and dare trust in his providence; and be quiet; and go a Angling.'

> 'Of recreation there is none
> So free as fishing is alone.'

PRAYER
Thank you, Lord, for the open air, the countryside and for all recreations that bring quietness and contentment. Amen

See also 3 and 4 March

9 August

On 10 August, 1950 Fred Lemon had a vision of Jesus in his prison cell. A life of violence and crime had eventually brought him to Dartmoor prison, without hope and full of anger and bitterness.

'This is Jesus'

Fred Lemon was sleeping the fitful sleep of a man who has spent a day without exercise or satisfying work. Since his last unappetising meal, the evening had stretched endlessly. The light from the gas-lamp was too dim to read by, and bed had been the only alternative. Fred stirred slightly and turned on his prison bunk.

Then he saw them. Three men stood quietly at the foot of his bed – ordinary men in ordinary suits. One of them spoke.

'Fred,' he said, 'this is Jesus', and he pointed to the man in the centre.

Then Jesus began to talk to him. He spoke about Fred's whole past life – the drinking, the violence, the bad friends and the crime that had brought him at last to Dartmoor, on a charge of robbery with violence. He spoke of the good things too, of Fred's small kindnesses and his efforts to reform. There was no harshness in the words, only love. Fred understood that God could and did forgive him.

Afterwards, Fred could remember clearly only Jesus' parting words: 'Fred, if you want to be a Christian, you must drive the hatred from your heart.' Then, with a palpable click, the three men passed through the thick stone walls and out of his cell. Fred lay back and slept peacefully.

Next morning, he knew that what had happened had not been a dream. Jesus Christ had appeared to him just as surely as he had appeared to Saul on the Damascus road nearly 2,000 years before. But as for those words – 'Drive hatred from your heart' – that was impossible.

Continued on 10 August

10 August

Fred Lemon had not forgotten the night in August when
Jesus Christ had visited him in his prison cell at Dartmoor.
But bitterness and hatred still gripped his heart.

Forgiveness

Four long months passed. One morning, a fellow prisoner
murmured 'Compliments of the season' through half-closed lips.
It was Christmas Day.

Fred went back to his cell to await the call to the traditional
carol service. As he waited, he flicked through his Bible and read
the well-known story. Suddenly it took on new meaning. The one
who came to the smelly, dark stables as a baby was the one who
had visited his cell. He too had been unfairly treated but he held
no hatred in his heart. His prayer had been, 'Father, forgive
them'.

Fred longed to be free from the icy hatred that gripped his
heart, hatred for the prison officers who had treated him badly.
He knelt on the cold cell floor and prayed, 'Lord, I want to give
you my heart. Get rid of this hatred inside me. I want to forgive
them all.' Then he repeated the nicknames of the prison officers,
faltering a moment before he could name the one who had
wronged him most.

He felt the love of God flow into his heart, dispelling the
long-harboured bitterness. 'Peace on earth' the angels had sung.
For Fred they seemed to sing the words again, in Dartmoor
Prison.

PRAYER
Father, it is easier to hate than to love, to remember real or
imagined wrongs than the kindness shown to us. Drive the
hatred from our hearts. Open our lives to accept your love
for us in Jesus Christ, so that we may forgive others as you
forgive us. For Jesus' sake. Amen

See also 9 August

11 August

The Reverend Augustus Toplady died on 11 August 1778.

Hymn on a playing-card

The story is told that Augustus Toplady was out walking a few miles from his Somerset home when a sudden and severe storm broke. He looked round the open countryside for somewhere to shelter and saw that the sheer mass of rock beside him had a crack running down the middle in which he could stand, protected from the downpour of rain.

His mind turned to the spiritual shelter that Christ provides, and, stooping down, he picked up a playing-card that had been dropped at the spot so that he could jot down the words that came into his mind. The hymn that he wrote – 'Rock of Ages' – became famous in English and has been translated into other languages too. The original playing-card has been preserved in America.

When Prince Albert, husband of Queen Victoria, lay dying, he often repeated the words of the hymn, saying, 'If in this hour I had only my worldly honours and dignity to depend upon, I should be poor indeed.'

Rock of Ages, cleft for me,
Let me hide myself in thee.
Let the water and the blood
From thy riven side which flowed
Be of sin the double cure,
Cleanse me from its guilt and power.

Nothing in my hand I bring;
Simply to thy cross I cling;
Naked, come to thee for dress,
Helpless, look to thee for grace;
Foul, I to the fountain fly:
Wash me, Saviour, or I die!

12 August

William Blake died on 12 August 1827.

Blake longed to be an artist, but, knowing his parents could not afford the training, asked instead to be apprenticed to an engraver. When he had learned the trade he did not use it only to reproduce others' drawings, but created his own original and striking works of art. Only one fragment of Blake's many copperplates survives. Many were destroyed by a puritanical friend, for Blake's ideas and his portrayal of them were very different from others of his time.

Mystic and visionary

The happiest times for young William Blake were when the great doors of the abbey were closed and he was left entirely alone to his work. His master, Basmire, an engraver, had given William the job of drawing the many monuments in Westminster Abbey and other London churches, so that engravings could be made from them for the Antiquarian Society. Blake loved nothing better than to move quietly about the abbey, sometimes standing on top of a monument to get a better view of the recumbent figures below.

But the boys of Westminster School were allowed in the abbey for their free time and had fun playing hide-and-seek round the tombs as well as teasing the life out of the young artist. When they ran off to lessons, Blake was at peace, and in the stillness of the abbey he saw the visions that had been common to him since, at the age of about eight, he had seen angels in a tree at Peckham Rye. In the abbey, he saw a vision of Christ and his apostles. These visions were the stuff of which his poems and engravings were made.

See also 28 November

13 August

Octavia Hill died on 13 August 1912.

The National Trust was founded largely through the efforts of Octavia Hill. Beautiful homes, gardens, moors, cliffs and open spaces are preserved for everyone in Britain, as well as visitors to the country, to see and enjoy.

A little bit of paradise

Plaster had peeled from the damp, dirty walls, and on the stairs a well-placed bucket caught the unremitting drips of rain falling from a hole in the ceiling. The banister had gone. Water for the whole house was stored in a large, dirty, leaking water-butt. But Octavia, now seventeen, felt proud of her new possession in Paradise Place in London.

At last she had somewhere to lodge some of the quarrelling, filthy, drunken, homeless people she cared for. As a good landlord, she saw that passages were scrubbed, the water-butt replaced and leaks repaired. But she never interfered with well-meant kindness. Her tenants were free to lead their own lives. She treated them as she treated all her friends, with courtesy and respect.

Octavia believed that Paradise Place should include more than a roof over the head – it should provide gardens, fresh air and open spaces. She longed for her new friends to enjoy these pleasures too. At last she discovered an old dumping-ground, cleared the rubbish and made a garden where the children could play and their parents sit and watch.

It was through Octavia's contact with the Reverend Maurice, when she was only fourteen, that she began to help city-dwellers and the homeless. She understood the human need for the countryside as well as for a home. Through her reforms and her vision, everyone in Britain today can enjoy a little bit of paradise.

14 August

On 14 August 1885, the Royal Assent was given to the Criminal Law Amendment Act, for which Josephine Butler had campaigned so long.

Josephine Butler campaigned for a cause which Victorians considered unfit for ladies to mention. She determined to abolish the law which gave a special group of non-uniformed police absolute powers to arrest any woman they might think guilty of prostitution and enforce medical examination. Josephine abhorred the attitude which condemned 'fallen' women as irredeemable while dismissing men's vice as excusable. She believed in the equality of men and women before God.

Oakum picking

Mrs Butler's soft white fingers struggled unsuccessfully to disentangle the tarry rope fibres. The other oakum-pickers in the damp, stone-floor shed laughed at her efforts. To their surprise and delight, this quiet, beautiful lady joined in their laughter.

The women wondered why she had come. They knew themselves to be despised – either so poor that a reluctant state was forced to support them, or else condemned to this life because of petty crimes. Instead of preaching or condemning them, she had chosen to work alongside them.

The spontaneous laughter broke the ice. Josephine Butler began to talk to them, telling first of her own tragedy in the death of her little daughter. Then, eagerly, they began to tell her of their troubles and she was deeply touched. They were not hardened criminals, but women fallen on bad times, often through no fault of their own.

She began to visit the shed often, sometimes reading to them from the Bible and one day, quite naturally, pouring out her heart in prayer for them all as they knelt on the cold floor. Then she took Mary, a dying prostitute, back to her own home in the respectable quarter of Liverpool and nursed her with love and care. Mrs Butler had found the work God was calling her to do.

15 August

James Keir Hardie was born on 15 August 1856.

James Keir Hardie was the illegitimate son of Mary Keir, a Scottish farm servant. His stepfather, David Hardie, was a ship's carpenter. He was a miner till he was 23. He became a Scottish miners' representative, a political writer and a Labour Member of Parliament. He was the founder of the British Labour Party.

The man in the cloth cap

Even the police on duty at the House of Commons did not recognize Keir Hardie as an MP.

'Do you work here, mate?' one of them asked him. Hardie said that he did. 'Where, on the roof?' the policeman went on.

'No, on the floor,' Hardie replied.

Certainly Hardie in his loud check suit and bright red tie, looked very unlike his soberly well-dressed fellow MPs. Instead of the customary top hat he wore a Sherlock Holmes-type deer-stalker, which gave rise to the nickname 'the man in the cloth cap'. Even his bushy red beard convinced his colleagues in the House that he was a fierce revolutionary.

Keir Hardie certainly entered politics to champion the cause of the under-privileged and down-trodden. Almost penniless himself, he was determined that their cause should be led not by aristocratic sympathisers or by well-wishers infiltrating Conservative or Liberal ranks, but by self-confessed Labour Members, who themselves belonged to the working class.

But if Hardie looked like a revolutionary, the House was to find that he had no ambitions or plots for class war or violent change. Although his parents were atheists, Hardie himself found inspiration and comfort from reading his Bible. He was never an orthodox Christian but he took as his ideals the teaching of Jesus Christ in the Sermon on the Mount. He wanted justice for the overworked and underpaid – especially in the mines – but he insisted on bringing it about by peaceful means.

The outbreak of war in 1914 seemed to Keir Hardie a verdict of failure on all his efforts for peace and international understanding. But the fact that today we take for granted the justice of many of the things he fought for – fair wages, women's rights and racial equality – is proof that Keir Hardie's life and work were not in vain.

16 August

In August 1896, gold was discovered in the Klondike,
Yukon, Canada, and the famous gold rush began.

Bible gold

God said: 'All the silver and gold of the world is mine.'
From *Haggai 2*

'When your . . . silver and gold . . . have increased, make sure
that you do not become proud and forget the Lord your God.'
From *Deuteronomy 8*

'The judgements of the Lord are just; they are always fair.
They are more desirable than the finest gold.'
From *Psalm 19*

'I love your commands more than gold, more than the finest gold.
And so I follow all your instructions.'
From *Psalm 119*

'[Wisdom] cannot be bought with silver or gold. The finest gold
and jewels cannot equal its value. It is worth more than gold.'
From *Job 28*

'Choose knowledge rather than the finest gold.'
'It is better – much better – to have wisdom and knowledge than
gold and silver.'
'An idea well-expressed is like a design of gold, set in silver.'
'A warning given by an experienced person to someone willing to
listen is more valuable than gold rings or jewellery made of the
finest gold.'
From the *Book of Proverbs*

'It may now be necessary for you to be sad for a while because of
the many kinds of trials you suffer. Their purpose is to prove that
your faith is genuine. Even gold, which can be destroyed, is tested
by fire; and so your faith, which is much more precious than gold,
must also be tested, so that it may endure.'
From *1 Peter 1*

17 August

William Carey, pioneer missionary, translator, botanist, was born on 17 August 1761.

The prayer God didn't answer

'Would you rather have a sixpence or a shilling?' the ironmonger asked.

Young William Carey, delivering goods for his shoemaker master just before Christmas, could not believe his ears. A Christmas box of a few pence might have been expected – but a whole shilling seemed too good to be true.

And it was! When William went to spend it on a much-longed-for treasure, he discovered that it was a counterfeit coin. Temptation was strong. He substituted the bad shilling for a good one in his master's takings. Then he felt frightened. The penalty in those days for theft of anything over a shilling was death. Conviction for stealing less than a shilling carried a sentence of transportation to the West Indies or America.

'I made this deliberate sin a matter of prayer as I passed over the fields home,' Carey wrote. 'I promised that if God would but clearly get me over this, I would certainly for the future leave off all evil practices. A gracious God did *not* get me safe through!'

His master discovered the false coin and sent the other apprentice back to the ironmonger with it. The whole story came out. The tradesman had been playing a practical joke on young Carey. Carey was forgiven, but deeply ashamed. At sixteen, he joined with Christians whose faith was real and whose lives were upright.

PRAYER
Please, Lord, do not always give us what we want, but answer our prayers as you see is best for us. Amen

See also 18 August,

18 August

William Carey began his working life as a shoe-maker. His studies led in time to his becoming a village schoolmaster. But he had dreams of a quite different vocation.

Geography without tears?

'His pupils saw sometimes a strange sight, their master moved to tears over a geography lesson, as pointing to continents, islands and peoples he would cry, "And these are pagans, pagans!"'

Perhaps this description of the young shoemaker turned teacher and preacher, is a bit far-fetched. It was written in a biography by his great-grandson. Carey was not an emotional man. But he did have an intense compassion and concern for people in other lands who had not heard the gospel, at a time before the great missionary movements were formed. On his wall he hung a large map of the world, made out of sheets of paper pasted together. He filled in the names of the countries and wrote beside them all the information he could gather about the people, their customs, population and religion.

Carey determined to go himself and preach the gospel in India. Taking a reluctant wife, with a brand-new baby and three small boys, and facing the hazards of a five-month voyage in the midst of wars between France and England, Carey set out. His efforts to survive lasted seven years, without one single convert to the Christian faith. His wife was now dangerously mad, and funds from England took many months to arrive.

But Carey never gave up. 'Expect great things from God – Attempt great things for God' was always his motto. In time, Carey saw God turn his vision into reality.

POSTSCRIPT
Carey – self-taught – eventually became a distinguished college professor in India. He translated the Bible into Bengali, and parts of it into as many as twenty-four different languages and dialects.

See also 17 August

19 August

On 19 August 1959, Cliff Richard turned professional.

Cliff Richard, born Harry Webb, grew up in a council house outside London. He had a lightning rise to stardom – he was hailed as Britain's 'golden boy of pop' at eighteen, and is still at the top over twenty years later.

'Fifteen fabulous years'

Cliff argued endlessly with his Christian friends. For a start, he didn't think that the idea of the Trinity made sense. Yet for all his stubbornness, he recognized that they had a personal relationship with Jesus Christ which he knew nothing of.

Cliff's moment of decision came during a filming session at Pinewood Studios. He was staying in the home of a Christian friend. Back there one evening, Cliff was lying on his bed when he asked Jesus to come into his life instead of standing knocking outside. It wasn't an emotional experience. Cliff realizes that like most stage people he is emotional by nature, yet there was no particular emotion on this occasion. It was a cool and reasoned decision made after months of hassle. He needed Jesus.

That day marked the turning-point in Cliff's life. 'Today, fifteen years on,' he wrote in his autobiography in 1977, 'there's the overwhelming evidence that Jesus accepted the invitation – fifteen fabulous years of getting to know him.'

Today Cliff Richard can say, 'What I really want is to be seen as the Christian I claim to be. Not so that people will say, "What a sincere bloke Cliff Richard is" but simply so that Jesus will get noticed. What other people think of me is becoming less and less important; what they think of Jesus because of me is critical.'

See also 20 August, 10 March

20 August

Staying on

The papers all reported it – in their own way. Cliff Richard was definitely quitting show business and becoming a monk – or was it a missionary? Opinions varied. Cliff himself had thought that now he was a Christian he should leave his singing and film career and concentrate on something more obviously 'Christian' – like teaching.

Then God moved in. Without any effort on Cliff's part, he was asked to do a gospel album, religious television shows and a film called *Two a Penny*, produced by the Billy Graham film company. Cliff got the message. He had thought of throwing over his career as being of no use to God. But he had a ready-made audience and a huge number of fans ready to listen to him. All this he could use for God – so why get out?

Cliff reckons that *Two a Penny* is far and away the best film he has done, and through it thousands of people have met Jesus Christ. One was a girl from the provinces who came to London after running off with £200 of her firm's money. She went to see the film and was so moved by it that she made straight for the Billy Graham office in Camden Town, told them of her theft and asked for their help. As a result, the whole matter was cleared up with her employers and she soon became part of a local church fellowship.

See also 19 August, 10 March

21 August

Jean Waddell was arrested in August 1980.

August 1980 was the month in which many foreign and national Christians were arrested in Iran. Jean Waddell, secretary to the Bishop of Iran, was imprisoned for six months and released at the same time as Dr and Mrs Coleman (see 2 August).

Coincidence?

If Diana Hunt had not gone upstairs to Jean Waddell's flat at that precise moment . . . *If* she had not taken the children with her . . . *If* the surgeon hadn't arrived on the scene when he did . . . Jean Waddell would have certainly died. Paul Hunt, chaplain at that time to the Bishop of Iran, doesn't think that all those 'ifs' were pure chance. He believes, as William Temple said, that 'coincidences begin to happen when you pray'.

Paul and Diana Hunt, having breakfast with their two little girls on that holiday morning, had been planning a picnic. They heard no sounds from the upstairs flat, where gunmen had entered, interrogated then beaten and shot Jean Waddell, leaving her tied up.

But when Diana went up, accompanied by two excited children, to invite Jean to join their picnic, she encountered armed men coming out of the flat. Iranians love children, and their faces softened when they saw the two little girls. They hustled the three of them into the bathroom, where Diana waited, afraid to move and give away her husband's whereabouts. At last she stole quietly downstairs, summoned neighbours and raised the alarm. The gunmen had fled without finding Paul, their real quarry.

Jean was rushed to hospital and as she arrived a surgeon – one of the few available – came downstairs. He immediately cancelled his next operation and set about saving Jean's life. In an hour, he said, she would have been dead.

Paul and Diana knew that Christians, both in Iran and in other countries, had been praying for them. Diana had been strongly conscious of their prayers as she waited fearfully in Jean's bathroom. People were praying – so coincidences began to happen.

22 August

Roy Castle was born in August 1932.

Roy Castle has been in show business for over thirty years.
He is a past master of many kinds of entertainment –
straight actor, singer, instrumentalist, dancer and presenter
of television programmes.

Keep smiling

Roy Castle always seems to have a smile on his face. He explains what puts it there.

'I have discovered,' he says, 'that whenever I obey what the Bible tells me to do I feel free, happy and contented. I've got a smile on my face! When I disobey the rules (and we all do) then I am unhappy and under a cloud. Say the devil dangles a little carrot and you know perfectly well it's a little bit wrong – not a lot wrong – but it's still a worry. It's like a small stone in your shoe. The time I get a real experience of Jesus is when I say "No, I'm not going to do that". It's like shaking that little stone out, putting your shoe on and marching along. It's a great feeling of peace.'

PRAYER
Lord, help us to be honest with you. Help us to obey you
when you speak inside us and tell us that something is even
a little bit wrong. Keep a smile on our faces because we are
doing what you say. For Jesus' sake. Amen

See also 23 August

23 August

On 23 August 1980, Roy Castle's son had a serious accident.

Danny Boy

The whole Castle family had arrived on the Isle of Man for the start of Roy's three-week season at the Gaiety Theatre. Fifteen-year-old Daniel went for a walk, exploring along the coast. He slipped and fell a horrifying thirty feet down a steep slope to the rocks below, where he lay unconscious.

The only route to the hospital at Douglas was by lifeboat, over choppy seas, then by car across the island for eleven miles. It was confirmed that Daniel had a perforated lung, cracked skull, fractured bones and severe bruising. He was put into intensive care. If he lived, he might be paralysed or suffer brain damage.

Roy dashed back across the island with only minutes to spare before his opening show that night. The crowd, all set to enjoy themselves, had no idea of the tragedy. 'During the request spot some holidaymakers asked me to play – would you believe it – *Danny Boy*,' Roy recalls. 'It was difficult, but I think I played it the best ever.'

Next day, the Castles' church pastor flew across and, together with Daniel's parents, knelt at his hospital bedside and prayed. 'You can imagine our joy when, at the end of the prayer, Daniel said "Amen",' Roy says.

That was the start of Daniel's long, slow recovery. The lung has healed and fears about paralysis and brain damage were set at rest. Looking back on that near-tragedy, Roy Castle could say, 'I just can't imagine what it must be like to go through that kind of experience without the strength that comes from being a Christian. The whole thing has proved to be a wonderful witness to the power of God.'

See also 22 August

24 August

In an age when privileged people were allowed to appoint their own domestic chaplains, the Countess of Huntingdon appointed eighty-four evangelical chaplains, by the simple expedient of building that number of small houses, all with a chapel attached. After her death, the chapels were formed into the Countess of Huntingdon's Connexion – a small denomination which still exists.

'Our dear Selina'

The Countess of Huntingdon's handsome front door opened again, and a fresh party of people entered. The guests were ushered upstairs, while their servants were led into the large kitchen. Their eyes must have lighted up to see the well-spread table. First they would enjoy a hearty meal, along with the other servants whose employers had come visiting, then they would be treated to a sermon. And it *would* be a treat – for the preachers they listened to were the Wesleys, George Whitefield and other compelling voices of the day.

Upstairs in the drawing-room, their masters and mistresses were being received by the countess. She was a remarkable woman in every way. She cared nothing for fashion, and dressed just as *she* pleased. But she did care about passing on to others the new life she had found in Jesus Christ. What better scheme than to use her own London home – 'upstairs' and 'downstairs' too? People of quality, who would never have listened to John Wesley in the open air or in country barns, were quite willing to come to 'our dear Selina's' drawing-room and listen to the good news that could change their lives too.

25 August

Michael Faraday died on 25 August 1867.

Michael Faraday belonged to a small, strict Christian group called the Sandemanians, who believed fervently in the Bible and faith in Christ alone for salvation. They also believed that money should be given away. Faraday saw a display of God's truth and wonder in the science he loved. He and his wife lived simply, refusing honours and giving away any money he earned.

The making of a scientist

School-days had been fun for Michael Faraday because of the chance to play marbles in the street rather than to learn much beyond reading, writing and arithmetic. At thirteen, he became an errand-boy, but was later given the chance to be an apprentice to a bookseller and learn the book-binding trade.

Michael often glanced through the books he was given to bind, and one day became engrossed in a large encyclopedia on electricity. His lifelong love for science had begun. He tried to get a job at the Royal Society, and at last managed to become laboratory assistant to the great Sir Humphrey Davy, who was its president. At first he had the job of rebinding his books, but soon his work became more scientific, and he even travelled abroad with his boss meeting many famous scientists of the day.

Soon Faraday began to research and make discoveries for himself in electricity, chemistry and metallurgy. He made the first electric motor, the first dynamo and the first transformer. He was a brilliant lecturer. He could make science interesting to ordinary people. Even more than his science, he loved Sarah Bernard, the woman he married, and above all else was his love for God.

26 August

James Woodforde was born in 1740 and for much of his life was vicar at Weston Longeville in Norfolk. He kept a diary of everyday happenings for forty-four years. In 1778, plans were made for his nephew Bill, who lived with him, to join the navy.

Entry for 26 August 1778

'Mr Baldwin called on us this morning and talked with us concerning a Midshipman's place for Bill. In the afternoon took a walk with Bill to Mr Baldwin's and there drank a dish of tea with him, Miss Vertue Baldwin and Mr Hammerton. Had a good deal of chat with Mr Hammerton about Bill. Bill is to go to London when Mr Hammerton goes to show himself to a Captain of a ship and Mr Hammerton will use all his interest for him. I have been most uneasy and most unhappy all day about one thing and another. When Bill goes away I shall have no one to converse with – quite without a friend.

28 August

'Mr Hammerton said that he would do what he could and would advance him money to rig himself out if he succeeds, upon my promise of paying him again soon. It was so friendly in Mr Hammerton that I could not but comply. Bill is therefore to go in the London coach on Sunday evening and wait at *The Swan and Two Necks* in Lads Lane, London, till Mr Hammerton calls on him. Very low and ill withal, especially going to bed.'

30 August

'I read prayers and preached this afternoon at Weston. About 8 in the evening I took a ride with Bill to Norwich and there took a place in the coach for him. I stayed with Bill till 12, saw him safe into the Machine and then I went to *The King's Head* where I slept but very little. I was very restless and uneasy all night.'

PRAYER
Father, we too know the sense of unease and foreboding as the time draws near to say goodbye to someone we love. We remember how we feel when the plane or train departs. We understand the feelings of loneliness and emptiness that follow such partings. We pray today for all who face such an experience. Please give them your comfort and friendship, through Jesus Christ. Amen

27 August

The English league football season begins in August.
Ian Bolton plays centre-half for Watford Football Club.

Journey into Life

There was no denying that things looked bad. Footballers can't afford to have back trouble, and as Ian lay in hospital, he wondered what the future held. Perhaps his football career was at an end.

It was good to see visitors, but he didn't feel exactly relieved when he saw the figure of Baptist minister John Boyes coming purposefully across the ward to his bed. Ian admired John and respected his Christian faith, but it made him feel uncomfortable. And the snag about being in bed with a bad back is that you can't get up and walk away. Only a few weeks before, John had given Ian a Bible which he'd brought into hospital. But that was as far as he wanted to go. He'd always shied away from anything more.

John talked, then said, 'May I pray?' Ian resisted the temptation to say 'Get out!' and politely agreed.

That night, Ian couldn't sleep. For one thing, he was to see the specialist next morning and, after special tests, hear his verdict. For another, John's visit had upset him. He began to read the Bible by his bed then turned to the booklet – *Journey into Life* – that John had left him. He read: 'Accept Jesus Christ into your life to be your Lord to control you, your Saviour to cleanse you, your Friend to guide and be with you.' Ian's defences went down. He followed that advice and committed his life to Christ.

God met Ian at every level of need. Amazingly, the specialist's report was 'No problem'. Ian was discharged the following day, and three days later was playing for Watford in their Boxing Day match.

28 August

28 August is the Feast Day of St Augustine.

St Augustine is one of the Fathers of the Christian church.
He was born in AD 354. He used his learning and brilliant
mind to combat the heresies that beset the early church. He
founded a small community from which the Augustinian
Orders take their rule and was afterwards appointed Bishop
of Hippo, in North Africa.

'Take up and read'

Augustine was beside himself. He could not bear even to stay
inside the house. In a frenzy of anguish and distress he rushed out
into the garden, throwing himself down under the shade of a fig
tree. Then he began to cry, pouring out his troubles to God. He
could not go on any longer, torn between the life he was living and
the beckoning of God towards a life of holiness and devotion to
Christ. After a while, as his sobs subsided, he seemed to hear a
voice saying, 'Take up and read, take up and read.'

Augustine went quietly indoors for a Bible. His eyes fell on
verses in Paul's letter to the Romans: 'Let us conduct ourselves
properly as people who live in the light of day – no orgies or
drunkenness, nor immorality or indecency, no fighting or
jealousy. But take up the weapons of the Lord Jesus Christ and
stop paying attention to your sinful nature and satisfying its
desires.'

Augustine realized that these words summed up God's
challenge to his way of life. 'I had no desire or need to read
further,' he wrote. 'As I finished the sentence it was as though the
light of peace had been poured into my heart, all the shadows of
doubt dispersed. Thus have you converted me to you.'

See also 13 November

29 August

Sir John Betjeman, Poet Laureate, was born on 29 August 1906.

Human beings are different of course!

Here among long-discarded cassocks,
Damp stools, and half-split open
    hassocks,
Here where the Vicar never looks
I nibble through old service books.
Lean and alone I spend my days
Behind this Church of England
    baize.
I share my dark forgotten room
With two oil-lamps and half a broom.
The cleaner never bothers me,
So here I eat my frugal tea.
My bread is sawdust mixed
    with straw;
My jam is polish for the floor.

Christmas and Easter may be feasts
For congregations and for priests,
And so may Whitsun. All the same,
They do not fill my meagre frame.
For me the only feast at all
Is Autumn's Harvest Festival,
When I can satisfy my want
With ears of corn around the font.
I climb the eagle's brazen head
To burrow through a loaf of bread.
I scramble up the pulpit stair
And gnaw the marrows hanging there.

It is enjoyable to taste
These items ere they go to waste,
But how annoying when one finds
That other mice with pagan minds
Come into church my food to share
Who have no proper business there.
Two field mice who have no desire
To be baptized, invade the choir.
A large and most unfriendly rat
Comes in to see what we are at.

He says he thinks there is no God
And yet he comes . . . it's rather odd.
This year he stole a sheaf of wheat
(It screened our special
    preacher's seat),
And prosperous mice from
    fields away
Come in to hear the organ play,
And under cover of its notes
Ate through the altar's sheaf of oats.
A Low Church mouse,
    who thinks that I
Am too papistical, and High,
Yet somehow doesn't think it wrong
To munch through
    Harvest Evensong,
While I, who starve the whole
    year through
Must share my food
    with rodents who
Except at this time of the year
Not once inside the church appear.

Within the human world I know
Such goings-on could not be so,
For human beings only do
What their religion tells them to.
They read their Bible every day
And always, night and
    morning, pray,
And just like me, the good
    church mouse,
Worship each week in
    God's own house,

But all the same it's strange to me
How very full the church can be
With people I don't see at all
Except at Harvest Festival.

Diary of a Church Mouse by Sir John Betjeman

30 August

Barry Maguire is one of several American gospel singers who perform at the Greenbelt Christian Rock Festival held during the last weekend in August in England.

Barry Maguire was born in 1935. After school he joined the US Navy, worked in fishing and construction industries, then bought a guitar and began singing at clubs. He met with success and was a member of the New Christy Minstrels in the sixties. He played male lead in the original Broadway production of the musical *Hair*.

A matter of life or death

'Man, there's no sense in this; I've done everything there is to do.'

That's how life seemed to Barry Maguire. 'My life was like an amusement park and I'd done all the rides. The ones I dug I'd gone on a couple of times until they lost their thrill. There was just no more rides left.' He'd experimented with drugs of every kind, he'd tasted fame and all that went with it. There seemed nothing left for him but death.

One day, Barry met a Christian and recognized him as the one person who was 'alive' in a city full of 'dead' people. He explained to Barry that Jesus had allowed himself to be killed in order to absorb the death that our selfishness brings. Jesus brings life. Barry was faced with a choice between suicide and giving his life to God.

'That's when God really spoke to me,' he explains. 'He said, "Man, if you give your life to me, I will heal it. I will make you a brand new person." I didn't think that could ever happen because of the snake-pit of my life. I said, "OK, if you want me, you've got yourself a boy."'

Barry believes that we all have the same choice to make: 'If we live for God: we live. If we live for ourselves: we die. If a person turns his back on God the only choice left to him is *how* he wants to die.'

PRAYER
Thank you, Lord Jesus, for your offer of abundant and eternal life to all who trust in you. Amen

31 August

John Bunyan died on 31 August 1688.

John Bunyan was born in 1628, the son of a tinker. His best-known book, *The Pilgrim's Progress*, was written in Bedford jail, where he spent many years for preaching as a non-conformist. He describes his own spiritual pilgrimage in *Grace Abounding to the Chief of Sinners*.

Days to remember

After months of despair, Bunyan began to feel that God did love and accept him.

'Now was my heart filled full of comfort and hope and now I could believe that my sins should be forgiven me; I was now so taken with the love and mercy of God that I thought I could have spoken of his love and mercy to me even to the very crows that sat upon the ploughed lands before me, had they been capable to have understood me; wherefore I said in my soul with much gladness, "Surely I will not forget this forty years hence"; but alas! within less than forty days I began to question all still.'

Later, he recorded:

'I remember that one day, as I was travelling into the country and musing on the wickedness and blasphemy of my heart, that scripture came into my mind, "He hath made peace through the blood of his cross". By which I was made to see, both again and again and again that day, that God and my soul were friends by this blood; yea, I saw that the justice of God and my sinful soul could embrace and kiss each other through this blood. This was a good day to me; I hope I shall not forget it.'

See also 1 September

1 September

The Pilgrim's Progress is John Bunyan's dream story about the joys and difficulties of the Christian life, told in the form of a journey made by Christian from the City of Destruction to the Celestial City (see also 31 August).

Enter the foul fiend

'Now, in this Valley of Humiliation, poor Christian was hard put to it; for he had gone but a little way before he espied a foul fiend coming over the field to meet him; his name is Apollyon. Then did Christian begin to be afraid. The monster was hideous to behold; he was clothed with scales, like a fish (and they are his pride), he had wings like a dragon, feet like a bear, and out of his belly came fire and smoke, and his mouth was as the mouth of a lion. He beheld Christian with a disdainful countenance: "I perceive thou art one of my subjects." Christian answered, "I was born in your dominions, but I have let myself to another, even the King of princes."

'Then Apollyon broke out in a grievous rage, saying, "I am an enemy to this Prince; I hate his person, his laws, his people."

'Apollyon straddled quite over the whole breadth of the way, and said, "Prepare thyself to die; here will I spill thy soul."

'Then did Christian draw, for he saw it was time to bestir him. Apollyon as fast made at him, throwing darts as thick as hail, wounding him in his head, hand and foot. Christian's sword flew out of his hand. Then said Apollyon, "I am sure of thee now." But, as God would have it, while Apollyon was fetching of his last blow, Christian nimbly stretched out his hand for his sword, and caught it, saying, "Rejoice not against me O mine enemy; when I fall, I shall arise", and with that gave him a deadly thrust. Christian made at him again saying, "Nay, in all these things we are more than conquerors through him that loved us." And with that Apollyon spread forth his dragon's wings and sped him away, that Christian for a season saw him no more.'

Abridged from *The Pilgrim's Progress*, by John Bunyan, 1678

2 September

On 2 September 1666, the Great Fire of London broke out.

London's burning!

'On September 2, after midnight, London was set on fire and on September 3 the Exchange was burnt; and in three days almost all the city within the walls and much without them. The season had been exceedingly dry before and the wind in the east, where the fire began. The people having none to conduct them aright could do nothing to resist it, but stand and see their houses burn without remedy, the engines being presently out of order and useless. The streets were crowded with people and carts, to carry away what goods they could get out. And they that were most active and befriended (by their wealth) got carts, and saved much; and the rest lost almost all.

'Almost all the booksellers in St Paul's Churchyard brought their books into vaults under St Paul's Church, where it was thought almost impossible that fire should come. But the church itself being on fire, the exceeding weight of stones falling down did break into the vault and let in the fire, and they could not come near to save the books.

'At last some seamen taught them to blow up some of the next houses with gunpowder, which stopped the fire.

'It was a sight that might have given any man a lively sense of the vanity of this world, and all the wealth and glory of it, and of the future conflagration of all the world. To see all the flames mount up towards heaven, and proceed so furiously without restraint; to see the air as far as could be beheld so filled with smoke that the sun shined through it with a colour like blood; but the dolefullest sight of all was afterwards to see what a ruinous confused place the city was. No man that seeth not such a thing can have a right apprehension of the dreadfulness of it.'

From *The Autobiography of Richard Baxter*

See also 19 November

3 September

Thomas More (1478-1535) wrote this letter when part of his house and barns had been burned through a neighbour's carelessness.

'Be merry in God'

'Mistress Alice, in my most hearty wise I recommend me to you. And whereas I am informed by my son Heron of the loss of our barns by fire, with all the corn that was therein; albeit, saving God's pleasure, it is great pity of so much good corn lost, yet since it hath liked him to send us such a chance, we must and are bounden not only to be content but also to be glad of his visitation. He sent us all that we have lost, and since he hath by such a chance taken it away again, his pleasure be fulfilled. Let us never grieve thereat, but take it in good worth and heartily thank him as well for adversity as for prosperity. And peradventure we have more cause to thank him for our loss than for our winning. For his wisdom better seeth what is good for us than we do ourselves. Therefore I pray you be of good cheer, and take all the household with you to church and there thank God for that he hath given us and for that he hath taken away from us and for that he hath left us.

'And thus as heartily fare you well, with all our children, as ye can wish.

'At Woodstock, the third day of September, by the hand of your loving husband,

'Thomas More, Knight.'

Quoted in Thomas Stapleton's *Life of Sir Thomas More*

BIBLE VERSE
Job said: 'The Lord gave, and now he has taken away. May his name be praised!'
From *Job 1*

PRAYER
Help us, dear Lord, to accept disappointment and loss as part of your wise giving. Don't let us become bitter and resentful when things go badly, but teach us to love and trust you all the more. For Jesus' sake. Amen

See also 1 and 6 July

4 September

Albert Schweitzer – missionary, doctor, musician and winner of the Nobel Peace Prize – died on 4 September 1965.

Reverence for life

'In the evenings, after praying with his mother, he [Albert] would add his own silent prayer for all living creatures: "Dear God, protect and bless all things that breathe, guard them from all evil and let them sleep in peace."

'Sometimes the fact of pain shocked him into violent and repeated resolves to so order his life that he would inflict no pain on anything that lives or breathes. When he was seven or eight he went out bird-hunting with a friend. Like his friend, he was armed with a catapult. At the moment when young Schweitzer stooped to gather a stone to insert in the catapult, the Easter bells rang out. It was like a sign from heaven. He began to shout and wave his arms, shooing the birds away, then he fled home. He had discovered the commandment that was to weigh increasingly on him over the years: "Thou shalt not kill."'

From *Schweitzer, Hero of Africa*, by Robert Payne

See also 14 January

5 September

Jonas Hanway died on 5 September 1786.

Take your Hanway – it looks like rain!

It was a beautiful object. The handle was of ebony delicately carved with leaves and flowers. The outside was pale green silk and the lining of stone-coloured satin. Jonas Hanway held his splendid umbrella high above his head as he strode through the streets of London in the rain. Small boys jeered and coachmen complained that he was ruining trade. No one would hire their cabs if he could shelter under an umbrella instead. There were those who complained for religious reasons too. Hanway was defying the heavenly purpose of rain – to make us wet!

But Hanway went on his way unperturbed. One onlooker described him: 'When it rained a small parapluie defended his face and wig; he was the first man who ventured to walk the streets of London with an umbrella over his head; after carrying one near thirty years he saw them come into general use.' Not only were they used, but for some years they were known as 'hanways'.

But the small memorial tablet to Jonas Hanway in Westminster Abbey makes no mention of umbrellas. It tells of Hanway's real life-work, once he returned from being a merchant overseas in Russia and Portugal (where he first observed the 'umbrello'). He gave all his time and money in Christian caring for those who had no champions. The tablet reads: 'The helpless infant nurtured through his care. The friendless prostitute sheltered and reformed. The hopeless youth rescued from misery and ruin and trained to serve his country. In one common strain of gratitude they bear testimony to their benefactor's virtue.'

6 September

Bible wisdom – about friends

'Friends always show their love. What are brothers for if not to share trouble?'

'Some friendships do not last, but some friends are more loyal than brothers.'

'People learn from one another, just as iron sharpens iron.'

'Gossip is spread by wicked people; they stir up trouble and break up friendships.'

'A friend means well even when he hurts you. But when an enemy puts his arm round your shoulder – watch out!'

'Do not forget your friends or your father's friends. If you are in trouble, don't ask your brother for help; a neighbour nearby can help you more than a brother who is far away.'

From the *Book of Proverbs*

Jesus said: 'You are my friends if you do what I command you.'

From *John 15*

PRAYER
Thank you for friends. Help me to be a good friend – loyal, honest, dependable and true. For Jesus' sake. Amen

7 September

Group Captain Leonard Cheshire was born on 7 September 1917.

Leonard Cheshire studied Law at Oxford before joining the Royal Air Force. As a bomber leader during the Second World War, he gained the Victoria Cross, as well as other awards for bravery.

A home for Arthur

Arthur badly wanted to go home, and the matron of the hospital agreed entirely. When Leonard Cheshire came to visit Arthur Dykes, she took him aside and told him the truth.

'He hasn't long to live and we can do no more for him. We need the bed.'

It sounded reasonable enough, except that Arthur had no home to go to and no remaining relatives to care for him. Cheshire had room enough to take him, but not the least notion how to care for a seriously sick man. He tried without success to find someone to take on the job but when a friend said, 'You've decided to look after him yourself, haven't you?', he made up his mind to do so.

Arthur was plucky and made light of his illness, but when he arrived, he was far too weak even to walk. Cheshire soon found that he had everything to do for the dying man.

As they spent time together, the two became very close. Cheshire was greatly impressed by Arthur's serene faith in God. 'I got more from him than from all the learned books I had been reading,' he said.

Continued on 8 September

8 September

There are now nearly 200 Cheshire Homes in Britain and abroad.

'It is better to trust in the Lord'

As Leonard Cheshire nursed the dying Arthur Dykes with gentleness and love, they talked of many things. Cheshire had been searching for God, and now Arthur showed him by his peace and serenity that Jesus Christ is real. But Arthur had more to say. He wanted others in need to have the same opportunity of being cared for and given a home. He was certain that caring for such people was the vocation that God had given to his benefactor and friend.

Leonard Cheshire was not so sure. Friends dismissed such an idea as ridiculous and put up all kinds of objections. One night, at random, he read the verse in the Bible that says, 'It is better to trust in the Lord than to put confidence in man.' He decided to trust the whole matter to God.

Shortly afterwards, the telephone rang. It was a request for him to take in an old lady of over ninety. It seemed that God was showing the way ahead.

Arthur was now very near death. As Cheshire sat beside him, he read a book lying by the bedside. It resolved his last doubts. Like Arthur, he decided to become a member of the Roman Catholic Church.

On the day of Arthur's funeral, his third resident arrived. The work of the Cheshire Homes had begun in earnest.

'If you want to work for peace, work for justice.'
Leonard Cheshire

See also 7 September

9 September

Chairman Mao Tse-tung of China died on 9 September 1976.

Arabs in the desert carry them, merchants in the bazaar tune to them, women grinding maize listen to them – everyone everywhere has a transistor radio. Well, not quite everyone – but in hot, friendly countries where doors stay wide open, those outside can listen to a neighbour's radio. If you can't read or write, you can still listen. All over the world, Christian radio stations are broadcasting the good news of Jesus Christ to places where missionaries cannot go. The Far East Broadcasting Company can beam programmes to mainland China.

Secret hearers

Ever since their marriage during the nightmare years of the Communist Revolution in China, Ping and her husband had harboured a secret. They were Christians. They possessed no Bibles, and relied on each other for help and strength. In time, they had an agonizing decision to make. Their two young sons were taught to report anything heard at home that was contrary to the ideals of the revolution. Should Ping and her husband share their faith with the boys, or spare them the pressure of having to inform on their parents? They decided to keep their secret and commit the boys to God's care.

When they were a bit older, both boys became proud owners of radio sets. Each evening they climbed into their bunk beds, adjusted their earphones and settled down to listen. Kung, the elder of the two boys, remembers those days:

'When I lay on my top bunk and listened with my earphones, my family thought I was listening to propaganda broadcasts. But the truth was that I was listening to programmes from "The Voice of Friendship" from Manila.'

Kung listened for many months, and began to learn about God's holiness and his own need of Jesus as Saviour. One night, he committed his life to Christ.

Continued on 10 September; see also 10 May

10 September

Kung, the elder of Ping's two sons, had come to trust in Jesus Christ through listening secretly to the broadcasts of the Far East Broadcasting Company. For the beginning of the story in full, see 9 September.

'Streams in the Desert'

Kung said nothing to his family about his decision to become a Christian. He was afraid of what they would say.

One day Ping, his mother, was alarmed to find that her one Christian book, called *Streams in the Desert*, had gone missing from its familiar hiding-place. Someone might have discovered that she was a secret believer and she would be taken away for questioning. A few weeks later, Ming, the younger son, asked her what she knew about something called 'streams in the desert'. In much fear she admitted to him that it was a Christian book.

Then Ming pulled out the tattered book from under his bunk and gave it to her. He threw his arms round his mother and told her how he had been listening to the gospel programmes of the Far East Broadcasting Company as he lay on his bottom bunk. They had been teaching from that same book called *Streams in the Desert*. When he found the copy hidden among his mother's treasures, he had taken it to read over and over again as he waited to hear more on the daily radio programme. Now he had decided to be a Christian too.

Today, the Bai family are united in serving Jesus. They are members of the huge radio church brought together by the Far East Broadcasting Company.

See also 9 September, 10 May

11 September

On 11 September 1974, Joni Eareckson was invited to
appear on the New York television programme, *Today*.

'Please, God, do something in my life'

She had *read* about it – in the story of *Black Beauty*, a man had
fallen from a horse and broken his neck. And he had died. Now it
had happened to her. Less than one minute in time had ended for
ever the happy, carefree life of an American schoolgirl. When
they lifted Joni from the water after that tragic dive, all feeling had
gone from legs, arms and body up to her shoulders. Weeks of
intensive care followed, when she was unable to feed herself or
even wipe away the tears that flowed so freely.

Only a short while before the accident she had prayed: 'Lord,
do something in my life that will change me and turn me round.'
Gradually, she began to wonder if this could be the answer.
Although she was a Christian, her life had been largely a matter of
pleasing herself. God might work through this accident. When
the surgeon talked of an operation to fuse the bones again, Joni
began to hope once more. Others with her injuries had died. God
had let her live. Surely now he would heal her. The operation was
performed and pronounced successful.

'How long will it be before Joni walks?' her mother asked.

'I'm afraid you don't understand,' the surgeon replied. 'She
will never walk again.'

And there was worse to come. Surely, Joni hoped, her hands at
least would regain feeling. But the day came when she was told
that she would never use her hands again.

During the dark days and nights of depression and despair that
followed, one thing comforted Joni. Jesus was close and *he*
understood. When Jesus hung on the cross, she thought, he too
was helpless. He was unable to wipe off the sweat, to brush aside
the flies. He knew just how she felt. He was close. And he was
turning her life round for some special purpose.

Continued on 13 September

12 September

Archaeologist Alan Millard has been involved in 'digs' in
Syria, Iraq and Jordan. 12 September is his wedding
anniversary.

Stranger than fiction?

'Solomon began work on the Temple . . . the inside was covered
with gold. The whole interior of the Temple was covered with
gold. Even the floor was covered with gold.'
From *1 Kings 6*

'The natural reaction to that account is: "I can't believe he had so
much gold!" Walls, ceiling and even floor of the temple plated
with it. It seems impossible to the modern mind. Many scholars
have suggested that the account is exaggerated. Perhaps gold was
applied to the carved woodwork, rather as gold leaf is used on
plaster moulding in stately homes today. Or perhaps the whole
account springs from wishful thinking by homesick Jewish exiles
remembering in too glowing terms the temple once loved and
now destroyed.

'As a student of the world where the Bible was born, I am
interested in discoveries that relate to the Bible. For years I had
known that other kings proudly recorded that they had decorated
their temples with gold. Further investigation revealed that
Babylonian and Assyrian and Egyptian kings also claimed to plate
the walls of temples with sheets of gold. These accounts occur in
contemporary inscriptions and there is no reason to doubt them.
On examining ruined temples in Egypt, in fact, rows of small
holes can still be seen in the stone blocks left in position. These
were cut for the nails that held the precious metal in place.

'The Bible relates that enormous quantities of gold entered
Solomon's exchequer. The Queen of Sheba brought him about
four tons! So there was no shortage of gold and no reason to
doubt that Solomon, like the rich kings of surrounding countries,
lavished his gold on the temple built for God's glory.

'Once again, there is no need to reject the Bible record –
except through ignorance or prejudice. That is important, for
God's call to faith can be heard more clearly because in both Old
and New Testaments faith is firmly bound to historical truth.'
Alan Millard

13 September

'Now you're happy?'

It was five years since the diving accident which had left Joni Eareckson paralysed from the neck down. One sunny day, Joni was driven down to the Town and Country Restaurant in Baltimore. A colleague of her father had arranged an exhibition of all the drawings that Joni had learned to do, using her mouth to hold pencil or brush. She and her friends were surprised to see roads blocked and police directing traffic. When they arrived, a brass band was playing and a huge banner across the building proclaimed 'Joni Eareckson Day'. The exhibition was a huge success. One thing puzzled a reporter who interviewed Joni.

'Why do you put the initials "PTL" on all your drawings?'

'It stands for "Praise The Lord",' Joni explained. 'God loves us, and for those who love him everything – even what happened to me at seventeen – works together for good. He has given me contentment and developed my patience and purpose in life. My art is a reflection of how God can empower someone to rise above circumstances.'

'Now I'm really happy,' Joni assured another young girl who questioned her. 'I wouldn't change my life for anything. I even feel privileged. I'm really thankful God did something to get my attention and change me. You don't have to get a broken neck to be drawn to God. But people don't always listen to the experiences of others and learn from them. I hope you'll learn from my experience and not have to go through the bitter lessons of suffering which I had to face in order to learn.'

See also 11 September

14 September

Bible wisdom – about anger

'When a fool is annoyed he quickly lets it be known. Sensible people will ignore an insult.'

'If you stay calm you are wise, but if you have a hot temper, you only show how stupid you are.'

'Don't make friends with people who have hot, violent tempers. You might learn their habits and not be able to change.'

'People with quick tempers cause a lot of quarrelling and trouble.'

'If you churn milk you get butter. If you hit someone's nose, it bleeds. If you stir up anger, you get into trouble.'

'A gentle answer quiets anger, but a harsh one stirs it up.'

From the *Book of Proverbs*

PRAYER
Help me, Father, by your Spirit, to calm down and know
your quietening and control when I get angry. Teach me to
keep back words and actions that upset and hurt others. For
Jesus' sake. Amen

15 September

In September 1979, Dave Markee was invited to play bass guitar in Eric Clapton's band.

Phone call to despair

'God, I don't care who you are. I don't care whether you're a Buddhist, a Muslim, a Jehovah's Witness or a dustman. If you're interested, will you please show me who you are?'

The sunshine on the beach at Nassau was brilliant, and the blue sea and shining white sands completed a picture of carefree happiness. But the phone had rung for Dave Markee – all the way from his suburban home in Surrey to the plush hotel where he had just been talking to the Rolling Stones – and disaster had struck. The successful, pot-smoking rock and roll artiste felt as though his world had ended. His wife wanted a divorce – and suddenly success and glamour meant nothing.

That was why he turned in desperation to the God he had heard about from fellow musician Bryn Haworth. Then he returned home and persuaded his wife, Ze, to give the marriage another chance.

A few weeks later, Dave knelt on the kitchen floor and asked Jesus to forgive him and take control of his life. 'I cried like I'd never cried before,' he says. 'It was as if Christ had been standing outside in the freezing cold wanting to enter so badly, yet waiting till he was asked. Then he rushed in. There was such a feeling of joy and light.'

Ze, meanwhile, was seeing to a manager who had arrived from New York to arrange a deal. Dave wasn't 'stoned', as she first suspected. He had found peace at last, a peace in Christ which Ze herself discovered a few months later.

267

16 September

Canon J.B.Phillips was born on 16 September 1906.

Ring of truth

One of the first to translate the New Testament into modern everyday language was Canon J.B.Phillips. Some years ago he was asked by the BBC to talk about his work with another translator of the Gospels, Dr E.V.Rieu.

'Towards the end of the discussion Dr Rieu was asked about his general approach to the task, and his reply was this:

'"My personal reason for doing this was my own intense desire to satisfy myself as to the authenticity and the spiritual content of the Gospels ... I approached them in the same spirit as I would have approached them had they been presented to me as recently discovered Greek manuscripts ... " A few minutes later I asked him, "Did you get the feeling that the whole material is extraordinarily alive? ... I got the feeling that the whole thing was alive even while one was translating. Even though one did a dozen versions of a particular passage, it was still living. Did you get that feeling?"

'Dr Rieu replied: "I got the deepest feeling that I possibly could have expected. It ... changed me; my work changed me. And I came to the conclusion that these words bear the seal of ... the Son of Man and God" ...

'I found it particularly thrilling to hear a man who is a scholar of the first rank as well as a man of wisdom and experience openly admitting that these words written long ago were alive with power. They bore to him, as to me, the ring of truth.'

From *Ring of Truth*, by J.B.Phillips

See also 17 September

17 September

One outstanding example of J.B.Phillips's translation of the New Testament is the passage below, from Romans 12.

'Let God remould you'

'With eyes wide open to the mercies of God, I beg you, my brothers, as an act of intelligent worship, to give Him your bodies, as a living sacrifice, consecrated to Him and acceptable by Him. Don't let the world around you squeeze you into its own mould, but let God remould your minds from within, so that you may prove in practice that the plan of God for you is good, meets all His demands and moves towards the goal of true maturity . . .

'Let us have no imitation Christian love. Let us have a genuine break with evil and a real devotion to good. Let us have real warm affection for one another as between brothers, and a willingness to let the other man have the credit . . . Share the happiness of those who are happy, and the sorrow of those who are sad. Live in harmony with each other. Don't become snobbish but take a real interest in ordinary people. Don't become set in your own opinions. Don't pay back a bad turn by a bad turn, to *anyone* . . .

'Don't allow yourself to be overpowered by evil. Take the offensive – overpower evil with good!'

From *Letters to Young Churches*

See also 16 September

18 September

In September 1877, *The Christian Herald* carried a report
of Dr Barnardo's trial.

Today we are used to seeing photographs of people in need
as part of the publicity for charity organizations. Dr Barnardo
was the first to use photography in this way. It was fitting
that his funeral was one of the first events to be recorded
on cine-film.

'Before' and 'After'

Now that Thomas Barnardo had established his home for
destitute boys, he could go out on more midnight forays to rescue
the homeless. He would often photograph the children as they
were when he found them, and publish the photos in pamphlets
or Christian magazines, alongside another taken after they had
been fed and cared for in his home. He entitled them *Before and
After*.

Barnardo was accused of faking or setting up these photographs and in court, where he faced this and other charges, Mrs
Williams, a West Indian widow, was called to give evidence. She
earned what she could, sewing sacks at home, for which she was
paid one shilling and eightpence (about eight new pence) per
hundred. She had no furniture, and neighbours spared scraps
of food for her family. Her children had no clothes – they kept
warm under the pile of sacks their mother had sewn. When she
took the finished sacks to the factory, the children were left in
the cold until she returned with the next consignment. When
Dr Barnardo visited her, he pulled back the pile of sacks and
discovered her three children asleep.

When Mrs Williams described this in court and verified the
photo Barnardo had taken, the whole court was moved.
Barnardo's defence counsel suggested that he had no need to
fake photographs when the truth itself was so tragic.

PRAYER
We pray for all who use photography, film and television to
bring home the need of others. May they work honestly and
with integrity. Save us from becoming hardened to scenes
of suffering, but make us willing to give practical help
wherever we can. For Jesus' sake. Amen

See also 17 and 18 July

19 September

George Cadbury was born on 19 September 1839.

Bitter chocolate

Business was bad. The two young brothers – George only twenty-one – took over the firm from their ailing father and determined to pay off debts and improve trade. They sold tea, coffee and 'cocoa nibs, a most nutritious beverage for breakfast'. They worked six days a week from eight in the morning till seven-thirty at night, and George economized enough to live on ten shillings (fifty new pence) a week.

But the public would not drink chocolate. It was too bitter! All kinds of additives were tried to disguise the bitterness of the cocoa butter, but the end result was no better than what George described as 'a comforting gruel'.

Then George heard that a Dutch chocolate manufacturer had invented a machine to press out the cocoa butter and 'I went off to Holland without knowing a word of Dutch,' he said, 'saw the manufacturer with whom I had to talk entirely by signs and a dictionary and bought the machine.'

So it was that in 1866 Cadbury's put on the market the first pure cocoa essence that tasted sweet. Business soon boomed. Tablets of chocolate as well as the 'nutritious beverage' were manufactured.

But George Cadbury cared for more than business. Every Sunday – his one day off – he set off at 6.30 a.m. to take Class 14 in the newly-formed Adult School. He took a flower for each member of his class. He described this school as 'a sort of co-operative system of carrying on class where one is our Master, even Christ'. And in true Quaker style, all were treated as equals, though many were down-and-outs. All denominations joined in. Reading and writing came first on the programme and Bible study followed.

Later in life, George Cadbury held reunions for past members of his class twice a year in his large house and garden. Almost 1,000 people would turn up, grateful to George for the start he had given them in learning and living.

See also 20 September

20 September

A village called Bournville

Each day in the Cadbury factory began with Bible reading and prayers for all. But no one could call the Cadbury brothers hypocrites. Their Christianity never stopped at fine words. In an age when most owners cared little about conditions for their factory-hands, George believed in providing first-class facilities. When the premises became too small, he determined to build a factory in the country. The brothers purchased a site a few miles out of Birmingham near the tiny stream of Bournbrook, which suggested the factory's new name.

George loved open space. He provided football fields for the men, and a playground and garden with a lily-pond for the girls. Inside, there were warm cloakrooms for drying off wet clothes and a warming cupboard for the girls to heat their own food.

The brothers kept in touch with factory conditions personally. 'Mr Richard and Mr George would go down on their knees and crawl under the tables to see if the water-pipes were hot enough,' one worker said.

But working out of town presented transport problems. George decided to buy land round the factory and build a village for his work-force. There was to be no jerry-building and every house would have a spacious garden big enough to grow vegetables. Fruit trees were planted and the garden dug over before each new owner moved in. Trees were planted profusely along the wide roads. Later, George Cadbury built schools and a shopping area. In friendly proximity stood an Anglican church and a Friends' Meeting House. The needs of the whole person were catered for.

See also 19 September

Bible wisdom – about the tongue

'Thoughtless words can wound as deeply as any sword, but wisely spoken words can heal.'

'Kind words bring life, but cruel words wound your spirit.'

'Kind words are like honey – sweet to the taste and good for your health.'

'A person's words can be a source of wisdom, deep as the ocean, fresh as a flowing stream.'

From the *Book of Proverbs*

'If a person never makes a mistake in what he says, he is perfect and is also able to control his whole being . . . Man is able to tame and has tamed all other creatures – wild animals and birds, reptiles and fish. But no one has ever been able to tame the tongue.'

From *James 3*

Paul said: 'Do not use harmful words, but only helpful words, the kind that build up and provide what is needed, so that what you say will do good to those who hear you.'

From *Ephesians 4*

PRAYER

'Lord, place a guard at my mouth, a sentry at the door of my lips.' Amen

From *Psalm 141*

22 September

On 22 September 1586, Sir Philip Sidney was mortally wounded in battle at Zutphen in the Netherlands.

Philip Sidney, born at Penshurst Place in Kent in 1554, was a courtier, poet and soldier. He was so loved and admired that, after his death, 200 poems were written in memory of him. One, by his friend Sir Fulke Greville, described him as 'a spotless friend and a matchless man'.

A spotless friend – a matchless man

When Philip Sidney rode to battle at Zutphen, he was not wearing greaves – the piece of armour that soldiers wore to cover their legs. He had taken them off on impulse, out of consideration for a fellow soldier who was without his. A bullet hit him on his unprotected thigh.

Fulke Greville describes how, as he lay wounded and desperately thirsty from fever and the hot sun, he passed his water-bottle with its meagre ration of water to a soldier lying near. 'Thy necessity is yet greater than mine,' he said. A few weeks later, Sidney died from his wound.

> Leave me, O Love which reachest but to dust,
> And thou, my mind aspire to higher things!
> Grow rich in that which never taketh rust:
> Whatever fades but fading pleasure brings.
>
> Then farewell, world! Thy uttermost I see:
> Eternal love, maintain thy life in me!
> *Sir Philip Sidney*

PRAYER
Give us, Lord, love and unselfishness in the little things of life, so that we may be ready to think first of others in the big moments of life. Amen

23 September

The Reverend Francis Kilvert died on 23 September 1879
when he was only thirty-eight. He had been married just
five weeks.

Kilvert's diary

'Why do I keep this voluminous journal? I can hardly tell. Partly because life seems to me such a curious and wonderful thing that it almost seems a pity that even such a humble and uneventful life as mine should pass altogether away without some such record as this, and partly too because I think the record may amuse and interest some who come after me.'

It was many years later that the twenty-two closely-written notebooks, containing the diary Francis Kilvert had kept for twenty-nine years, were finally published. Nothing very exciting or spectacular did happen to this country clergyman. He walked the hills between Herefordshire and Wales, intent on visiting the parishioners who lived around Clyro, where he was curate.

But Kilvert had eyes to see – eyes that noted the beauty of the countryside as well as the charms or quirks of the people he met. His kindness, shrewdness and imagination bring to life for us the people and countryside of a century ago. We are still 'amused and interested'.

PRAYER
Father, give us eyes today to see the beauty of the world
you have made and all that is best in the people we meet.
Amen

See also 24 September, 18 June

24 September

An extract from the diary of the Rev. Francis Kilvert, a nineteenth-century country curate.

The old soldier

'Called on the old soldier. He was with his wife in the garden digging and gathering red potatoes which turned up very large and sound ... The great red potatoes lay thick, fresh and clean on the dark newly turned mould. I sat down on the stones by the spring and the old soldier came and sat down on the stones by me while his wife went on picking up the red potatoes. We talked about the war and the loss of the *Captain*. Mary Morgan brought me some apples, Sam's Crabs and Quinin's. The spring trickled and tinkled behind us and a boy from the keeper's cottage came to draw water in a blue and white jug.

'It was very quiet and peaceful in the old soldier's garden as we sat by the spring while the sun grew low and gilded the apples in the trees which he had planted, and the keeper's wife moved about in the garden below, and we heard the distant shots at partridges.

'I dug up the half row of potatoes for him which he had left unfinished. Then we went indoors and I read to the old man the story of Philip and the Eunuch.'

PRAYER
Thank you, Lord, for all the gentle and quiet pleasures of life. Thank you for those willing to serve you in small and unobtrusive ways, not seeking the limelight and excitement but doing your will in the daily uneventful round. Amen

See also 23 September, 18 June

25 September

Poet Steve Turner's birthday is 25 September.

Read it out loud!

At school poetry had been boring. One well-tried method of punishment was to write out a poem – a long one – for detention. Then there was poetry-learning. What the poem *meant* didn't seem to matter – it was the memorizing that was important. Enough to kill poetry stone dead – as it had for Steve Turner when he left school with two O-levels to work in a clothing factory.

Then he came across the lyrics of the Beatles and Bob Dylan, and he began writing poetry himself. But the big change came when he heard poetry read out loud at a nearby pub. After much trepidation, Steve plucked up courage to read out some of his own poems and perhaps that was how Steve Turner the poet really took off.

Steve now reads his poems in churches, prisons, schools, art centres and at festivals, as well as in pubs. He believes it's the sound of the poems heard out loud that makes people keen to read and think about poems for themselves.

Poets are people who perceive what the rest of us don't notice. Steve Turner sees our world sharply and clearly and, because he is a Christian, he sees it with the insights that his faith brings. What he has to say makes people sit up. He doesn't aim to be popular, and the off-beat humour of his poems doesn't disguise their bite. Steve Turner's poetry gets under our skin even while it's making us smile.

History Lesson
History repeats itself.
Has to.
No one listens.

See also 7 January, 10 December

26 September

Wilson Carlile, founder of the Church Army, died on
26 September 1942.

From riches to rags

Wilson Carlile lay still, the pain in his back too bad for him to move. But he could think – think back over twenty-six years of success followed by total failure. He had always been clever with money. At seven years old, he had been given a little book for accounts along with his weekly pocket money, which his father audited each month. When he joined his grandfather's firm at fourteen, he had had a fair idea of money matters. He set himself a goal: he would make £20,000 by the age of twenty-five. That's rather like aiming to become a multi-millionaire today.

Although he was not strong – he had had trouble with his spine – Wilson was determined and he reached his target. But when the great financial crash of Black Friday came, he lost nearly £30,000 overnight. The shock, after years of overwork, brought on his old back trouble. His life seemed in ruins.

While he lay helpless, his forthright Christian aunt came to visit him. She told him plainly that he needed Jesus Christ as his Saviour. Wilson was angry at first, but as he read one of the books she had given him, a change came over him and he determined to give his life to Christ and to bring the good news of the gospel to others.

He became a curate but was horrified to find that the people sitting in his pews were wealthy and expensively dressed. Those who really needed him were tramping the streets outside or living in wretched nearby slums. Carlile determined to bring relief and help to them. He rallied some helpers and founded the Church Army. Today, 100 years later, it still exists to bring help and hope to those in greatest need.

POSTSCRIPT
The officers of the Church Army today organize seaside and other missions, run hostels for the lonely and homeless, and work in prisons and among the Forces. They help single parents, schoolgirl mothers, the elderly and many others with special needs. Young people can work for a year in their Christian Service Scheme in many of these activities.

See also 4 November

27 September

God will provide!

The door-bell rang and George Müller went to answer it. No visitor was standing on the step, but there *was* something there. He stared hard, then bent down and picked up a large fender (used to protect children from an open fire) and a dish. Müller thanked God for another answer to prayer, and added the objects to his growing collection. Fenders and dishes, as well as cups, plates, knives, forks and yards of calico and sheeting continued to arrive at the home of Mr and Mrs Müller. And George Müller was not really surprised. After all, he had asked God for them.

Appalled by the shocking conditions in Victorian workhouses – where orphans with no money or family connections were despatched – Müller determined to open an orphanage where love, care and Christian teaching would be given. But he had no money. One evening he read in his Bible, 'Open thy mouth wide and I will fill it.' He took God at his word. He would ask God for everything he needed for his orphans, without letting a soul know what was required. Then he would wait with patience for God to provide.

Müller had another reason for wanting to run his orphanage 'by faith'. He felt sad to see how many Christians spent their lives worrying and fretting over how to make ends meet. 'If I can show that God can supply the needs of all my orphans,' he thought, 'others will learn to trust their Father to supply their needs.'

From a small home for thirty girls, Müller's Homes grew to provide for 2,000 children. The homes still flourish in Bristol today.

See also 5 December

279

28 September

28 September is the Feast Day of St Wenceslas.

Good King Wenceslas

He was the kindest and best of kings. Brought up by his Christian grandmother, Wenceslas became king of Bohemia in his own right when he was of age. He bravely told the pagan ruling party, 'Till now I have been under your control. Today I throw it off and shall serve God with all my heart.'

At once he tried to get rid of the slave-trade which had its centre in Prague; he also reformed the corrupt legal system. But his enemies hated his justice and mercy. At the age of twenty-two, in the year 929, Wenceslas was assassinated and the country reverted to pagan rule. But the king was revered as a saint and many stories were told of his goodness.

One described how he would cut down trees on his royal estate to carry wood under cover of darkness to his poorest subjects. An incensed head forester reported the thefts to the king, never for one moment suspecting the true identity of the 'robber'.

'Don't stop the thief,' the king commanded. 'Give him a hard beating and let him go on his way.'

The forester was mystified both at the strange command and the unusual severity of the orders, but he carried them out and Wenceslas took his beating cheerfully.

Dr John Neale, writing a 'moral tale' for his children in Victorian times, may have based it on this legend. He later turned it into the carol that everyone knows and sings at Christmas.

29 September

On 29 September 1955, David Sheppard was ordained to the Church of England ministry.

David Sheppard, now Anglican Bishop of Liverpool, is known particularly for his concern for the inner city and for church unity. In the fifties, his main claim to fame was as an England Test cricketer.

From batsman to bishop

What does it feel like to walk from the pavilion across the grass to take up your stand and bat in a Test Match? It can be nerve-racking, as David Sheppard, former Sussex and England cricketer admits. 'There are times', he writes, 'especially in big cricket, when it feels more like an ordeal by fire than a game.'

David Sheppard began like hundreds of other schoolboys, by playing his own complicated games of solo cricket against the coal-shed door. He would bat whole sides, carefully imitating the stance and strokes of the various well-known cricket stars. He reckons those games taught him more about batting than anything else did.

This is his answer to the question of whether religion and cricket can mix: 'As a Christian . . . I believe that health, strength, quickness of eye all come from God. Success comes from God – and so too can failure. If I say my prayers faithfully, this is no guarantee that I shall make a hundred next time I go in to bat. I may make a duck. But I can make a duck or a hundred to the glory of God – by the way I accept success or failure.'

PRAYER
Thank you, Father, for the enjoyment to be found in playing games as well as watching them. Help us to take defeat and success in the right way, both for ourselves and for the teams we support. For Jesus Christ's sake. Amen

30 September

30 September is the Feast Day of St Jerome.

St Jerome lived from about 347 to 420 AD and was one of the greatest biblical scholars and translators of all time. As a student in Rome he spent his Sundays in the catacombs, discovering and deciphering the tombs of the early Christian martyrs. Later in life he founded a free school in Bethlehem, where he taught the local children Latin and Greek. Some have said he was canonized for his work, not for his saintly character, for 'it was almost impossible for Jerome to be long anywhere without falling into a dispute'!

The people's version

Jerome was unwilling to take on the job. But it was the pope himself, whose secretary he had been for a short while, who ordered him to do so. Pope Damasus had recognized Jerome's considerable talents and gave him the task of revising the Latin version of the New Testament. The New Testament was originally written in Greek, but as most people were more familiar with Latin, which was the language used in all church services, there were also scores of Latin versions of it around – 'almost as many distinct versions as copies of Scripture,' Jerome himself remarked.

Jerome set to work unwillingly because he knew that people dislike change and that he would meet with criticism. The Gospels soon appeared, followed by the rest of the New Testament. Then Jerome set to work on the Old Testament.

Although the Old Testament was originally written in Hebrew, most previous translators made use of the Greek version made by Jewish scholars some two hundred years before Christ. Jerome was a rarity among his contemporaries in knowing Hebrew, which he had studied with the help of Jewish rabbis. He decided to go back to the original Hebrew.

As he had anticipated, his 'new-fangled' translation came in for a storm of criticism. It was new and different and on that score it was disliked. Jerome called his critics 'two-legged donkeys', who 'think that ignorance is holiness'.

In spite of opposition, Jerome's version of the Bible endured because it was so fine and so infinitely superior to any others. It was used by the church for more than a thousand years and in 1546 it was declared at the Council of Trent to be the one authoritative Latin text. It became known as the Vulgate, the common version, because it was the version of the people.

1 October

Ashley Cooper, later Lord Shaftesbury, died on 1 October 1885.

Throughout a long parliamentary career, he was impelled by his love for Christ to relieve suffering and distress wherever he found it. He championed the cause of nearly every philanthropist of his age.

Bedlam!

'The unhappy patient was no longer treated as a human being. His body was immediately encased in a machine which left it no liberty of action. He was sometimes chained to a staple. He was frequently beaten and starved and at best kept in subjection by foul and menacing language.'

From *Lunacy, Law and Conscience*, by Kathleen Jones

The 'unhappy patient' was none other than King George III of England. But the king's illness led to public airing of a topic that had been previously hushed up. Young Ashley Cooper was invited to serve on a committee of inquiry about treatment of the mentally ill and was shocked by what he found. He went to see conditions for himself and found patients chained hand and foot to a straw-lined bedstead in a crowded room. They were left there naked, with only a blanket for cover, and taken out once a week to be cleaned down at an outside tub in icy water. The doctors admitted that no cure or treatment was attempted.

Ashley's maiden speech to parliament was on the subject and, in spite of his strong feelings, nervousness made him speak so softly that he could hardly be heard. 'My first effort has been made for the advance of human happiness. May I improve hourly!' he wrote in his diary.

And he did. Many exhausting hours were spent in the next fifty-seven years of his life helping the cause of those most neglected and helpless in the community – the mentally ill.

See also 8 October, 18 March, 28 April

2 October-

Harvest Thanksgiving Services are usually held at this time of year.

Good advice
'If you wait until the wind and the weather are just right, you will never sow anything and never harvest anything . . . Do your sowing in the morning and in the evening, too. You never know whether it will all grow well or whether one sowing will do better than the other.'
From *Ecclesiastes 11*

God's promise
'As long as the world exists, there will be a time for planting and a time for harvest. There will always be cold and heat, summer and winter, day and night.'
From *Genesis 8*

A harvest hymn
'May the peoples praise you, O God;
  may all the peoples praise you!
The land has produced its harvest;
  God, our God, has blessed us.
God has blessed us;
  may all people everywhere honour him.'
From *Psalm 67*

PRAYER
Father, we thank you for the seasons and for your promise that the pattern of the year will never fail. Thank you for this year's harvest. Help us not to be greedy or wasteful with your gifts. Make us always ready to share with those less fortunate than ourselves. Amen

3 October

St Francis of Assisi died on 3 October 1226.

Search for a beggar

Young Francis Bernadone stood in the little market booth of the Italian town of Assisi, selling bales of cloth for his father, who was a respected citizen and member of the guild of cloth merchants in the town. While he was busy serving a merchant, a beggar came up, pulling at his sleeve and whining for money. Francis was too busy unrolling bale after bale of cloth for the customer to attend to him. The purchase completed, he turned to look for the beggar but he had disappeared.

Francis leaped from the booth, leaving the precious bales of velvet and embroidered cloth unguarded, and began a chase across the market-place and up and down every alley of the labyrinth of Assisi's little streets. At last, he found the beggar and loaded him with money.

As he turned to go back to the market, Francis made a vow before God that he would never in all his life refuse to help a poor man. And he kept his promise.

PRAYER
Father, make us tender-hearted and generous to all who are in need. Amen

See also 5 October

4 October

Miles Coverdale's Bible, the first to be printed in English, was published on 4 October 1535. The *Great Bible* followed in 1539.

Chained for safety

Miles Coverdale was fortunate to have a friend in high places. Thomas Cromwell, 'Secretary of State' to Henry VIII, was sympathetic towards Coverdale's scheme to provide a Bible in English at long last. Coverdale based the New Testament and Pentateuch (the first five books of the Old Testament) on Tyndale's translation of 1525, and set about translating the rest himself. Unlike Tyndale, he was not a Hebrew or Greek scholar, but he could write splendid English.

Cromwell then commissioned Coverdale to produce another version, and although the printing of it was banned in Paris, press, paper and compositors were shipped to England and the work completed there. The king gave his blessing to this Bible and ordered a copy to be placed in every church. This so-called *Great Bible* was large and expensive. Parish councils did not want their precious copies stolen, so they often bought a chain and fastened the Bible to the lectern.

Psalm 23 in Coverdale's Bible

The Lorde is my shepherde, I can want nothinge. He fedeth me in a grene pasture, and ledeth me to a fresh water. He quickeneth my soule and bringeth me forth in the waye of rightuousnes for his names sake. Though I should walke now in the valley of the shadowe of death, yet I fear no euell, for thou art with me: thy staff and thy shepehoke cōforte me.

See also 6 and 7 October

5 October

A year or two before his death (in October 1226), St Francis
of Assisi was told that he was going blind.

Brother Fire

'If the faintest hint has been given of what St Francis felt about
the glory and pageantry of earth and sky, about the heraldic shape
and colour and symbolism of birds and beasts and flowers, some
notion may be formed of what it meant to him to go blind. Yet the
remedy might well have seemed worse than the disease. The
remedy . . . was to cauterize the eye, and that without any
anaesthetic. In other words it was to burn his living eyeballs with a
red-hot iron . . . When they took the brand from the furnace, he
rose as with an urbane gesture and spoke as to an invisible
presence: "Brother Fire, God made you beautiful and strong and
useful; I pray you be courteous with me."'
From *St Francis of Assisi*, by G.K.Chesterton

> Thou fire so masterful and bright,
> That givest man both warmth and light,
>   O praise him, O praise him,
>   Alleluia, Alleluia, Alleluia!
> From the *Canticle of St Francis*

See also 3 October

6 October

On 6 October 1536, William Tyndale was strangled at the stake, and his body afterwards burnt.

God's smuggler – to England

About 100 years had passed since Wyclif and his followers had translated the Bible into English and copied it so laboriously by hand. In the intervening years, printing had been 'discovered', having been first invented by the Chinese in the eleventh century. There was scope now for producing many hundreds of copies in a fraction of the time.

William Tyndale was a scholar who shared Wyclif's ideal of bringing the Bible to ordinary people in their own language. He went back to the original Hebrew Old Testament and Greek New Testament to make his translation. But the church was still bitterly opposed to an English Bible and England grew too hot for Tyndale and his unpopular views.

He fled to the Continent to finish translating and oversee printing, but enemies were constantly tracking him down. On one occasion he snatched up the precious manuscript only just in time, when the place where he kept his papers was set on fire as a result of someone informing on him.

Once the printing was done, the New Testaments had somehow to be shipped to England. All kinds of ingenious ways were devised. Wine-casks were made with false bottoms; Bibles were cunningly concealed inside bales of cloth. Sympathetic merchants smuggled the Bibles along with their wares. Once in England, the Testaments spread throughout the country. It looked as if Tyndale's prophecy that 'a boy who drives the plough in England shall know more of the Bible than many priests' might yet come true.

Continued on 7 October; see also 4 May

7 October

Books for burning

New Testaments in Tyndale's translation were arriving thick and fast in England, but were not always falling into the hands of sympathetic readers. Whenever a copy came to the notice of church leaders, they burned it, and there were public bonfires outside St Paul's Cathedral in London for that very purpose. The Bishop of London offered to buy up copies to burn, little realizing that the merchant who sold them to him was returning the sales money to Tyndale to finance further printing. But the opposition *was* winning – only one complete copy of the first edition has survived.

Undefeated, Tyndale kept moving his hiding-place to avoid arrest. He began on the Old Testament. He lost the whole of his translation of the book of Deuteronomy when he was caught in a storm off the Dutch coast.

At last enemies found him, when he was betrayed at Antwerp by a priest he had befriended. After months of torture in prison, he was condemned to death and strangled, then burnt at the stake. But in spite of seeming failure, his dying prayer was answered. 'Lord, open the King of England's eyes,' Tyndale prayed, and when the first complete Bible was printed in England, it had Henry VIII's blessing.

Luke 11:2-4 in Tyndale's New Testament

Oure Father, which arte in hevē, halowed be thy name. Lett thy kyngdō come. Thy will be fulfillet, even in erth as it is in heven. Oure dayly breed geve us thos daye. And forgeve us oure synnes: for even we forgeve every man that traspaseth us; and ledde us not into tempatciō, butt deliver us from evyll. Amen

See also 6 October, 4 May

8 October

The funeral service of Lord Shaftesbury took place on 8 October 1885.

A bed for the night

The lodging-houses throughout the towns and cities of England were a disgrace. A city missionary of the time described those in London:

'These houses are never cleaned or ventilated; they literally swarm with vermin. It is almost impossible to breathe. Missionaries are seized with vomiting or fainting upon entering them.'

'I have felt the vermin dropping on my hat like peas,' another missionary said.

These descriptions were quoted by Lord Shaftesbury in his speeches on the subject in parliament. He had already been concerned in a project to build two model lodging-houses that could be run at a profit. Next, he got two bills through parliament, one allowing local authorities to build lodging-houses and the other providing for all houses to be registered and inspected.

Recent investigation of hostels for down-and-outs has shown that conditions are still shocking and degrading. Does the Christian church need another Lord Shaftesbury today?

See also 1 October, 28 April

9 October

Lord Coggan, former Archbishop of Canterbury, was born on 9 October 1909.

Why so much suffering – if God really cares?

'All I can say in an almost one-sentence answer is that so often God is to be found in the heart of that suffering. There are many people who do not escape suffering but in the midst of their suffering find God there. St Paul had some appalling physical affliction. He did not say what it was. He did what any normal Christian would do, he asked God to remove the thing. He asked him not once, nor twice but three times. And God answered his prayer with a very clear "No". "No, you're to go through it, but in the midst of it you will find my grace." That's not an answer to the problem of suffering, but it is I think a light on it.'

From an interview with Lord Coggan in *Simple Faith?*

PRAYER
Lord, hear our prayer for all who suffer. Help them to find you with them in their pain. Take away bitterness and resentment, and ease pain of body and mind. Help us to face suffering with courage and trust in you. For Jesus' sake. Amen

10 October

Bible wisdom – about honesty

'If you are good, you are guided by honesty. People who can't be trusted are destroyed by their own dishonesty.'

'The Lord hates people who use dishonest scales. He is happy with honest weights.'

'Anyone who thinks it isn't wrong to steal from his parents is no better than a common thief.'

'It is better to have little, honestly earned, than to have a large income gained dishonestly.'

'The wicked run when no one is chasing them but an honest person is as brave as a lion.'

'Be honest and you show that you obey the Lord; be dishonest and you show that you do not.'

'You may think that everything you do is right, but remember that the Lord judges your motives. Do what is right and fair; that pleases the Lord more than bringing him sacrifices.'

From the *Book of Proverbs*

11 October

George Williams was born on 11 October 1821.

Help for apprentices

The London drapers' shops were eye-catching. Plate glass had transformed the windows, giving large, uninterrupted displays of fashion, and the new gas-lighting illuminated the ill-lit streets and made passers-by stop and look. And they could go in – for shops stayed open late and service was excellent.

Drapers prospered and everyone was happy – except the apprentices. Young George Williams, up in London from his father's farm in the country, discovered at first hand what conditions were like. Apprentices not only worked long hours, but there was little for them to do – besides gamble and drink – when they were free. Drapers provided accommodation for their own lads and often they were shepherded straight from the shop to bed and from bed to shop, with perhaps one evening off a week for courting. They were herded together in dormitories with no sitting-room or library. If they were ill, they were given the sack.

George Williams made good and bought his own draper's shop. He and other Christians in the trade enjoyed meeting together to talk and pray, and wanted to help the apprentices to do the same. On 6 June 1844, a group of twelve or thirteen men, including Williams, met 'for the purpose of forming a society the object of which is to influence young men to spread the Redeemer's Kingdom among those by whom they are surrounded'. The Young Men's Christian Association (YMCA) was under way.

See also 1 May

12 October

The complete *Good News Bible* was first published in
Britain in October 1976. It came out two months later in
the USA. One million copies were sold before the end of
the year.

Drawing Good News

'The Bible seemed so dull, so black – two columns of text with
little numbers at the side. The gap between people and the Bible
seemed to be growing. I asked myself, "If I really believe that love
and hope is in the Bible, what should I do?"'

Annie Vallotton, Swiss-born artist, soon had the answer to her
own question. She was invited to provide the 500 illustrations
needed for the *Good News Bible*. Wherever the new, lively,
everyday version was read, Annie's pictures would be studied too.

Her line-drawings may look simple and unelaborate, but she
drew them with great care. Annie made about eighty preliminary
sketches for every drawing, and she herself acted out many of the
poses in front of the mirror in order to get them just right.

She says that she aims her drawings at 'the child-like part that
remains in each adult'. She tells the story of a child who had to
give the Scripture reading in church. Instead of prefacing it with
words such as 'Here beginneth the lesson', she said, 'I have a
lovely story for you today – it's from . . . '

Annie Vallotton aims to bring the same freshness and
enjoyment through her drawings.

See also 13 October

13 October

'And we know that our old being has been put to death
with Christ on his cross, in order that the power of the
sinful self might be destroyed, so that we should no longer
be the slaves of sin.'
From *Romans 6*

'I have found it!'

The Australian Bible Society tell a story about the Annie
Vallotton drawing which accompanies the verse quoted above in
the New Testament of the *Good News Bible*.

A Bulgarian prisoner was attending Bible studies organized by
a visitor to an Adelaide prison. He was serving a sentence for
murder, after killing his wife because of the terrible after-effects
of Nazi ill-treatment which she was suffering. He had tried to kill
himself too, without success. For six years he had tried to find
peace and forgiveness – but failed.

One day, when the group was studying Romans chapter 5,
using the *Good News Bible*, the man suddenly cried out: 'I have
found it!'.

But he was not reading the verses – his attention had been
caught by Annie Vallotton's drawing of a man laying down a heavy
load at the foot of Christ's cross and walking away free. Through
that picture, he realized for the first time that his own heavy
burden of guilt, remorse and bitterness could be put down and
left once and for all at the cross where Jesus died to take away sin.

See also 12 October

14 October

William Penn was born on 14 October 1644.

The 'holy experiment'

Penn tried in vain. It was impossible for Quakers to gain religious tolerance in England. Perhaps they could make a fresh start in a new country. Some Quakers had already settled in America, and Penn approached the king with a request to buy land there which belonged to the English crown.

Charles's answer surprised even the hopeful Penn. He insisted on giving him a charter to the whole large territory known today as Pennsylvania. In return, Penn must pay 'two beaver skins to be delivered at our castle at Windsor on the first day of January every year', and one fifth of any gold and silver mined in the province. Penn would be free to build towns and harbours, make laws, and rent and sell the land. The only thing he might not do was to declare war – but, as a devout Quaker, Penn was also an ardent pacifist who had no intention of doing that.

Penn began to plan what he called his 'holy experiment'. At the centre of his new land, he would have a splendid city. The streets would not run higgledy-piggledy in all directions, but be laid out in neat rectangles. Houses would not be huddled miserably close together. Each would have 'ground on each side for gardens or orchards or fields, that it may be a green country town, which will never be burnt and always wholesome'.

This town of his dreams was to be called 'Philadelphia'. Penn composed the name from two Greek words, *philia* (love) and *adelphos* (brother). Not only should his town be pleasant and healthy to live in, but if he had his way it would be a town of brotherly love.

POSTSCRIPT
The king chose the name 'Pennsylvania' – literally, the Forests of Penn – as a tribute to Penn's late father, a famous admiral.

PRAYER
Help all those, dear Lord, who plan our towns and cities. May they endeavour to meet the needs of all ages and races, of the handicapped, the lonely and families. May we be friendly and peaceable members of the communities in which we live. Amen

See also 27 October

15 October

In October 1953, Britain declared a state of emergency in Kenya because of the activities of the Mau Mau terrorist movement.

Andrew Kaguru was one of many Christian Kikuyu who was murdered for his faith. Because of persecution, the number of Christians in the Kikuyu tribe fell from 22,000 to 800. But those who stood firm bore such a witness to their faith that the Christian church is now flourishing.

Kept faithful

Andrew Kaguru enjoyed life in the beautiful Kikuyu tribal reserve, where he preached at the small, grey church – though everything had changed since the days when it paid to be a Christian.

In the past, people had wanted a Christian name, and found it useful to produce a reference from a missionary when applying for a job. But now the Mau Mau movement, based on ancient Kikuyu beliefs and born of hatred for white domination and a foreign religion, was growing fast. In the forest clearings, at dead of night, Mau Mau leaders forced oaths of allegiance from terrified tribesmen. Horrible rites accompanied the oath-taking, which included a promise to kill all who resisted the Mau Mau.

Andrew bravely denounced the Mau Mau from his pulpit. He knew the danger he faced, but was certain that death could only come if God permitted it. One morning, at about two o'clock, there was a battering at Kaguru's hut. He was ordered to take the oath, but refused to do so though he was repeatedly beaten.

'I have no other decision,' he told them. Then he was beaten again and his body hacked to pieces. His twelve-year-old son crept out, found his father's body, and ran for help for his mother, soon to have a baby, who was badly wounded too.

The Kikuyu Christians asked their brothers and sisters in Christ: 'Do not pray that we may be kept safe. Pray that we may be kept faithful.'

16 October

Bible wisdom – about sharing

Jesus said: 'When someone asks you for something, give it to him; when someone wants to borrow something, lend it to him.'

From *Matthew 5*

'If you lend only to those from whom you hope to get it back, why should you receive a blessing? Even sinners lend to sinners, to get back the same amount! No! Love your enemies and do good to them; lend and expect nothing back. You will then have a great reward, and you will be sons of the Most High God. For he is good to the ungrateful and the wicked. Be merciful just as your Father is merciful.'

From *Luke 6*

'Suppose there are brothers or sisters who need clothes and don't have enough to eat. What good is there in your saying to them, "God bless you! Keep warm and eat well!" – if you don't give them the necessities of life?'

From *James 2*

'All the believers continued together in close fellowship and shared their belongings with one another.'

From *Acts 2*

'The group of believers was one in mind and heart. No one said that any of his belongings was his own, but they all shared with one another everything they had . . . There was no one in the group who was in need.'

From *Acts 4*

17 October

On 17 October 1979, Mother Teresa was awarded the
Nobel Peace Prize for her work among the outcasts and
dying in Calcutta.

The 'call within a call'

Mother Teresa held the tiny baby girl in her arms. 'See!' she exclaimed with joy and wonder. 'There's life in her!'

Every baby rescued from the dustbins or gutters of the Calcutta streets is a miracle to her. There can never be too many. Each is welcomed and loved as if it were the Christ-child.

Most visitors to India's great city avert their eyes from the suffering and squalor of the poor and dying. Mother Teresa lives among them, shares their poverty and brings them the love of Christ.

Born of Albanian parents, and brought up in Yugoslavia, Mother Teresa heard God's call to become a nun and give her time to prayer and meditation. She was sent to teach in the pleasant and congenial Loreto Convent School in Calcutta. One day, she had to go to the poor part of the city, and at once she recognized that this was where she really belonged. She received her 'call within a call' – to serve Christ in the filth, starvation and suffering of the Calcutta slums, not the refreshing green environment of the convent school.

A Calcutta temple built to the Hindu goddess, Kali, was turned into her Home for the Dying. From there, Mother Teresa and her Sisters of Charity go out into the streets and bring in those who are dying so that they may 'die within sight of a loving face'. People of all ages are rescued, and some recover. All are clean, cared for and at peace for the first time in their lives. The light of God's love fills the house.

Every human being matters to Mother Teresa, because all are loved by God and because Christ died for each one.

See also 19 October, 24 March

18 October

18 October is St Luke's Day. St Luke was a doctor as well
as being the author of Luke's Gospel and the Book of Acts.
He is the patron saint of doctors.

Ahead of the times

Dr James Simpson realized that enthusiasm and persuasive
pamphlets were not always enough to change the thinking of
doctors and politicians. But statistics might! He was appalled by
the number of patients who died as the result of being in hospital.
He reckoned that the Battle of Waterloo was a safer place than an
operating theatre! He also knew the remedy. So he set about
producing facts and figures to prove his case. He carefully
collected evidence from records kept by hospitals throughout
Britain. They supported his theory.

Patients in small cottage hospitals were far more likely to
recover than were those in big city infirmaries. Only one in eighty
patients died in the small hospitals; one in thirty died in the big
ones. Simpson believed that large hospitals, with as many as fifty
or sixty beds to a ward, spread disease and infection. He wanted
small hospitals, with every bed kept as a separate unit.

He did not believe, either, that hospitals should be massive,
permanent buildings. He recommended easily-built units that
could be demolished and replaced regularly without great
expense. If meccano-like frames could be used instead of bricks
and cement, the framework could be pulled to pieces and put
together again on a new site every few years. In an epidemic, a
hospital could be put up in a matter of days.

Simpson prescribed light, space and an abundance of fresh air
for every patient. Over 100 years later, with prefabricated
buildings easily available, Simpson is still ahead of the times!

See also 7 and 8 June

19 October

Mother Teresa's way of love

'We need to find God and he cannot be found in noise and restlessness. God is the friend of silence. See how nature – trees, flowers, grass – grow in silence; see the stars, the moon and sun, how they move in silence . . . The more we receive in silent prayer, the more we can give in our active life. We need silence to be able to touch souls. The essential thing is not what we say, but what God says to us and through us. All our words will be useless unless they come from within – words which do not give the light of Christ increase our darkness.'

'Be kind and merciful. Let no one ever come to you without coming away better and happier. Be the living expression of God's kindness: kindness in your face, kindness in your eyes, kindness in your smile, kindness in your warm greeting . . . To children, to the poor, to all who suffer and are lonely, give always a happy smile – Give them not only your care, but also your heart.

'Make sure that you let God's grace work in your souls by accepting whatever he gives you, and giving him whatever he takes from you.

'True holiness consists in doing God's will with a smile.'

From *Something Beautiful for God*, by Malcolm Muggeridge

See also 17 October, 24 March

20 October

Christopher Wren, mathematician, astronomer and architect, was born on 20 October 1632.

'Look around you'

The Great Fire of London broke out on 2 September 1666. Only five days later, Christopher Wren presented his plans for a new London. Charles II had announced that a new city would be built in which houses would no longer be made of timber, but of more fire-resistant brick and stone. But the splendid new London that Wren envisaged, with broad streets and open squares, a fine waterfront and promenade by the River Thames, was never to be. Objections were quickly made by the merchants and tradespeople, whose interests would not be served by the new open spaces.

However, Wren had greater success with his plans for St Paul's Cathedral. He had already been asked to undertake repairs and new design work for the cathedral, whose tall spire had been damaged in a small fire nearly 100 years before. Design after design was submitted and many building difficulties overcome before the great Thanksgiving Service was held in the new cathedral at the end of 1697. Regular services began a few days later.

Wren planned a cathedral where all the congregation could *hear* what was going on. The days when services were muttered in Latin behind screens were over. All wanted to be involved in the worship of God and in listening to the sermons. The cathedral must be designed so that everything could be clearly heard.

Wren's epitaph, written up in the cathedral, was composed by his son: *Si monumentum requiris, circumspice*: 'If you would see his monument, look around!'

PRAYER
We thank you, God, for those who planned and built the great cathedrals and churches that remind us of your greatness and majesty and bring us a sense of your presence. Amen

21 October

On 21 October 1854, Florence Nightingale and her nurses
were on their way to the Crimea.

Lady with the lantern

When Florence Nightingale was commissioned by the government to go out to the Crimean war-front in charge of nursing, she found conditions too horrible to imagine. Sewers were choked, water supplies were polluted and rats were everywhere. There were shortages of everything – including food. The wounded were crammed together in filthy conditions, and those not killed in battle often died from starvation or disease caught in hospital.

Florence worked without rest, ordering supplies, organizing administration and caring personally for the wounded. She was sometimes on her knees for eight hours at a time, bandaging wounds. Whenever a soldier was seen to be dying, she stayed with him to the end, easing his pain. She estimated that she witnessed 2,000 deaths during one winter. Although she was disillusioned by the selfish and heartless attitudes of many army leaders and administrators, she was full of admiration for the men whose gentleness and chivalry shone through the awful conditions. 'Before she came there was cussing and swearing,' one soldier said, 'but after that it was as holy as a church.'

At nights, Florence Nightingale went round the ward. One nurse who went with her said, 'It seemed an endless walk and one not easily forgotten. As we passed along the silence was profound; very seldom did a moan or cry from those deeply suffering fall on our ears. Miss Nightingale carried her lantern which she would set down before she bent over any of the patients.'

And this is how a soldier writing home described it: 'What a comfort it was to see her pass even. She would speak to one and nod and smile to as many more; we lay there by hundreds; but we could kiss her shadow as it fell and lay our heads on our pillow again content.'

See also 25 October, 12 May

22 October

Thomas Sheraton, English furniture-maker, died on 22 October 1806.

The preacher and his pulpit

'The plan of this pulpit is a regular hexagon which to me is the most beautiful and compact of all . . . Fix the whole [pulpit] firm so that it may not by shaking produce a disagreeable sensation to the preacher.'

Thomas Sheraton gave those directions to country cabinet-makers who might be asked to design a pulpit, in his *Cabinet Maker and Upholsterer's Drawing Book*. He probably knew from experience that 'disagreeable sensation' that a preacher could get from an unsafe pulpit, because as well as designing and making beautiful furniture, Sheraton spent his life preaching. He made no money at either calling. He was brought up in Stockton-on-Tees, but moved to London for a while where he lived in a poor street above his shop and looked 'like a worn-out Methodist minister with threadbare black coat'.

But Sheraton cared little about his own comfort. His mind was full of the furniture he designed and made, and of the gospel he wanted to preach in church or in the open air. He returned to Stockton to become assistant minister at a Baptist church, and died as he had lived – poor. His furniture – and his books – now sell for a fortune, but Sheraton was content with 'a wooden-bottom chair' and 'common food and raiment wherewith to pass through life in peace'.

PRAYER
Thank you, Lord, for men and women like Thomas Sheraton, who put you first, the needs of others next and himself last. Thank you too for the beauty and usefulness of the things he designed and made. May we serve you in all that we do. For Jesus' sake. Amen

23 October

23 October is United Nations Day.

The United Nations is an international organization formed to keep peace in the world. Corrymeela is a Christian community in Northern Ireland dedicated to the work of peace and reconciliation. Both Protestants and Roman Catholics are involved, and while there are branches in Belfast and elsewhere, the centre itself is a beautiful house on the Antrim coast. It provides a holiday for children and adults away from bombs and fighting, where they can learn to live with those they once thought enemies. The community centre was officially opened at the end of October 1965.

Corrymeela – hill of harmony

'You comin' out, Boxer?' his friends asked. 'There's a patrol of Brits movin' down the street. We got a few stones to bounce off their skulls.'

Boxer and his gang were ordinary boys living in a tough, working-class area of Belfast, in sunless red-brick streets, with few green playing-fields. Games of cops and robbers had been replaced by live war-games – stoning the British troops on patrol in the area. It was a fairly safe game as the army couldn't hit back provided the boys stuck to stones and nothing worse.

Boxer, a leading spirit, usually enjoyed the glamour of the game as much as his friends. But now he stood silent.

'What's the matter?' they asked. 'Gettin' scared?'

'No – but if I stone the Brits, I shan't be allowed back at Corrymeela.'

One week of glorious holiday at Corrymeela had had its effect on Boxer.

See also 22 June

24 October

Geoffrey Chaucer died in October 1400.

Chaucer's plowman

There was a plowman with him there, his brother,
Many a load of dung one time or other
He must have carted through the morning dew.
He was an honest worker, good and true,
Living in peace and perfect charity,
And, as the gospel bade him, so did he,
Loving God best with all his heart and mind
And then his neighbour as himself, repined
At no misfortune, slacked for no content,
For steadily about his work he went
To thresh his corn, to dig or to manure
Or make a ditch; and he would help the poor
For love of Christ and never take a penny
If he could help it, and, as prompt as any,
He paid his tithes in full when they were due
On what he owned and on his earnings too.

From Nevill Coghill's translation of *The Canterbury Tales*, by Geoffrey Chaucer

PRAYER
Lord, teach us today to do all our work cheerfully and well –
the pleasant as well as the boring or tiring jobs. May we
help others willingly and live in peace and charity. For
Jesus' sake. Amen

See also 3 April

25 October

Florence Nightingale determined to make a career out of nursing the sick, and travelled in Europe studying methods of nursing in the 1840s. She became famous for her courage and devotion in tending the casualties of the Crimean War. In 1860, she set up a nurses' training school in London.

Notes on nursing

'More interesting than a novel' was one reader's comment on Miss Nightingale's new book, *Notes on Nursing*. It was soon to be seen on coffee-tables everywhere, though not everyone agreed with the author's new-fangled ideas on soap-and-water hygiene. 'That about the skin and washing and hot water. I don't believe a word of it,' one young lady confided. 'I'm quite satisfied with my skin and I don't want it better than it is.'

Florence Nightingale had some very definite opinions:

Patients' needs
Patients need a bunch of flowers – a view out of a window. A pet of some kind, even a bird in a cage. Freedom from irritating noises like the constant rustle of a nurse's dress. Someone to understand their many fears and worries and to guess their needs, because they are shy of asking.

Invalids' food
Milk is the most nourishing food but invalids should not be kept short of vegetables. Tea may not be nourishing but 'nothing is a substitute to the English patient for his cup of tea'.

Serve food carefully. 'Do not give too much, do not leave any food by the patient's bed. Take care nothing is spilt in the saucer.'

Women's work
Women should neither strive to do something because it is usually a man's job nor hold back from a job because it is not considered women's work. 'You want to do the thing that is good whether it is suitable for a woman or not.'

See also 21 October, 12 May

26 October

Alfred, King of Wessex, is thought to have died on 26 October 900.

Alfred was born in about AD 848, fourth son of Aethelwulf, King of Wessex. As well as successfully defending his country against the Danes, he was a scholar, writer and devout Christian. He is said to have translated part of the Bible into English and longed to spread learning in the land.

Alfred – the Greatest!

Alfred never expected to become king, but when his father and two older brothers had died, he began to take a hand in resisting the Danish marauders. He fought eleven battles in one year alone.

After he became king, he was celebrating Christmas one year at Chippenham, in Wiltshire, when the Danes, whose fleet had slipped past unnoticed, attacked and killed many people. The *Anglo-Saxon Chronicle* tells us that Alfred, 'with a little band made his way by wood and swamp and after Easter he made a fort at Athelney. From that fort he kept fighting the foe.'

Alfred was not skulking in a peasant's hut (burning the cakes!) afraid and beaten. He was busy planning his next campaign against the enemy. At length, the two sides met in battle and Alfred was victorious.

Today the thought of compelling an enemy to convert to the victor's religious faith is shocking and horrifying to us, and rightly so. But the fact remains that if Alfred had lost that battle the strong tide of paganism would have swept again across Britain and the Christian faith would have been driven underground.

27 October

On 27 October 1682, the ship carrying Penn and his Quaker emigrants arrived in America.

Arrival of the 'Welcome'

It had been a terrible voyage, lasting two months. Nearly a third of the original passengers had died of smallpox, which broke out in the cramped and unhygienic conditions on board. Storms and lack of fresh food made matters worse. But, at last, the *Welcome* sailed up-river to the Dutch settlement of New Castle. On shore, an advance welcoming party awaited them. There were Dutch, Swedes, English – and Indians. A table and chair were carried into the clearing, and quills and ink-well provided. Then the documents giving Penn rights over the land were duly signed. The settlers promised allegiance to their new ruler.

But the rightful owners of the land were the Indians – and Penn never forgot it. Previous settlers had taken the land from them by force or fraud. If the Indians retaliated, they had been killed. But Penn insisted on treating the Indians with complete fairness. Although the king had granted him full rights to the land, he recognized their prior rights and refused to take territory from them. The land must be bought, and on fair terms. He would not let his agents bargain for a low price, nor would he be taken in by any cunning Indian demand for high payment.

The Indians never forgot Penn's fairness, and legends about him were passed down for generations. His love of running made him popular with them too. At thirty-eight, he could still outrun some of the Indian braves. He visited them in their homes, unarmed and unguarded, believing that his surest defence was 'God's spirit within the Indians' hearts'.

See also 14 October

28 October

Ivan Turgenev, the Russian writer, was born on 28 October 1818.

Turgenev had a favourite game that he played with friends, called 'the portrait game'. He describes it: 'I would draw five or six profiles, whatever came into – I don't say my head – into my pen; and everybody would write underneath each profile what he thought of it. Some very amusing things resulted. I have saved all these sketches and shall use some of them for future stories.'

'A face like all men's faces'

'I saw myself a youth, almost a boy, in a low-pitched wooden church. The slim wax candles gleamed, spots of red, before the old pictures of the saints. There stood before me many people, all fair-haired peasant heads. From time to time they began swaying, falling, rising again, like the ripe ears of wheat when the wind in summer passes over them. All at once a man came up from behind and stood beside me. I did not turn towards him, but I felt that the man was Christ.

'Emotion, curiosity, awe overmastered me. I made an effort and looked at my neighbour. A face like everyone's, a face like all men's faces. The eyes looked a little upward, quietly and intently; the lips closed, not compressed; the upper lip as it were resting on the other; a small beard parted in two; the hands folded and still; and the clothes on him like everyone's.

'"What sort of Christ is this?" I thought. "Such an ordinary, ordinary man. It cannot be." I turned away but I had barely turned my eyes from this ordinary man when I felt again that it was really none other than Christ standing beside me. Suddenly my heart sank and I came to myself. Only then I realized that just such a face is the face of Christ – a face like all men's faces.'

Ivan Turgenev

BIBLE VERSE
'Of his own free will [Jesus] gave up all he had, and took the nature of a servant. He became like man and appeared in human likeness. He was humble and walked the path of obedience all the way to death.'

From *Philippians 2*

29 October

Gemma-Jadvyga Stanelyte was born on 29 October 1931.

'Gemma, we love you!'

The bus driver called as witness stood up in court and bravely insisted that the procession had *not* held up traffic. Well, the bus had arrived on time, that was fair proof. But that was not the evidence the court wanted, and the driver was threatened with prosecution.

Gemma stood in the dock quite unrepentant of the crime she was accused of committing. She agreed that she had organized the traditional religious procession because she loved her country and longed to see its young people brought back to God. Meanwhile many Christian friends, banned from the court, stood outside in the cold and the rain, the sound of their prayers coming through the windows into the court-room.

Sentence was passed: three years in a labour camp.

'I am a firm believer,' were Gemma's last words to the court. 'Even though freedom is very dear to me, my faith is still more precious.'

The streets were crowded when Gemma was led out and bundled into the steel police van. The Christians shouted, 'Gemma, little Gemma, we're with you! We love you!' They threw flowers after the departing van.

'Please pray for me,' Gemma wrote from prison camp. 'My greatest comfort is to join my small sacrifice to Christ's great sacrifice – life demands many sacrifices, even in freedom. They are just small prickles from Christ's crown of thorns. I am grateful for all.'

POSTSCRIPT
Gemma belongs to the Lithuanian Catholic Church. She was sentenced in December 1980. The *Lithuanian Catholic Church Chronicle* wrote: 'Her sacrifice will encourage Lithuanian young people to stand closer to the Jesus she loved. People like her can be eliminated – but never defeated.'

30 October

**On 30 October 1974, George Foreman lost his world
heavyweight title to Mohammed Ali.**

George Foreman grew up in the black ghettos of Houston,
Texas. He was soon in trouble with the law and ended up in
a reformatory. But he could box, and in 1973 beat Joe
Frazier to become world heavyweight champion. During his
career he earned £7 million. He bought three luxury homes
and lived in a hotel where he could get his favourite cheese
omelettes by phoning room service! Now, he doesn't even
own a colour television.

'My fingers won't make a fist!'

When the six-feet-four, eighteen-stone black man strode across
the restaurant to greet him with smile and outstretched hand,
Alan Hart, boxing correspondent of *The Sun* newspaper, could
hardly believe his eyes. He'd known Foreman only too well in the
days when he'd been world champ. There was only one way to
describe him – 'mean-minded, rude, arrogant and downright
belligerent'. The menacing monster of a few years back had been
transformed into a serene, warm person.

Over a meal, George told Alan his story:

'The ring is the loneliest place in the world. It was after a fight
in Puerto Rico in 1975 when I lost to Jimmy Young. I got back to
my dressing-room and felt my life was slipping away. It was the
saddest, darkest tunnel – I could smell death. I told God I'd give
him money if he'd let me live. "I don't want your money," God
told me, "I want *you*."' George went through a grim time before at
last he gave himself to God, and peace and joy flooded his life.

At first he plannned to go on fighting and 'bring glory to God in
the ring'. But he couldn't do it! 'My fingers won't make a fist,' he
told Alan. 'When I try, it turns into a wave!' So George has
become pastor of a church in the area where he grew up, bringing
to black and white youngsters the purpose and happiness he now
knows.

31 October

On 31 October 1521, Martin Luther nailed his *95 Theses* to the door of the Castle Church at Wittenberg, Germany.

By faith alone!

Tomorrow would be All Saints' Day – the signal for a rush to buy the indulgences that the Emperor Frederick always sold on that day. Townsfolk had only to pay the entrance fee to the Castle Church and view the holy relics on display to obtain 1,443 years' remission from purgatory and total absolution for all repented sins. It was more than Martin Luther could bear.

Soon after noon, he crossed from his Augustinian cloister to the church and nailed his printed placard to the door that served as a notice-board. The *Theses* set out his arguments against the use of indulgences, and attacked the church's preoccupation with wealth. He offered to have a public discussion on the subject with any volunteer.

In the past, Luther too had been burdened by guilt that would not budge however often he went to confession or did penances. On a visit to Rome, he had dashed madly from one sacred relic to another and had climbed, kneeling, the sacred staircase said to have been brought from Pilate's palace in Jerusalem. All in vain. His fear of God and sense of guilt remained.

Then, one day, light from the Bible had dawned. 'The just', he read, 'shall live by faith.' By faith! He could not *buy* indulgence from punishment or cancel out his sin by penances or good works. God's forgiveness was *freely given* in response to faith. Luther wanted the world to share the freedom and release that justification by faith had brought to him. He wanted too to put an end to the wicked practice of making money for the church by selling pardons and indulgences. So he nailed his *Theses* to the door. Before long, the church had something to say in reply.

See also 18 February, 18 April

1 November

1 November is All Saints' Day.

Saints alive!

What *is* a saint? Someone martyred for his faith or reproduced in a stained-glass window? The apostle Paul had quite a different meaning for the word. When he wrote to the mixed bag of Christians living at Rome, Ephesus or Corinth, he addressed them *all* as saints. To be a saint literally means to be 'set apart' for God, and for Paul and his fellow Christians, everyone who committed life and soul to Jesus Christ became a saint and part of Christ's 'Body' – the church.

On All Saints' Day, the church remembers not only the great and famous who have earned the title of saint in the eyes of the world, but also the multitude of unknown, unheard-of Christians who have served their Master down the ages to this day. This book is really an 'All Saints' book'. It tells the stories of people of every country and age who have put their faith and their lives into the keeping of Jesus Christ.

Everyone who makes Jesus their Saviour and Lord joins the great host of saints – the unseen church that stretches from the days of Paul down to our own day and reaches across the whole world.

Thanksgiving
For all the saints who from their labours rest,
Who thee by faith before the world confessed,
Thy name, O Jesus, be for ever blessed:
Alleluia, Alleluia!
William Walsham How (1823-97)

2 November

On 2 November 1953, Chad Varrah first offered his phone number to anyone in despair.

The befrienders

'I am being pushed around from institution to foster-home. No place to go; no place to stay where you're at; nothing to do, nothing to want to get up in the morning for. So I figure, why should I live, you know? What is there in life? As hard and as clearly as I'm trying to look – I can't see one thing to live for.'

That's how one fourteen-year-old girl feels, and plenty of teenagers can understand and even share her feelings. Every month of the year, three people of sixteen or under commit suicide in Britain. Some don't mean to kill themselves – only to let family and friends know how miserable they are. But their attempt proves fatal just the same.

Chad Varrah, a London clergyman, recognized that those in despair badly need help. He offered his telephone number to anyone feeling at the end of their tether, and set up a counselling centre at his church. But he soon found that many waiting to see him went away feeling better for a chat with one of the receptionists in the office. So he decided to have a centre manned not by psychotherapists or clergy, but by volunteers, trained to help, who would listen and befriend in complete confidence.

Today, there are over 170 branches of the Samaritans in Britain – the counselling service founded by Chad Varrah. The telephone number is advertised in public places and is in the local phone directory. Wherever the Samaritans have opened a branch, the suicide rate has fallen.

PRAYER
We pray for all those who take time to listen to others' troubles, and especially for all Samaritan volunteers. Help us not to be too full of ourselves to notice when others are lonely and sad, or too selfish to offer them friendship. For Jesus' sake. Amen

3 November

On 3 November 1978, Delia Smith presented the first in a
series of cookery programmes on BBC television.

Testing ... testing ...

When Delia Smith appears on the television screen, all goes
smoothly with her mouth-watering recipes. But that's because
there has been plenty of hard work and testing beforehand. 'Each
cookery class takes two days to prepare,' she says, 'one day of
rehearsal and one in the studio.' She uses no autocue as her eye
has to be on what's cooking. She memorizes and perfects her
recipes before presenting them on television.

Delia tests more than recipes. As a Christian, she knows that
she must have some way to test out all the different ideas and
beliefs that bombard us. Her testing-point is the Bible. 'My faith
is very much based on the Word. One has to test everything by
Scripture.'

Below is one of Delia Smith's own tested recipes: 'It is
unbelievably simple to make – it's dark and sticky and gets much
better with a few days' keeping.'

Sticky Teabread

¼ pint water	1 tsp. bicarbonate of soda
4 oz. sultanas	6 oz. plain flour
5 oz. caster sugar	1 egg
¼ lb. butter	1 tsp. baking powder

Preheat the oven to Gas Mark 4 /350°F.

First grease a 1lb loaf tin and line it with greaseproof paper,
also greased. Then take a large thick-based saucepan and put
into it the water, sugar, sultanas, butter and bicarbonate of soda.
Place the pan on medium heat, stir the ingredients together and
bring them up to the boil. Then boil for ten minutes exactly –
but don't go away, watch it like a hawk, because if the temperature isn't controlled, it might boil over. When the ten minutes
is up, remove the pan from the heat and allow the mixture to
cool. Then add the beaten egg and the baking powder and sifted
flour. Give it a good mix then place the mixture in the prepared
tin and bake it for about 1½ hours on the middle shelf.

From *Frugal Food*, by Delia Smith

4 November

Nigel Perrin was born on 4 November 1947.

Nigel Perrin was one of the King's Singers, a group started by six former students of King's College, Cambridge. Nigel shared the singing of the two top lines. He left in 1980 to become Adviser on Music in Evangelism and Worship for the Church Army.

Close harmony

'A single, six-voiced instrument' – that's how the King's Singers describe their particular sound.

Nigel explains more about singing in harmony: 'No one singer can go out and just sing to please himself. Singing in harmony means accepting the discipline of being one of a group. The individual doesn't come first – what matters is the sound made by us all. We have to keep exactly the same tempo – it's no good rushing ahead of each other – and, of course, we have to be in the same key. The only way to achieve the single sound is to practise listening to one another.'

Nigel sees the shared life of Christians as being very like this. Living in harmony means putting others' interests before your own, caring more about the whole group than doing your own thing, and above all, *listening* sensitively to one another, recognizing both the needs and gifts of other people.

The apostle Paul put the same idea into a prayer:

'May the God of steadfastness and encouragement grant you to live in such harmony with one another, in accord with Christ Jesus, that together you may *with one voice* glorify the God and Father of our Lord Jesus Christ.'

From *Romans 15 (Revised Standard Version)*

See also 26 September

5 November

In Britain, 5 November is Guy Fawkes' Night, usually celebrated with bonfires and fireworks.

The Reverend Ronald Lancaster is clergyman, schoolmaster and licensed maker of fireworks. He makes and supplies fireworks and also masterminds spectacular firework displays. He devised the firework display for the Queen Mother's eightieth birthday celebrations and those for the opening of the London Barbican Centre and the Humber Bridge, among many others.

Licensed to make fireworks

Ronald Lancaster makes fireworks in the workshops behind his home in quiet Kimbolton in Cambridgeshire. His lifelong love of fireworks began as a boy when he was friendly with the owners of the firm of Standard Fireworks, whose factory was close to his childhood home in Huddersfield.

'Making fireworks is very much like cooking,' Mr Lancaster explains, 'adding ingredients, stirring, mixing and gently cooking to get the required result.' Gunpowder may not have changed much over the centuries, but colour is a newer, exciting addition. Quality control also makes safer and more accurate forecasting of 'recipes' possible.

Fireworks and religion have always gone together. The Chinese were probably the first to make and use them in religious ceremonies as far back as 2,000 years ago. In some Mediterranean countries, fireworks are part of Christian celebrations. In Italy, Masses followed by fireworks mark the patronal festivals of local saints. In Britain, 5 November bonfires and fireworks probably go back much further than Guy Fawkes, who was arrested in 1605 while planting explosives under the House of Lords. Country people used to celebrate All Saints' Day with bonfires, though they may have been continuing the pagan celebration of 1 November, which was then the first day of the new year.

Whatever the roots of the custom, fireworks are a splendid and exhilarating way to celebrate – and for Christians, celebrating always includes God!

6 November

On 6 November 1883, the final survivor of the first
generation of Pitcairn Islanders died.

The Bounty Bibles

Two Bibles were saved by the mutineers and taken ashore before
the *Bounty* itself was burned and the men and their Tahitian wives
settled down to enjoy the idyllic life of Pitcairn. No one from
England was likely to find them and take them back to justice
when their island was not even marked on sailors' charts.

But the idyll soon ended. Fighting, drunkenness and murder
broke out. When only two of the original men survived, one of
them, Edward Young, resolved to teach the new generation
different ways. But he was dying and his companion, John
Adams, could neither read nor write.

Using the rescued Bibles, Young began to teach him, with
amazing results. John Adams, 'short, pitted with smallpox and
very much tattooed', himself a murderer, not only learned to read,
but found that the Bible changed his life. Young died and Adams
became a father to the whole colony. He taught the Bible to the
children and became an example of goodness and loving care.
Thanks to him, the children of the mutineers grew up honest and
God-fearing.

JOHN ADAMS' PRAYER
(Composed on Pitcairn Island for use on 'the Lord's Day'.)
Suffer me not, O Lord, to waste this Day in Sin or Folly
But let me worship Thee with much Delight,
Teach me to know more of Thee and to Serve Thee
Better than I have ever done Before
That I may be fitter to Dwell in Heaven
Where Thy Worship and Service are everlasting. Amen

See also 23 January

7 November

On 7 November 1910, Count Leo Tolstoy, the great Russian
writer, died in the station-master's hut at the little railway
station of Astopovo.

Theory and practice

Tolstoy remembers an early attempt to write a list of 'daily tasks
and duties which should last me all my life':

'I took some sheets of paper, and tried, first of all, to make a list
of my tasks and duties for the coming year. The paper needed
ruling, but, as I could not find the ruler, I had to use a Latin
dictionary instead. The result was that, when I had drawn the pen
along the edge of the dictionary and removed the latter, I found
that, in place of a line, I had only made an oblong smudge on the
paper, since the dictionary was not long enough to reach across it,
and the pen had slipped round the soft, yielding corner of the
book. Thereupon I took another piece of paper and by carefully
manipulating the dictionary, contrived to rule what at least
resembled lines . . . I proceeded to write, "Rules of My
Life" . . . but the words came out in such a crooked and uneven
scrawl that for long I sat debating the question, "Shall I write
them again?" – for long, sat in agonized contemplation of the
ragged handwriting and the disfigured title page. Why was it that
all the beauty and clarity which my soul then contained came out
so misshapenly on paper (as in life itself) just when I was wishing
to apply those qualities to what I was thinking at the moment?'

From *Childhood Boyhood and Youth*, by Leo Tolstoy

BIBLE VERSE
Paul said: 'Even though the desire to do good is in me, I am
not able to do it. I don't do the good I want to do; instead, I
do the evil that I do not want to do . . . What an unhappy
man I am! Who will rescue me . . . ? Thanks be to God, who
does this through our Lord Jesus Christ!'
From *Romans 7*

See also 8 November

8 November

'My life suddenly changed'

'Five years ago I came to believe in Christ's teaching and my life suddenly changed . . . It happened to me as it happens to a man who goes out on some business and on the way suddenly decides that the business is unnecessary and returns home. All that was on his right is now on his left and all that was on his left is now on his right; his former wish to get as far as possible from home has changed into a wish to be as near as possible to it. The direction of my life and my desires became different and good and evil changed places . . .

'I, like the thief on the cross, have believed Christ's teaching and been saved . . . I, like the thief, knew that I was unhappy and suffering . . . I, like the thief to the cross, was nailed by some force to that life of suffering and evil. And as, after the meaningless suffering and evils of life, the thief awaited the terrible darkness of death, so did I await the same thing.

'In all this I was exactly like the thief, but the difference was that the thief was already dying while I was still living. The thief might believe that his salvation lay there beyond the grave but I could not be satisfied with that because besides a life beyond the grave life still awaited me here. But I did not understand that life. It seemed to me terrible. And suddenly I heard the words of Christ and understood them, and life and death ceased to seem to me evil, and instead of despair I experienced happiness and the joy of life undisturbed by death.'

From *What I Believe*, by Leo Tolstoy

See also 7 November

9 November

On 9 November 1620, sixty-four days after the *Mayflower* **had set sail, land was sighted.**

The Pilgrim Fathers were Puritan Christians who had been persecuted in England and determined to seek freedom to worship across the Atlantic in America. They were the first English settlers in New England. About 100 of them set sail from Plymouth in the *Mayflower.*

One large iron screw

Everyone realized that the ship was in serious trouble. Water was seeping in everywhere and even the crew looked scared. The captain admitted that the main beam of the ship, holding the hull firm, had cracked and could snap in the storm at any moment. If it did, the whole ship would break up.

They were about half-way across the Atlantic. Some were for turning back to England. At least the route was well charted and winds would run in their favour. But Captain Jones at last sent for the ship's carpenter and discussed how they could save the beam. What was needed was a metal collar that would hold the split together. Splendid in theory – but where to find such a piece of metal 1,000 miles from shore?

Now the Pilgrim Fathers witnessed the providence of God. Among the stores that had been brought aboard for use in the new colony was a large iron screw. It was unearthed and jubilantly presented to the captain. He and the carpenter superintended as the beam was strapped to a strong post and fastened under the collar to relieve further strain. Leaks were plugged, and amid stifling conditions below deck and gale-force storms and winds above, the *Mayflower* turned valiantly in the direction of the American continent.

10 November

John Milton died on 8 November 1674 and was buried on 11 November.

John Milton, one of England's greatest poets, also wrote pamphlets on political and religious matters. In the days before newspapers, radio or television, this was a most effective way of making views known.

Virtue needs exercise

'I cannot praise a fugitive and cloistered virtue, unexercised and unbreathed, that never sallies out and sees her adversary but slinks out of the race where that mortal garland is to be run for, not without dust and heat. Assuredly we bring not innocence into the world, we bring impurity much rather: that which purifies us is trial, and trial is by what is contrary.'

From *Areopagiticus*, a pamphlet against the enforced licensing and censorship of books.

Jesus speaks to his followers

'Listen! I am sending you out just like sheep to a pack of wolves. You must be as cautious as snakes and as gentle as doves.'

From *Matthew 10*

'The world will make you suffer. But be brave! I have defeated the world!'

From *John 16*

PRAYER

Father, help us not to run away from trials. Give us a sturdy faith and virtue that can stand firm in the midst of wrong and impurity. Help us not to be overcome by evil but to overcome evil with good. For Jesus Christ's sake. Amen

11 November

Between the First and Second World Wars, British people observed two minutes' silence each year at 11 a.m. on 11 November (the eleventh hour of the eleventh day of the eleventh month) in memory of those who had died. Remembrance Day is now observed on the Sunday nearest to 11 November.

Pleader for peace

Wilfred Owen was killed just one week before peace was declared. As well as being a soldier, he was a poet. He told his mother in a letter: 'I came out to help these boys – directly by leading them, indirectly by watching their sufferings that I may speak of them as well as a pleader can. I have done the first.' But he had done the second too. His poetry still pleads against the horrors of war.

In hospital on the Somme he wrote: 'Already I have comprehended a light which will never filter into the dogma of any national church: namely that one of Christ's essential commands was: Passivity at any price! Suffer dishonour and disgrace, but never resort to arms. Be bullied, be outraged, be killed; but do not kill . . .

'Christ is literally in "no man's land". There men often hear his voice: Greater love hath no man than this, that a man lay down his life for his friend. Is it spoken in English only and French? I do not believe so. Thus you see how pure Christianity will not fit in with pure patriotism.'

PRAYER
Teach us, Father, how terrible war is. Teach us first to keep peace in our own homes and then to work for peace in the world, and to look for the coming day when Christ, the Prince of Peace, shall rule. Amen

See also 12 November

12 November

The poetry is in the pity

'This book is not about heroes. English poetry is not yet fit to speak of them. Nor is it about deeds, or lands, not anything about glory, might, majesty, dominion or power, except War.

Above all, I am not concerned with Poetry.

My subject is War and the pity of War.

The poetry is in the pity.

All a poet can do today is warn. That is why the true poets must be truthful.'

From the preface to *The Poems of Wilfred Owen*

Anthem for doomed youth

What passing-bells for those who die as cattle?
Only the monstrous anger of the guns.
Only the stuttering rifles' rapid rattle
Can patter out their hasty orisons.
No mockery for them from prayers or bells,
Nor any voice of mourning save the choirs, –
The shrill demented choirs of wailing shells;
And bugles calling for them from sad shires.

Wilfred Owen

See also 11 November

13 November

St Augustine of Hippo was born on 13 November AD 354.

'Multiplied misery and toil'?

'God, my God, what a dog's life I was forced to undergo during my boyhood, after it was pressed on me as my duty that I must obey my teachers. It seemed that there was no other way to get on in the world . . . So I was packed off to school without understanding the reason for it, fool that I was, and if I proved slow at grasping the teaching, they whipped me . . . and so many others have followed that course since, making a track of multiplied misery and toil for the sons of Adam . . .

'We were not deficient, Lord, in either memory or ability . . . But our great love was playing at sports, and for this we were punished by grown men who were doing exactly the same thing themselves. They like to call their playing around "business" . . .

'And yet I did wrong, Lord my God . . . I did wrong in acting contrary to the precepts of my parents and those same teachers. The lessons they tried to force me to learn, from whatever motives, would have helped me later on.'

A PRAYER TO GOD
'Lord, my King and my God: I am offering you everything useful I learned as a boy, and everything I now speak and write and read and compute . . . I give thanks to you, my joy, my confidence, my God, thanks to you for your gifts – and will you please sustain them in me? For in this way you will keep me safe, and develop and mature that which you have given; and I shall be with you, who gave me life in the first place.'

From *The Confessions of Augustine in Modern English*

See also 28 August

14 November

On 14 November 1854, thirty ships bringing medical supplies, food and clothing to the Allied armies in the Crimea,
were destroyed in a storm. One of the heroines of the war
was Mary Seacole, a West Indian, who was an accomplished
nurse and had cared for British troops when they were
stationed in Jamaica.

When she arrived, she built a lodge house and grandly called it
'The British Hotel'. Mary imposed high standards. The 'hotel'
was never open on Sundays and cards and dice were forbidden
on the premises. Downstairs there was a restaurant providing
food and cheer for the troops, which included feather-light
sponge cakes, hot coffee and broth for the invalids. The upstairs
was laid out as a hospital ward, with medicines put ready for the
sick. She devoted her energies to able-bodied and wounded
alike. She thought of many ways of alleviating suffering, such as
making muslin nets to protect the sick from flies.

She became known as 'Mother Seacole' to the hundreds of
soldiers she called her sons. Often she would go out to the
trenches looking for the missing ones, narrowly escaping death
herself. Many soldiers died in her arms, comforted by her
motherly words. When the war was over, she planted lilacs on
the graves of all who had been her friends.

See also 14 May

15 November

Johannes Kepler died on 15 November 1630.

Johannes Kepler was a German astronomer who
formulated 'Kepler's Laws' to describe the movements of
the planets in the solar system. He also did important work
in the field of optics.

God waited 6,000 years

In 1594, when the brilliant young Johannes Kepler was given the
Chair in Astronomy at Gratz, he was expected to plot the
horoscopes of the great and mighty. What we now understand as
the study of stars and planets for scientific purposes was then
little more than the practice of astrology. Kepler obediently set
about his predictions, using common sense and shrewd judgement.

Meanwhile, he settled to his real life-work of studying sun,
moon and stars, looking and measuring to see how the heavenly
bodies behaved. His studies and the tables of measurement he
devised (using 'new-fangled' logarithms) laid the foundation for
the whole science of astronomy.

But he was no cold scientist. He was fired with enthusiasm to
discover the truth to the glory of God. He wrote: 'Eighteen
months ago the first dawn rose for me; three months ago the
bright day; and a few days ago the full sun of a most wonderful
vision; now nothing can keep me back. I have stolen the golden
vessels of the Egyptians to make out of them a holy tabernacle for
God. I am writing this book for my contemporaries or – what does
it matter – for posterity. Has not God waited six thousand years
for someone to contemplate his work with understanding?'

See also 16 November

16 November

In the midst of the Thirty Years' War in Europe, Kepler, the great German astronomer of the sixteenth to seventeenth century, wrote to his son-in-law: 'When the storms are raging there is nothing nobler for us to be done than to let down the anchor of our peaceful studies into the ground of eternity.'

The Bible looks at the stars

'[God said] to Job ... "Can you tie the Pleiades together
    or loosen the bonds that hold Orion?
Can you guide the stars season by season
    and direct the Great and the Little Bear?
Do you know the laws that govern the skies ... ?"'
From *Job 38*

'Look up at the sky!
Who created the stars you see?
    The one who leads them out like an army,
    he knows how many there are
    and calls each one by name!
His power is so great –
    not one of them is ever missing!'
From *Isaiah 40*

'When I look at the sky, which you have made,
    at the moon and stars, which you set in their places –
what is man, that you think of him;
    mere man, that you care for him?'
From *Psalm 8*

'Praise the Lord! ...
Praise him, sun and moon;
    praise him, shining stars.
Praise him highest heavens.'
From *Psalm 148*

See also 15 November

17 November

17 November is the Feast Day of St Hilda.

Hilda, a great-niece of King Edwin of Northumbria, was born in AD 614. She founded a double monastery – for men and women – at Whitby, in Yorkshire, high on the cliffs beside the sea, where the ruins of the abbey can still be seen. The Synod of Whitby took place there in 664.

Celebrating on the right day

It was the strange state of affairs at the palace of the King of Northumbria that brought matters to a head. Queen Eanfleda was observing Palm Sunday, which in those days meant fasting rigorously. On the same day her husband, King Oswy, was in the dining-hall, celebrating Easter with the usual lavish feasting!

The reason was that the queen, brought up in Kent, had been instructed to observe the Christian calendar imposed by St Augustine and his missionaries from Rome. They had landed in Kent and were preaching and teaching their way through England. Oswy, living in the north of the country, had been influenced by St Columba and the Celtic Irish missionaries. He had learned from them to keep Easter according to a different and now outmoded form of reckoning.

Today, such a difference in dates seems a trifling matter but it was a big issue at that time. But the dispute over the date of Easter brought into the open the clash between the Celtic and the Roman branches of the Christian church. Which was to be dominant in England?

To settle the matter a synod or church council was called at Whitby, with King Oswy himself presiding. Colman, abbot of Lindisfarne, was called on to speak first and he put forward the case for the Celtic reckoning. He insisted that the apostle John favoured this method. Wilfred of Ripon then spoke for the other side. Although he too was a northerner, he had travelled widely on the continent and favoured Roman customs. He said that St Peter approved his views.

King Oswy decided it was safer to keep in with St Peter who, he was assured, held the keys of heaven. So the Roman, not the Celtic dating was accepted and as a result the church in Britain did not go its own separate way but became firmly joined to Rome and Europe.

Continued on 18 November

18 November

St Hilda was abbess of a double monastery at Whitby from 657 AD. During her time of office, five future bishops were among her monks, as well as Caedmon, a lay brother, whose story is told by the Venerable Bede, in his *Ecclesiastical History*.

Singing the good news

It was a pleasant custom. When the evening meal was over, the brothers would pass round the harp, so that each in turn could play and sing for the enjoyment of the whole company. Caedmon alone dreaded the ordeal of taking his turn. He was employed in looking after the cows and had no skill in music.

One night, as he saw the harp getting nearer, he slipped quietly away to take refuge in his cow-shed. Soon he was asleep. Suddenly and clearly he heard his name called.

'Caedmon,' the voice said. 'Sing me something!'

In vain Caedmon protested that he could neither sing nor play, and that he had left the table for that very reason.

'Yet you must sing to me,' his visitor insisted.

'What shall I sing about?' Caedmon asked.

'Sing me the story of Creation,' he was commanded. Caedmon resolved to obey.

This is the song that Caedmon sang:
'O sing the praise of our Guardian King
The thoughts of the Lord who made everything!
(Eternal Lord, how great is your name!
Glorious Father, for ever the same!)
First he created for children of men
The heaven above as roof – and then –
Guardian King who does all things well –
He made the earth where men can dwell.'

Next morning, he was taken before the Abbess Hilda. In her wisdom, she was sure that God had given Caedmon this gift to use for him. The monks should teach Caedmon all the stories and truths of the Bible. Then he could sing about the love of God, about heaven and hell. In this way, many people would learn the good news of Jesus and join in the singing too.

See also 17 November

19 November

Richard Baxter, born on 12 November, was baptized on 19 November 1615.

Richard Baxter, a Puritan clergyman, lived through momentous days in England's history: the Civil War, the restoration of the monarchy, the Great Plague and Great Fire of London. He wrote over 130 books. In an intolerant age, he believed in 'loving all Christians of what sort soever, that may be truly called Christians'.

A narrow escape

'At seventeen years of age, as I rode out on a great unruly horse for pleasure, which was wont on a sudden to get the bit in his teeth and set on running, as I was in a field of high ground, there being on the other side a quickset hedge a very deep narrow lane about a storey's height below me, suddenly the horse got the bridle as aforesaid and set on running, and in the midst of his running unexpectedly turned aside and leaped over the top of the hedge into that deep lane. I was somewhat before him at the ground and as the mire saved me from the hurt beneath, so it pleased God that the horse never touched me, but he light with two feet on one side of me and two on the other, though the place made it marvellous how his feet could fall beside me.'

From *The Autobiography of Richard Baxter*

PRAYERS
Lord, it belongs not to my care
Whether I die or live;
To love and serve thee is my share,
And this thy grace must give.
Richard Baxter

Thank you, Heavenly Father, for your protecting care over us – at home, at work and as we travel. Help us to trust you when we are afraid. Through Jesus Christ our Lord.
Amen

See also 2 September

20 November

William Cowper, poet and hymn-writer, died on 20 November 1800.

Depths of despair

Nothing gave pleasure any more. Country walks, which had always delighted Cowper, now seemed drab and tasteless. He could not enjoy the sight of trees or wild flowers, or take pleasure in quiet evenings by the fire. Worse still, Cowper's happiness and joy in God had gone. He still went to church and taught in Sunday school, but he did it all automatically.

In an age when no one understood much about the workings of the mind and emotions, or knew how to try to treat depression and mental illness, the kindly-meant help given by friends only made him worse. One night, after a terrifying nightmare, his quiet despair turned to raving madness. His greatest horror was the belief that God had rejected him.

For two years his faithful friend, Mrs Unwin, nursed him as best she could. Although she did not understand the disease that caused his madness, she persevered in gentle, kind and firm treatment until the darkness passed.

Lines Written Under the Influence of Delirium
Man disavows, and Deity disowns me,
Hell might afford my miseries a shelter;
Therefore Hell keeps her ever-hungry mouths all
    Bolted against me . . .
Hatred and vengeance my eternal portion,
Scarce can endure delay of execution,
Wait with impatient readiness to seize my
    Soul in a moment.
William Cowper

PRAYER
Father, have mercy on all who are suffering from mental breakdown as the result of disease or circumstance. Help those who care for them. When we are depressed and think everyone is against us, may we know you still close to love and help us. Amen

See also 26 November

21 November

Bible praise

'I will proclaim your greatness, my God and King;
  I will thank you for ever and ever.
Every day I will thank you;
  I will praise you for ever and ever.
The Lord is great and is to be highly praised;
  his greatness is beyond understanding . . .
The Lord is faithful to his promises,
  and everything he does is good.
He helps those who are in trouble;
  he lifts those who have fallen . . .
The Lord is righteous in all he does,
  merciful in all his acts.
He is near to those who call to him,
  who call to him with sincerity . . .
I will always praise the Lord;
  let all his creatures praise his holy name for ever.'

From *Psalm 145*

'How great are God's riches! How deep are his wisdom and knowledge! Who can explain his decisions? Who can understand his ways? . . . For all things were created by him, and all things exist through him and for him. To God be the glory for ever! Amen.'

From *Romans 11*

22 November

Little is known about St Cecilia. She was probably a Roman Christian, murdered for her faith. She is the patron saint of musicians.

Jessy Dixon was born in San Antonio, Texas. He studied classical music, and at the same time began the career in gospel music for which he is now famous.

The singer and his song

'There are no textbooks from which you can learn gospel music,' Jessy Dixon says. When he was twelve or thirteen, and already playing in classical concerts, someone sat down with him and patiently taught him to play gospel music, note by note on the piano. His parents didn't think this craze would last, but Jessy kept up his gospel music at college and was spotted by James Cleveland, 'the King of Black Gospel', who offered him a job.

As Jessy went on singing gospel songs, he realized increasingly that he didn't know the God he was singing about. Outwardly he was successful, but he felt empty inside. He knew that if his career was to go on, he must experience for himself the gospel he was singing about.

Two sermons – one at a meeting at night, the other on the radio next morning – preached the same message about Christ as Saviour, and Jessy committed himself to Jesus Christ.'I just invited the Lord into my life ... It was what I really needed ... I felt like a shiny new diamond on the inside.'

From then on, he longed to sing about the Lord he knew for himself. Jessy believes that wherever he is – at home or on the road – he must still keep close to Christ. His personal knowledge and experience must keep step with his singing if he is to sing as he should and be ready to recommend the Person he sings about to others.

PRAYER
Thank you, Lord, for all Christian musicians and for the many kinds of music they help us to enjoy – from classical to rock. May they play and sing their best – to your glory. Amen

23 November

The third Sunday in November marks the end of Prisoners' Week.

The Reverend Peter Timms was until recently Governor of Maidstone Prison.

1980 was designated throughout the world as the International Year of the Child.

Lifer

It was quite in order for Noel to come to see the prison governor. Time was set aside every morning and evening for any prisoner to come.

Noel was a young man – in his twenties – a 'lifer', serving anything up to thirty years for murder. He came into the room, clutching something in his hand. He sat down, then handed it across the table.

It was a polished copper plaque, some fifteen inches in diameter, skilfully pressed out with a design of a child being rescued from water. Round the edge were the hands that were saving him.

Noel said, 'Mr Timms, I want to help towards the International Year of the Child. Could you give this plaque I made to someone outside the prison who has helped children?'

Peter Timms gladly agreed, and asked listeners on local radio to write in, describing their own contribution to the Year of the Child. He and Noel sorted through the answers and selected a local Women's Institute for the most original contribution. The chairman and secretary of the branch were invited to lunch, and so were Noel and his wife. Noel himself presented the plaque.

During their stay in prison, lifers have several long, in-depth interviews with their governor. When Noel came for interview, Peter Timms asked him about his feelings towards imprisonment.

'Since I came to prison,' he said, 'I've learned to know what Jesus Christ is about. I'll never undo the damage I did, that brought me here, but if I were here literally for the rest of my life, it would have been worthwhile, to find Jesus.'

24 November

From the age of ten, Grace Darling lived on the Longstone Lighthouse off the Northumberland coast. Her father, the lighthouse-keeper, was a man of deep Christian faith. He entertained the family by playing his violin – hymns on Sundays! – and reading to them from the Bible, and from the works of Bunyan, Baxter, Cowper and Milton.

'To the lighthouse'

On the morning of 7 September 1838, Grace rose and dressed quickly in her tiny room. She was used to the roar of wind and crash of waves, but the previous night's storm had brought disaster. The *Forfarshire*, bound for Dundee from Hull, had broken up on the rocks of the Farne Islands.

Most of the sixty-three on board had drowned, but Grace could make out a few survivors huddled on the rocks. At once, she offered to row with her father in their small boat to rescue them. Her father knew that they would barely have enough strength to reach the rock, let alone row a boat-load back. They would have to rely on the survivors' help.

They set off on their exhausting and dangerous mission. Grace was small and slight, but she was determined. They reached the rock and Mr Darling climbed ashore, while Grace kept the boat steady in the rough sea. Four men and one woman were helped aboard, and some of the men gladly took their turn at rowing on the return journey. Once safely at the lighthouse, Mr Darling and two volunteers went back to fetch the four remaining on the rock. All the survivors were eventually brought safely to Longstone.

Grace became a public heroine overnight, but did not live many years to enjoy fame. She died of tuberculosis at twenty-seven; a plaque on a little cottage in the seaside village of Bamburgh – once the home of the kings of Northumbria – marks the room on the mainland where she died.

25 November

John Flynn was born in Australia on 25 November 1880.

John Flynn was ordained in 1911 and was the first superintendent of the Australia Inland Mission. He became Moderator-General of the Presbyterian Church of Australia in 1939. It was Flynn's vision which led to the establishment of the Flying Doctor Service, whose first flight in 1927 saved a miner's life.

The back of beyond

Their nearest neighbours might live 200 miles away. That is the situation for those in the Australian outback – an area in central Australia that is as big as the whole of Europe. In the early part of the twentieth century, farmers were afraid to settle there because of the risk of being ill or injured so far away from medical help.

John Flynn badly wanted to bring help to the sick, as well as preach the gospel to the people in the outback. Setting up hospitals was no real answer. Carrying a sick person hundreds of miles over bumpy roads could well be fatal. Somehow the doctors must get to them.

But most forms of travel were too slow for emergencies. Aeroplanes were the only possible answer and they were most unreliable. John Flynn's scheme seemed no more than a fantasy. But the First World War encouraged the development of aircraft and made flying safer. Flynn's plan became a possibility.

As a tribute to what he achieved, the words on John Flynn's tombstone near Alice Springs read: 'He brought gladness and rejoicing to the wilderness and solitary places'.

See also 27 November

26 November

William Cowper was born on 26 November 1731.

Poems and pets

Slowly, painfully, William Cowper was emerging from the blackness and horror of madness. But he was so shattered that he could only sit, numb and still, unable to feel happiness or safety from the fleeting horror that still troubled his mind.

One day, a neighbour called holding in his arms a brown, large-eyed hare. 'I thought Mr Cowper might like it,' he said – and Mr Cowper did. He was delighted with his new pet, and spent hours trying to tame it.

Others in the village were so pleased that something had at last done their friend good that Cowper was inundated with presents of hares. He politely refused all but three – Bess, Puss and Tiny. These became his joy and constant interest. He watched their individual ways, noted their different dispositions and busied himself gathering food for them and making hutches with doors that led into the drawing-room. At last he was on the road to recovery.

Epitaph on a Hare

Here lies, whom hound did ne'er pursue,
Nor swifter greyhound follow,
Whose foot ne'er tainted morning dew,
Nor ear heard huntsman's halloo;

Old Tiny, surliest of his kind,
Who, nursed with tender care,
And to domestic bounds confined,
Was still a wild Jack hare . . .

I kept him for his humour's sake,
For he would oft beguile
My heart of thoughts that made it ache
And force me to a smile.

William Cowper

See also 20 November

27 November

'O Hell! O Harry!'

There was still a hitch in John Flynn's scheme to fly doctors to people who were ill in the Australian outback. Somehow those in need must be able to send an SOS.

In those days, wireless sets relied on heavy and expensive batteries that needed frequent recharging. It wasn't feasible to equip all the ranches with them. A friend of Flynn's, called Traeger, came up with the brilliant idea of a radio that needed no batteries. Electricity would be generated by the user. All he had to do was to sit in a chair and pedal with both feet. If he worked hard enough, he produced enough power to send his Morse message. The set cost only £33 and could be installed at all cattle-stations where at least one person could be taught Morse and set to pedal.

The station-manager's wife at Augustus Downs was the first to try out the new wireless set in 1929.

'Say "Hello Harry",' Traeger instructed.

In her flurry, she forgot her Morse and the message arrived as 'O Hell! O Harry!'

Today, a much more sophisticated link-up brings reassurance, immediate advice and flying help to the inhabitants of the Australian outback.

PRAYER
Thank you, Lord, for using spiritual vision and practical ingenuity in your service. May the discoveries of science be used more and more to benefit mankind and not to destroy.
Amen

See also 25 November

28 November

William Blake, artist and poet, was born on 28 November 1757.

'The notes of woe'

He died at the age of sixty-nine 'in a most glorious manner. He said he was going to that country he had all his life wished to see and expressed himself happy, hoping for salvation through Jesus Christ. In truth he died as a saint.'

In spite of this glowing account reported by an eighteen-year-old writer, William Blake was by no means a conventional Christian. But he hated hypocrisy and some of his poems – such as the one below – express anger at the outrages committed against human beings and animals by those who went piously to church. He bitterly opposed the treatment of the little chimney-sweeps of London.

The Chimney Sweeper
A little black thing among the snow,
Crying ''Weep! 'Weep!' in tones of woe!
'Where are thy father and mother, say?'
'They are both gone up to the church to pray.

'Because I was happy upon the heath,
And smil'd among the winter's snow,
They clothed me in the clothes of death,
And taught me to sing the notes of woe.

'And because I am happy and dance and sing,
They think they have done me no injury,
And are gone to praise God and his Priest and King,
Who make up a heaven of our misery.'

See also 12 August

29 November

C.S.Lewis, scholar, writer and story-teller, died in
November 1963.

Surprised by joy

All his life, C.S.Lewis had experienced moments of intense and
sudden joy, just when he least expected them. It began as a child,
on reading Beatrix Potter's *Squirrel Nutkin* or seeing a garden on
a tin tray; later, Norse myths brought the same stab of pleasure.
He tried to track the emotion to source through reading and
philosophy.

He did not want to become a Christian. In his case, Lewis
admits, to talk of searching for God would be as absurd as talking
of a mouse searching for the cat. Yet the truth of God's existence
came hammering home, and at last he admitted that God was
God, describing himself as 'the most reluctant convert in all
England'.

His belief in Jesus came later. 'I was driven to Whipsnade one
sunny morning,' he writes. 'When we set out, I did not believe
that Jesus Christ is the Son of God and when we reached the zoo I
did. Yet I had not exactly spent the journey in thought. Nor in
great emotion. "Emotional" is perhaps the last word we can apply
to some of the most important events. It was more like when a
man, after a long sleep, still lying motionless in bed, becomes
aware that he is now awake.'

At last he recognized his moments of joy for what they were –
pointers or signposts to the perfect joy that awaits us in the
presence of God.

BIBLE VERSE
'You will show me the path that leads to life;
 your presence fills me with joy
 and brings me pleasure for ever.'
From *Psalm 16*

See also 30 November, 10 January, 16 June

30 November

How do *you* imagine angels? With white swansdown wings and voluminous nightgowns? With long, golden hair? C.S.Lewis had a quite different idea, and in his science fiction trilogy he describes them and the effect their appearance had on his hero, Ransome, when he first encountered an angel – or 'eldil'.

Encounter with an angel

'What I saw was simply a very faint rod or pillar of light. I don't think it made a circle of light either on the floor or the ceiling, but I am not sure of this . . . So far, all is plain sailing. But it had two other characteristics which are less easy to grasp. One was its colour. Since I saw the thing I must obviously have seen it either white or coloured; but no efforts of my memory can conjure up the faintest image of what that colour was. I try blue, and gold, and violet, and red, but none of them will fit . . . The other was its angle. It was not at right angles to the floor. But . . . what one actually felt at the moment was that the column of light was vertical but the floor was not horizontal – the whole room seemed to have heeled over as if it were on board ship . . . I had no doubt at all that I was seeing an eldil . . . Here at last was a bit of that world beyond the world . . . breaking through and appearing to my senses.'

From *Perelandra*, by C.S.Lewis

See also 29 November, 10 January, 16 June

1 December

Edmund Campion was executed at Tyburn on 1 December 1581.

Edmund Campion was educated at Christ's Hospital and St John's College, Oxford, where he welcomed Queen Elizabeth I on her visit there. Although he became a deacon in the Church of England, his conscience was uneasy. He fled abroad, became a Jesuit priest in Prague and returned to England on the first Jesuit mission. He was arrested, taken to the Tower of London, tortured repeatedly and executed as a traitor.

'Your Queen and mine'

No one could be a more loyal subject of the queen, yet Campion had to enter his own country disguised as a jewel-merchant. He made his way to Stonor Park, a large house where the Roman Catholic owners worshipped secretly. He was smuggled in, dressed, innocently enough, as a workman, and hidden away in his tiny attic, four feet high. Here he could minister to the small groups of staunch Roman Catholics.

But it was not in Campion's nature to deceive or to lie low. He believed fiercely that true loyalty and patriotism involved a return to Rome and papal supremacy. He eagerly wrote down his reasons for such belief. A printing press was somehow smuggled into Stonor Park, and the persuasive *Ten Reasons* were printed. Four hundred copies were audaciously left on the benches of St Mary's Church in Oxford. There was an immediate hue and cry. Protestants refused to believe that any Jesuit could be a loyal patriot. He must be a spy and a political traitor.

Someone gave the game away. Stonor Park was raided, the printing press discovered and Campion arrested in London. Repeated racking failed to make him give up his faith or admit to treachery. 'If our religion do make traitors, we are worthy to be condemned,' he told the queen, 'but otherwise we are and have been as true subjects as ever the Queen had.'

On the scaffold, Campion maintained his love and loyalty. 'I beseech you to have patience and suffer me to speak for my conscience. I pray for Elizabeth – your Queen and mine.'

2 December

John Brown and four of his sons were hanged at Charleston on 2 December 1859.

John Brown was a direct descendant of Peter Brown, who had sailed from England in the *Mayflower* (see 9 November). John and his sons bent all their energies to helping slaves, organizing escape routes to Canada. The song, *John Brown's Body*, was written not long after his death.

'His soul goes marching on'

It was the day of his execution. 'I, John Brown,' he wrote, 'am now quite certain that the crime of this guilty land will never be purged away but with blood.' He handed the letter to his guards and set out on his last journey – to the gallows. The story goes that on his way he stopped to kiss a negro child. He remained firm to the end in his belief that slavery degrades humanity and contradicts the plain teaching of the Bible.

One day, he was leading a party of thirty slaves to freedom when he was attacked by a band of men. He overpowered them and forced their leader to conduct the slaves to safety himself – on foot, because he had put a negro woman and child on the leader's horse.

But John Brown's fearless tactics and ambitious plans led to arrest. He planned to free all slaves in the state of Virginia and began by attacking an armoury at Harper's Ferry, where he was arrested with four of his sons. At his court martial, he boasted of the slaves he had helped to safety and claimed, as he took the oath and kissed the Bible, that it 'teaches that in all things whatsoever I would that man should do to me I should do even to them'. His body may 'lie mouldering in the grave' but for all who share that belief, 'his soul goes marching on'.

PRAYER
Forgive us, Father, that we are often afraid to stand up for what we believe to be right, and for what the Bible teaches. Give us courage today. For Jesus' sake. Amen

3 December

Advent Sunday, which marks the beginning of the season of Advent, falls on the Sunday nearest to 30 November.

'The trumpet shall sound!'

Advent is the beginning of the Christian year. It is a reminder to get ready for the 'advent' or coming of Jesus Christ. It isn't just a reminder to start buying cards and presents or make the Christmas cake, or even to think only about Jesus' first coming at Christmas. Advent reminds us that Jesus is coming again. The first Christians expected Jeşus back at any time. Centuries have passed but Jesus' promise to return still stands firm.

'There will be the shout of command, the archangel's voice, the sound of God's trumpet, and the Lord himself will come down from heaven. Those who have died believing in Christ will rise to life first; then we who are living at that time will be gathered up along with them in the clouds to meet the Lord in the air. And so we will always be with the Lord.'

From *1 Thessalonians 4*

'[Jesus] says, "Yes indeed! I am coming soon!"

'So be it. Come, Lord Jesus!'

From *Revelation 22*

4 December

Sheila Cassidy arrived in Chile in December 1971 and was expelled in December 1975.

Sheila Cassidy, who trained as a doctor, went to Chile to escape the academic rat race and became closely involved in treating the poor and sick. Following an extreme right-wing coup, she treated a wounded guerrilla soldier and was arrested. After torture and imprisonment, she was expelled from the country.

Facing death

The car threaded its way slowly through the streets of Santiago, crossing and re-crossing the same network of streets and houses.

'Which street? Which house?'

The questions were repeated continuously, and Sheila Cassidy, sitting beside the man with the gun in the front of the car, could not answer.

When she had been arrested, Sheila had thought that a phone-call to the British Embassy would soon solve her problem. Instead, she was taken into a small bare room, told to strip naked, then, blindfold and gagged, she was strapped to a metal bed. The electric current was switched on and the questions began. At each question, an electric shock passed through her body, strengthening in intensity until she answered. Determined not to betray the nuns who had sheltered the wounded guerrilla, Sheila invented the area, street and house where she treated his wounds.

Now they were driving her there to verify the details she had given. At any moment they would guess she had been lying. One of the men said, 'It would be easier to kill her now.' She sat still, realizing she would probably die.

Suddenly, God seemed very far away and unreal. Had belief in him all been a fairy story? Then, after a moment, with no rush of emotion or feeling of exaltation, Sheila suddenly knew with absolute certainty that God *did* exist. She stretched out a hand of faith to the God who seemed so far away, but was *real*.

PRAYER
Help us to trust you, Lord, even when you seem unreal and far away. For you have promised never to leave or forsake us. Amen

See also 7 December

5 December

In the first few days of December 1857, George Müller
faced a problem. The central heating system in his
orphanage in Bristol needed major repairs.

The north wind doth blow!

There were no two ways about it. They wouldn't get through the winter without doing something about the troublesome boiler. Brickwork must be dismantled, the cause of the leak identified and the damage repaired. It could take several days. Meanwhile, the children would be without any kind of heating. Müller decided to trust God and go ahead with the work.

He had no sooner arranged for workmen to begin the following Wednesday than the north wind began to blow. Bitterly cold weather set in. He decided to ask God for two things. First, for the wind to change from north to south; second, for the workmen to 'work with a will'.

All weekend the north wind blew. On Tuesday, it was still blowing. By Wednesday morning, it had veered round completely and blew softly from the south. A spell of unexpectedly mild weather began as they let the huge boiler go out. The children noticed scarcely any drop in temperature.

The workmen arrived, the bricks were pulled out and – joy of joys – the cause of the trouble was quickly located. Repairs began. That evening, Müller went to see the foreman. 'They will work late this evening,' he promised Müller in the men's hearing, 'and again tomorow.' Then the plumber said, 'We would rather work all through tonight and get the job done.'

Müller wrote, 'I remembered the second part of my prayer, that God would give the men a mind to work. Thus it was: by the morning the repair was accomplished, the leak was stopped, though with great difficulty, and within about thirty hours the brickwork was up again and the fire in the boiler; and all the time the south wind blew so mildly that there was not the least need of a fire.'

See also 27 September

6 December

St Nicholas has always been a very popular saint – patron saint of children, sailors, merchants and pawnbrokers. He is reputed to have done many wonderful things, including bringing back to life three murdered children hidden in a brine tub. The only hard fact known about him is that he was Bishop of Myra, in Asia Minor, in the fourth century ' AD.

Santa Claus and all that

St Nicholas and the giving of presents have always been linked. Legend tells that Nicholas heard of the misfortune of three girls whose father had no money to give them dowries and so find them husbands. To save them from a life of prostitution, Nicholas determined to provide the money needed. So as to keep his generosity secret, he threw three bags of gold into their window at night.

Presents used to be given to children on St Nicholas's Day – and still are in some countries. But, more often, Christmas Day itself is associated with present-giving, and St Nicholas has been transformed into Santa Claus, complete with fur-lined hood, sledge and reindeer.

He travelled round the world before coming to Britain. Dutch settlers in the United States took with them their stories and customs of Sinte Klaas or Santa Claus, and he arrived from a cold climate to become a familiar figure in large stores and part of family Christmas routine.

But his supposed visit by night and the mysterious leaving of gifts still remind us of the unassuming generosity of St Nicholas – practised for the sake of Christ.

BIBLE VERSE
Jesus said: 'When you help a needy person, do it in such a way that even your closest friend will not know about it. Then it will be a private matter. And your Father, who sees what you do in private, will reward you.'
From *Matthew 6*

7 December

Learning to share

'All me own work' had been a saying in Sheila Cassidy's family. There is a great sense of achievement in beginning and completing something worthwhile on one's own.

In prison in Chile, she learned to share achievement. Workshops were set up to utilize every precious scrap of material and make soft toys, embroidered blouses and sandals. The team supervisor allocated work, and often something that Sheila had skilfully begun would be given to careless hands to finish. Or she might be asked to finish something poorly begun.

Sharing extended to food too. Whatever visitors brought, to extend the meagre ration of dry crusts and greasy soup, was added to a common pool and distributed to all 180 prisoners. Sheila longed to keep back the special English sweets the consul brought, in order to enjoy the pleasure of giving them to her special friends instead of throwing them on the common heap. The impersonal nature of the sharing stripped away the last traces of self-indulgence in giving.

But sharing could be personal too. When Sheila arrived at the prison, wearing the blood-stained, filthy clothing she had lived in day and night during torture, others gladly gave her their spare clothes, lovingly laundering hers. She had the opportunity to do the same for others, and when she was released she left behind all but the clothes she wore. Sheila also shared her faith with girls who had grown up to hate the church, but who asked the reason for her strength under torture and her steadfast commitment to Christ.

PRAYER
Help us to learn to share with others our possessions, our skills, our time and our love. For Jesus' sake. Amen

See also 4 December

8 December

Martin Rinkart, German clergyman, poet and musician, died on 8 December 1649.

Peace after thirty years

The city of Eilenberg in Saxony was crammed to capacity. The safe walls that surrounded it made it the ideal bolt-hole for refugees escaping the horrors of the war. Plague broke out in the city as a result of the overcrowding, and thousands died. The city superintendent had conveniently gone away for a while, and the other clergy had died themselves from the plague. Martin Rinkart was left to cope as best he could.

Some days he had to conduct forty or fifty funerals, and one day that meant taking his own wife's funeral when she too died of plague. Famine followed plague, and people began to die from starvation. It was a grim and bitter time and Rinkart worked tirelessly to try to bring help and comfort to those in the city.

There was great joy and celebration when the Thirty Years' War ended at last and the Peace of Westphalia was signed. Some say that Rinkart's well-known hymn was written for the peace celebrations; others believe that it was sung at his wife's funeral. Whichever is true, 'Now thank we all our God' reminds us that Christians have always been able to rely on and experience God's goodness and love even through suffering and hardship.

Now thank we all our God
With hearts and hands and voices,
Who wondrous things hath done,
In whom his world rejoices;
Who from our mothers' arms
Hath blessed us on our way
With countless gifts of love,
And still is ours today.

9 December

The new 'House of the Scugnizzi' was opened in December 1969.

One of the gang?

Big Head, Wooden Head, Cheese Head, Drain Rat, Tarzan, Little Mouse – these were some of the names of the gang. Not names that any right-minded parent would have given them, but the nicknames they invented for each other. These boys had left their homes in the shanty towns, where there were too many mouths to feed, and come to live on the streets of Naples, scrounging food and sleeping rough. They bent down a thousand times a day to salvage the wisps of tobacco in a tossed-away cigarette-end, in order to collect and sell it.

Father Mario Borrelli cared about these urchins, or 'scugnizzi', and longed to help them. But he knew that as a Catholic priest he would be treated with suspicion. So he decided to become a street-boy himself by night and join one of the gangs.

Once the boys learned to accept and trust him, he began to plan to house and feed them. He and a friend made use of a bombed-out church – cleaned and kitted out with bedding. There the boys could get three meals a day and a bed at night. Father Borrelli also found an honest way for them to make a living, by collecting and selling scrap metal.

POSTSCRIPT
When Father Borrelli's work among the street-boys of Naples became known, money was given in Italy and overseas so that a new community centre with school and clinic could be opened. Since the Italian earthquake in 1980, Borrelli's school has provided refuge and schooling for those still without schools of their own.

PRAYER
We ask your strength and encouragement today for all who work on behalf of the unloved and unprotected. Show us how we can help them too. Amen

See also 22 December

10 December

The United Nations declared 10 December as Human Rights' Day.

Georgi Vins is a Russian Baptist who was imprisoned many times for his faith. He now lives in the United States.

Poet Steve Turner recognizes that the right to be free is something more than a state or government can grant. The last two lines of his poem suggest that those of us in 'free' countries may make our own prisons.

For Georgi Vins, the day after his release

Already I'm beginning to wonder
when freedom will lose its bright glow for you.
Today you must be delirious with smiling faces,
open Bible, open street, open door, open gospel,
open church.
But already I'm beginning to wonder
when you'll notice that the palms are thinning out
on the dusty road from Siberia.
I'm beginning to wonder
when you'll see that there are never any fingerprints
in the hotel Gideon.
I'm beginning to wonder
when you'll walk the streets of New York
and whether you'll go out alone.
I'm beginning to wonder
whether you'll hear secret police
whistling tunes in elevators and supermarkets
in a carefully conceived plan
to stop the private ownership of thoughts.
I'm beginning to wonder
when you'll see your first millionaire evangelist
asking for more money to stay on TV
so that he can ask for more money to stay on TV.
I'm beginning to wonder
when you'll pass your first State church
closed by the people.
I'm beginning to wonder
when they'll let you meet the victims of freedom,
persecuted by apathy, exiled within themselves.

See also 7 January, 25 September .

11December

James Fairbairn was born on 11 December 1913.

Professor Fairbairn was professor of Pharmacognosy at
London University and an international expert on cannabis.

More than biochemistry

Marijuana, cannabis, hashish or just plain 'pot', is still banned in
Britain. James Fairbairn was one of the few people allowed to
grow it – for experimental purposes. For five years he studied its
effects and characteristics, and wrote and spoke about it all over
the world.

These are some of the reasons he gave for *not* legalizing pot:

The case is still open – no one has yet fully proved the safety of
pot. At one time, cocaine and opium were hailed as harmless
drugs – time and experience have proved otherwise.

Pot lessens concentration – and that spells danger to those who
work machinery or drive cars. Nor is there any kind of
'breathalyser' or check to spot 'high' operators and drivers who
could cause accidents to themselves and others.

People are more than animals, needing a quick dose of
'happiness'. James Fairbairn believed that man is 'more than
biochemistry – he is a creature made in the image and likeness of
God'. Therefore, a drug which can be taken to tranquillize, cheer
or put to sleep whenever life gets hard, is making him less than he
was meant to be. Difficulties, disappointment, sadness – all are
experiences through which people can grow and develop as
human beings. They are opportunities to know and find God.
Learning to deal with mental and physical stresses leads to a
fuller enjoyment of life – with its sharp tang as well as its
sweetness.

12 December

After his resurrection, Jesus told his disciples: 'Everything written about me in the Law of Moses, the writings of the prophets and the psalms had to come true.' The first Christians loved to find and quote Old Testament verses which described Jesus' coming, and there was probably an early written collection of these texts.

Bible foretelling – Jesus' birth

'The Lord himself will give you a sign: a young woman who is pregnant will have a son and will name him "Immanuel" ["God is with us"].'
From *Isaiah 7*

'A child is born to us!
   A son is given to us!
   And he will be our ruler.
He will be called "Wonderful Counsellor,"
   "Mighty God," "Eternal Father,"
   "Prince of Peace."'
From *Isaiah 9*

'The Lord says, "Bethlehem Ephrathah, you are one of the smallest towns in Judah, but out of you I will bring a ruler for Israel, whose family line goes back to ancient times."'
From *Micah 5*

How it happened

'Joseph went from the town of Nazareth . . . to . . . Bethlehem in Judaea, the birthplace of King David . . . to register with Mary, who was promised in marriage to him. She was pregnant, and while they were in Bethlehem, the time came for her to have her baby. She gave birth to her first son . . .

'The angel said to [the shepherds] . . . "I am here with good news for you, which will bring great joy to all the people. This very day in David's town your Saviour was born – Christ the Lord!"'
From *Luke 2*

See also 15 and 19 December

13 December

Samuel Johnson, writer, wit and dictionary-maker, died on
13 December 1784.

Peace at the end

Dr Johnson loved food, London, good talk and cats. His own cat
was called Hodge. In his *Life of Johnson*, James Boswell describes
how he had commented on what a fine cat Hodge was.

'Dr Johnson replied, "Why, yes, sir, but I have had cats whom I
liked better than this"; and then, as if perceiving Hodge to be out
of countenance, adding, "but he is a very fine cat, a very fine cat
indeed".'

Johnson suffered from violent attacks of depression and had
always feared death. But when the time came, he had peace. The
servant of his friend, who sat up with him during his last night,
said, 'No man could appear more collected, more devout or less
terrified at the thought of the approaching minute.'

PRAYER
(Written by Johnson a few days before he died)
Almighty and most merciful Father, I am now, to human
eyes it seems, about to commemorate for the last time, the
death of thy son, Jesus Christ, our Saviour and Redeemer.
Grant O Lord, that my whole hope and confidence may be
in his merits and in thy mercy. Forgive and accept my late
conversion and accept my imperfect repentance. Have
mercy upon me and pardon the multitude of my offences.
Bless my friends and have mercy upon all men. Support me
by the grace of thy Holy Spirit in the days of weakness and
at the hour of death, and receive me, at my death, to
everlasting happiness for the sake of Jesus Christ. Amen

See also 16 May

14 December

Dorothy L. Sayers died in mid-December 1957.

Dorothy Sayers, daughter of a clergyman, is best known for her Lord Peter Wimsey detective novels. She was also a scholar and translated a great part of Dante's *Divine Comedy* before her death. She wrote clearly about Christian theology and her play-cycle, *The Man Born to be King*, was something new and startling when it was first broadcast. Val Gielgud, her first BBC producer, described her as 'an enormously definite person'.

'Shocked? So they should be!'

When the first instalment of *The Man Born to be King* was broadcast in Britain in 1941, many listeners were shocked and horrified. Leaders from all the main churches had read the scripts in advance and were enthusiastic, but ordinary church-goers felt differently. Never before had an actor spoken the words of Christ – and besides, the language was modern, not like the Authorized Version of the Bible. At the time, the war was going badly for the Allies, and some protesters insisted that it was the result of God's displeasure at the broadcasting of such 'blas-phemous' plays. The BBC stood firm, and many listeners understood the Christian good news for the first time through the plays they heard.

This is some of what Dorothy Sayers herself had to say about the plays in her introduction to *The Man Born to be King*:

'God was executed by people painfully like us, in a society very similar to our own. He was executed by a corrupt church, a timid politician and a fickle proletariat led by professional agitators. His executioners made vulgar jokes about him, called him filthy names, taunted him, smacked him in the face, flogged him with the cat, and hanged him on the common gibbet – a bloody, dusty, sweaty and sordid business. If you show people that, they are shocked. So they should be. It is curious that people who are filled with horrified indignation whenever a cat kills a sparrow can hear the story of the killing of God told Sunday after Sunday and not experience any shock at all.'

See also 16 December, 6 January, 12 April

15 December

Bible foretelling – Jesus' life

Isaiah described the perfect Servant of the Lord in these words:
    'The Sovereign Lord has filled me with his spirit.
He has chosen me and sent me
To bring good news to the poor,
To heal the broken-hearted,
To announce release to the captives
And freedom to those in prison.
He has sent me to proclaim
That the time has come
When the Lord will save his people . . . '
From *Isaiah 61*

How it happened

'Jesus went to Nazareth, where he had been brought up, and on
the Sabbath he went as usual to the synagogue. He stood up to
read the Scriptures and was handed the book of the prophet
Isaiah. He unrolled the scroll and found the place where it is
written,
'"The Spirit of the Lord is upon me,
    because he has chosen me to bring good news to the poor.
He has sent me to proclaim liberty to the captives
    and recovery of sight to the blind;
to set free the oppressed
    and announce that the time has come
    when the Lord will save his people."
    'Jesus rolled up the scroll, gave it back to the attendant, and sat
down. All the people in the synagogue had their eyes fixed on
him, as he said to them, "This passage of scripture has come true
today, as you heard it being read."'
From *Luke 4*

See also 12 and 19 December

16 December

Jesus the Healer

ANDREW: There's a deputation of elders asking to see the Master.

SIMON: They must wait. He's gone down the village to a fever-stricken family.

THOMAS: Can somebody come at once to a dying woman?

JUDAS: Here's a lame man hobbled six miles on crutches.

JAMES: Here's a stretcher-case brought all the way from Bethsaida.

ANDREW: There's a man here wants Jesus – but he says Matthew will do.

MATTHEW: Right you are – coming in half a minute.

THOMAS: Here, let me go; you've had nothing to eat.

MATTHEW: It's all right Thomas, I know who it is.

JUDAS: There's an old woman here with a bad leg.

NATHANIEL: Oh, I can't *bear* to see any more bad legs! – Where is she?

CROWD (*pressing in upon the house*): We are here, we are here, we are waiting. Waiting upon the Lord. We are sick, we are blind, we are unclean. Heal us, help us . . .

ANDREW: Here's John back again.

JOHN: Let me sit down.

ANDREW: What's the matter?

JOHN (*almost in tears*): Nothing, but I'm so *tired* . . .

CROWD (*outside*): Jesus! Jesus of Nazareth! Touch me! Speak to me!

SIMON: The Master has come back.

JESUS (*outside*): Daughter, you are healed. Go home now and live better . . . Stand up, old man, and give thanks to God . . . Mother, give me the child . . .

JESUS (*entering briskly*): Fishers of men, you have toiled hard today . . . My poor children! John, you look ready to drop. Give me your hand. I see I must finish up by healing my own disciples. Andrew has a headache I fancy . . . And has nobody had any dinner? . . . We will go right away by ourselves into a quiet place up in the hills and rest.

From *The Man Born to be King*, by Dorothy L.Sayers

See also 14 December, 6 January, 12 April

17 December

Thomas Guy died on 17 December 1724.

Thomas Guy was born in 1644, the son of a lighterman and coal-dealer in Southwark, London. He was apprenticed to a bookseller before setting up in business himself. He dealt mainly in Bibles and at first imported most of these from Holland. Later, he obtained the right to print Bibles himself from Oxford University. He made an immense fortune both from his business and his shrewd investments. He paid for the building of Guy's Hospital in London.

Poor little rich man

It was evening when Thomas Guy's visitor arrived. He came to the little shop where Guy could be seen any day eating a dry crust at mealtimes and working at all other hours. But his visitor knew that, despite appearances, Guy was a rich man. He told him that he had come to ask the secret of his success in making money. Guy did not take offence, but suggested that they should talk in the dark to save the cost of the candles.

Thomas Guy looked so poor that once, as he stood looking over London Bridge, he was mistaken for a down-and-out and offered money by a kindly passer-by. Yet when he died, he left huge amounts of money for the upkeep of hospitals and almshouses – and still there was £80,000 left to be shared between relatives and friends. Guy recognized that the nearby St Thomas's Hospital was badly overcrowded, and had begun by paying to have three new wards added to it. Still he knew that there was too little help for the sick and poor around him, so he paid for a brand-new hospital, at a cost of £18,793-16s – an enormous sum at that time.

Thomas Guy had no wife or children and neglected only his own creature comforts. The question remains: was he mean, or was he one of the most generous men of his time?

18 December

Sundar Singh was born in India and brought up as a Sikh.
On 18 December 1904, he had a vision of Jesus and became
a Christian.

The warmth of love

Snow had begun to fall as Sundar Singh strode across the bleak mountain-pass on his return from a preaching mission to Tibet. He was joined by another traveller and as the snow turned to a blizzard, they were buffeted by blinding sleet and icy winds.

Suddenly they heard a cry. Someone had fallen from the narrow pass and was lying on the ledge below. Sundar at once stopped to help him, but his companion argued that it was impossible. They would both die themselves if they tried. They parted – Sundar carefully picking his way down the mountain-side, while the other man pressed on to the next village.

The injured traveller was unable to walk, so Sundar gently picked him up and with great difficulty dragged him up the steep slope. Once back on the path, he slung him on to his back and continued his journey. The going was twice as hard with the weight of the injured man as well as snow and wind to contend with. As they rounded a bend, they saw beside the path the still figure of the traveller who had gone on alone. Sundar called to him, then touched him. He was dead.

At last, Sundar struggled into the village with his burden. Both were safe. The man who had tried to save his life had lost it. Sundar Singh, who risked losing his life out of love for another, had saved his. The warmth of the two bodies, in close contact, had kept them both alive.

19 December

Bible foretelling – Jesus' death and resurrection
'He endured the suffering that should have been ours,
   the pain that we should have borne . . .
Because of our sins he was wounded,
   beaten because of the evil we did.
We are healed by the punishment he suffered,
   made whole by the blows he received.
All of us were like sheep that were lost,
   each of us going our own way.
But the Lord made the punishment fall on him,
   the punishment all of us deserved.
He was treated harshly but endured it humbly;
   he never said a word.
Like a lamb about to be slaughtered,
like a sheep about to be sheared,
   he never said a word.
He was arrested and sentenced and led off to die,
   and no one cared about his fate.
He was put to death for the sins of our people . . .
   His death was a sacrifice to bring forgiveness.'
From *Isaiah 53*

'You protect me from the power of death,
   and the one you love you will not
      abandon to the world of the dead.
You will show me the path that leads to life.'
From *Psalm 16*

How it happened
'Peter [declared]: "Jesus of Nazareth was a man whose divine
authority was clearly proven to you by all the miracles and
wonders which God performed through him . . . In accordance
with his own plan God had already decided that Jesus would be
handed over to you; and you killed him by letting sinful men
crucify him. But God raised him from death, setting him free
from its power, because it was impossible that death should hold
him prisoner."'
From *Acts 2*

See also 12 and 15 December

20 December

Donald Swann studied Russian at university before serving in the Middle East in the Second World War with the Friends Ambulance Unit. Perhaps best known as a musician and revue entertainer with the late Michael Flanders, he is still busy spreading music, humour and happiness.

A real Christmas?

'That Christmas night, Rachel, my daughter, cried most of the night and woke us up. Perhaps it was from excitement as she was not ill. Nothing "abnormal"; just a child of one year crying in the night. When we rose for good on Christmas morning (we had been "rising" all night) we were broken and weary. The prospect of a festival and a meal of any sort was appalling. I was in acute misery. I remember the service I went to, a children's one, where the vicar spoke all the time to the children (our pram was at the back with the now sleeping child) . . . His words had solace in them, it was solace I wanted for that awful night and for the certainty that Christmas was spoiled . . .

'Lying awake I had remembered the manger and the stable, and it occurred to me that Jesus might have been a wakeful baby, and screamed. I had never thought of this before. In the stress of my exhaustion I recalled that Christmas night was his actual birth . . . I saw him lying peacefully in the manger as he does in so many of the Nativity pictures, with the ox and the ass, and I thought: Now he's going to cry. And Mary won't know why because it's her first child and she'll be worried. This came to me as a shock and Christmas changed in my mind . . .

'Since this new revelation of Christ as a crying child, I have longed to work with a writer on a Nativity play that showed this "real" aspect of being a manger infant.'

From *The Space Between the Bars*, by Donald Swann

21 December

Joseph Stalin, Soviet head of state until his death in 1953, was born on 21 December 1879.

Svetlana Alliluyeva, daughter of Stalin, left Russia in 1967, and now lives in Princeton, USA. She wrote to Malcolm Muggeridge and spent a week with him in England in 1981, when a television programme was made of their conversation.

Their church – and ours

She was thirty-six – but no details of her name or age were entered in the church register. The baptism of Svetlana Alliluyeva was conducted quietly and secretly, as are all adult baptisms in Russia. But the old priest in the Moscow church was wise. He did not flinch from baptizing a daughter of the dreaded and cruel Stalin. 'He did not say that Christ cannot love me, Stalin's daughter. He knew that Christ can love me because he is Christ. He heard my voice calling him and he answered me.'

Now in the West, Svetlana still worships in church – but in a very different setting. She could not believe her eyes when she first saw soft little cushions for kneeling on. In Russia, they kneel on the hard, cold, stone floor, and stand for hours listening to what God will say to them. Everyone in the West seems to go to church in pretty hats and dresses. In Russia, Svetlana says, they go to meet God, not to show off to one another. Where it is almost forbidden to go to church, men and women are drawn there by suffering, pain and tears.

But for Svetlana, the country or the church are not the most important factors. She carries the feeling of home with her wherever she goes, like a snail with its shell on its back. She knows that Jesus Christ is alive and is with her wherever she may be. Not only in church on Sundays – but in her home in Princeton, just as he was with her even in Soviet Russia.

22 December

After opening his home for *scugnizzi* (urchins), Mario Borrelli moved into one of the shanty towns of Naples to discover for himself the conditions that their families had to live in (see 9 December).

New homes for old

The rain poured down and Mario Borrelli, lying in bed and listening, realized that it was dripping steadily and relentlessly through the tin roof over his bed. His blanket was wet, and soon his pyjamas would be soaked. His first instinct was to get up and mend the roof, but he stopped and thought again. He had come to live here, where the shacks were made of hardboard, packing-cases and scrap metal, in order to experience the hardships their owners suffered. They put up with leaking roofs – he would too.

The whole township was a disgrace. Earth floors became mud pools when it rained. The rubbish was piled high outside, smelling dreadfully and spreading disease. Mario wanted his urchins to be able to live at home where they belonged, coming to him only for meals and schooling, but unless living conditions were improved, that was impossible.

He began what he called 'Operation Removal of Suffering'. Local authorities ignored his attempts to get water laid on and drains cleared, so he and his helpers threatened to go on hunger-strike if the shanty-dwellers were not transferred to decent houses by a given date. The press got hold of the story, and the authorities had to act. When one shanty town was cleared, Borrelli moved into another and repeated his action.

In six years, all 25,000 shanty-dwellers had been rehoused, and the old shanties bulldozed. Borrelli began to help the families to settle into their new homes, teaching them hygiene, reading, writing and child-care. For a while at least, their troubles were eased.

23 December

St Boniface of Crediton was born in about AD 675. He preached to the heathen tribes of Germany, enlisting other English men and women to help him. He was massacred as he sat quietly reading in his tent. The Christmas tree legend is founded on Boniface's felling of the oak at Geismar, which led to the conversion of the Bortharians.

The first Christmas tree

The villagers of Bortharia had been suffering from storms and plague. They intended to appease the god Odin by offering him a human sacrifice. Led by their chief, they assembled in the forest clearing at midnight. The priest tied the boy – the appointed victim – to the sacred oak and prepared to kill him.

At that moment, the breathless silence was broken by a shout. Dark-clad figures of Christian monks approached the scene of sacrifice, and their leader, Boniface, called out, 'Stop, in the name of Jesus Christ!'

The villagers were terrified. What new reprisals from their god would such blasphemy bring forth?

But Boniface reasoned, 'If Odin is really god, he can defend himself and prove himself. Let the boy go.'

There was no thunderbolt, no vengeance hurled at the Christian monk. The boy was untied, and Boniface began to tell the Bortharians the good news of God's love and mercy in Jesus Christ.

Then he offered them a young fir tree in place of the oak, planting it and placing his candle on it. His companions added their candles, and the fir tree shone out in the dark forest, a picture of God's ever-living love and of the light that has come into the world in Jesus Christ.

24 December

The carol *Silent Night* was first sung on Christmas Eve 1818.

Sadly, Joseph Mohr, who wrote the words, died in poverty
and distress, never knowing that his carol had become
famous and much loved in many countries of the world.

Silent organ – 'Silent Night'

It was Christmas Eve 1818 in the little Austrian village of
Oberndorf and that night the church would be full for the
customary midnight service. But there would be no music from
the organ. The constant dampness from the nearby river had
finally made it impossible for Franz Gruber, the organist, to
squeeze a single note from it. But the assistant vicar, Joseph
Mohr, decided to provide some item that would make the
service special in spite of the lack of organ music. Sitting down,
he quickly wrote a new carol, then sent it across to Gruber, so
that he could compose a tune to fit the words. Together they
would sing the new carol for the Christmas congregation,
accompanied instead by a guitar.

The carol was greatly enjoyed and there its story might have
ended. Christmas came and went. Then an organ builder
arrived to mend the organ. Perhaps Gruber showed him the new
carol, or perhaps he came across the sheet of music somewhere
in the church in the course of his work. He played it over and
took a great liking to it.

Wherever he went he played the carol and in time two
strolling families of singers learned it and added it to their
repertoire. One group travelled to the United States and played
and sang it there. The other sang it before the King of Prussia.

Silent Night soon became known far and wide. It was
translated into many languages and today, over one hundred and
fifty years later, it will be sung again in churches, schools, in the
open air and by the fireside in countries all over the world.

> Silent night, holy night!
> Sleeps the world; hid from sight
> Mary and Joseph in stable bare
> Watch o'er the Child beloved and fair,
> Sleeping in heavenly rest,
> Sleeping in heavenly rest.

25 December

In the year 1652, Christmas Day in England was officially cancelled.

25 December has always been celebrated, perhaps to mark the darkness and death of the old year and to encourage the birth of light and the new year – or perhaps because people in the northern hemisphere need some kind of half-way merry-making to help them endure the whole winter. In Britain, early missionaries transformed the pagan rites of Yuletide, by designating 25 December as the birthday of Christ.

Christmas is cancelled!

The Puritans ruled the country, and they strongly disapproved of keeping any day special – except Sunday, 'the Lord's Day'. So they passed an act of parliament to cancel Christmas 1652, and to show they meant it, they decided that parliament would sit just as on any other day of the year. Everything was banned – from mince-pies to church attendance.

John Evelyn, the diarist, defied the ban and went with his wife to church. He recorded what happened. As they were receiving communion, a party of musketeers broke in. They waited till the service was over, then arrested the worshippers. They soon let them go, unsure how to punish people for going to church.

No one is likely to cancel Christmas again, but perhaps for many the real Christmas *is* cancelled. The true cause for celebration has been forgotten.

> Rejoice and be merry in songs and in mirth!
> O praise our Redeemer, all mortals on earth!
> For this is the birthday of Jesus our King,
> Who brought us salvation – his praises we'll sing.

PRAYER
Thank you, Lord Jesus, for today's celebrations. Help us to put you at the centre of them and not to spend a 'cancelled' Christmas because we have left you out. Amen

26 December

26 December is the Feast Day of St Stephen, the first
Christian martyr.

'Father, forgive!'

There was a rising murmur of anger and scarcely-restrained indignation in the court-room. The voice of the prisoner, Stephen, rang out clearly.

'Look!' he cried. 'I can see the heavens open and Jesus Christ standing at the right hand of God!'

His accusers cried out in horror. How dare he speak like that about the impostor they had crucified so short a time before!

The nearest men seized Stephen, hauling him unceremoniously out of the court and into the street. The rest followed, carrying their victim along with them until they were outside Jerusalem's sacred walls. Then they threw him down and the first eager councillor picked up a huge stone and hurled it at him. It caught him a glancing blow and he staggered but kept his footing.

Cloaks were hurriedly loosened and stacked beside young Saul, leaving the men free for action. They picked up the boulders and rocks strewn by the roadside and threw them at Stephen with all their might. Half-stunned, he fell to his knees, blood streaming down his face.

'Lord Jesus,' he called out, 'receive my spirit!' Then he fell full-length. He spoke once more: 'Lord,' he prayed, 'forgive them this sin.'

It was over. Their hatred and energy spent, the men turned to pick up their cloaks. One of them remembered hearing words like that before. Jesus, who Stephen had claimed was alive and glorious at God's right hand, had said as he was dying, 'Father, forgive them, they don't know what they are doing.'

Adapted from *Acts 6 and 7*

27 December

Louis Pasteur was born in France on 27 December 1822.

Until he was eighteen, Louis Pasteur intended to be an artist. Then he turned to science, first physics and chemistry, then crystallography, where he made startling discoveries by the age of twenty-five. He became a professor at Lille University, where he was also expected to apply science to local industrial problems. Experiments in fermentation led to the discovery that living organisms cause decay and disease. 'Pasteurization' of milk, partial sterilization to destroy bacteria, was another result of his experiments. A deep faith in God lay behind Pasteur's whole life, as a man and a scientist.

Something nasty in the beet juice

Monsieur Bigo was a very worried man. He made his living in Lille by producing alcohol from beet juice. He was applying the yeast, as usual, to convert the juice to alcohol, but for some unknown reason the juice refused to be converted. He hurried along to the new professor for help.

Pasteur knew nothing at all about fermentation, but he went to Monsieur Bigo's factory and took samples of the offending juice back to his laboratory to examine under the microscope. He discovered that, in addition to the small globules of yeast, other small particles were present in the juice. He suspected that these strangers were the villains of the piece.

Up to that time, scientists had believed that the yeast was merely a catalyst – a substance which by its presence somehow made spontaneous fermentation occur. Pasteur recognized that the yeast was in fact a living organism. Somehow, the foreign bodies – also living – were invading the mixture and inhibiting the fermentation process.

Pasteur proved his point to a sceptical scientific public by demonstrating that once air was excluded and scrupulously clean containers used, fermentation was successful. A happy Monsieur Bigo had only to exclude the foreign bodies and his beet juice would ferment once more and his business thrive.

See also 28 December

28 December

Louis Pasteur said: 'There are two opposing laws – one, a law of blood and death, forces nations always to be ready for battle. The other, a law of peace, work and health, whose only aim is to deliver man from calamities. The one places a single life above all victories, the other sacrifices hundreds of thousands of lives to the ambition of a single individual.'

Mad dogs – and Joseph Meister

The year was 1940 and Joseph Meister, gatekeeper at the Pasteur Institute in Paris, was ordered by the German invaders to open Louis Pasteur's burial crypt. Rather than obey, he committed suicide.

There was good cause for his loyalty to Pasteur's memory. Fifty-five years earlier, he had been savagely bitten on his hands, legs and thighs by a mad dog. His case was hopeless – he would die a horrific and terrifying death, though it might be a month before the first signs of hydrophobia appeared. There was only one person who might save him – and he was not a doctor.

Louis Pasteur had been experimenting with his theory of inoculation against rabies, through giving repeated doses of vaccine taken from a rabid dog. So far he had experimented only on other animals – but always with success. Yet he dared not risk his vaccine on a human being. Friends and relatives appealed to him to help Meister. He had been so severely bitten that he was certain to contract the disease. There was nothing to lose.

After much mental anguish, Pasteur agreed to inoculate Joseph. Sixty hours after the accident, he had the first, weak dose of vaccine. Twelve more followed – each stronger than the last. At the end of them all, the patient showed no signs of the disease and returned home, full of health and gratitude to Pasteur.

His case made history. Only fifteen months later, 2,490 people had received the life-saving anti-rabies vaccine.

See also 27 December

29 December

Thomas à Becket was murdered on 29 December 1170.

Thomas à Becket, born in Cheapside, London, in 1118, was a brilliant courtier, friend and chancellor of Henry II. When the king made him Archbishop of Canterbury, Becket changed, as he put it, from 'a patron of play-actors and a follower of hounds, to being a bishop of souls'. Becket's conflict with the king led Henry to speak angry and reckless words. Four knights set off for Canterbury and murdered Thomas in his own cathedral.

Murder in the cathedral

Thomas and his priests are inside the cathedral – the knights outside:

PRIESTS: Bar the door. Bar the door . . .

THOMAS: Unbar the doors! throw open the doors!

I will not have the house of prayer, the church of Christ,

The sanctuary, turned into a fortress . . .

The church shall be open, even to our enemies. Open the door! . . .

(The door is opened. The knights enter, slightly tipsy) . . .

KNIGHTS: Where is Becket, the traitor to the King?

Where is Becket, the meddling priest?

Come down Daniel to the lion's den,

Come down Daniel for the mark of the beast . . .

Where is Becket, the Cheapside brat?

Where is Becket, the faithless priest?

Come down Daniel to the lion's den,

Come down Daniel and join in the feast.

THOMAS: It is the just man, who

Like a bold lion, should be without fear. I am here.

No traitor to the King. I am a priest,

A Christian, saved by the blood of Christ,

Ready to suffer with my blood.

This is the sign of the Church always,

The sign of blood. Blood for blood.

His blood given to buy my life,

My blood given to pay for his death,

My death for his death . . .

For my Lord I am now ready to die,

That his Church may have peace and liberty.

From *Murder in the Cathedral*, by T.S.Eliot

30 December

On 30 December 1976, *The Times* newspaper carried this story.

King of Sweden saves woman from snow death

'King Carl Gustave of Sweden saved a 23-year-old Chinese woman from freezing to death in the snow outside a royal palace in Stockholm on Christmas Eve, a court spokesman said today.

'A hospital spokesman said that another half-hour would have brought the woman to the critical point beyond which she would probably not have lived.

'The king's black labrador dog, Ali, is given half the credit for saving the woman's life. This is the rescue story, as recounted by the court spokesman and other official sources.

'"King Carl Gustave was walking with Ali through Ulriksdal Palace park after dinner, when the dog stopped in front of a snow-drift, sniffing. The king saw the woman lying in the snow; she was unconscious.

'"He carried her into the home of his sister, Princess Christina, who lived nearby and with whom he had been dining earlier that night. He wrapped her in blankets and called an ambulance. She was taken to hospital and was discharged the following day."'

BIBLE VERSE
'God's mercy is so abundant, and his love for us is so great, that while we were spiritually dead in our disobedience he brought us to life with Christ.'
From *Ephesians 2*

PRAYER
Jesus, our King, you loved us so much that you came to earth to rescue us from death and make us alive for ever. We thank you and ask you to make us your loyal subjects for ever. Amen

31 December

Bible endings

'The end of anything is better than its beginning.'
From *Ecclesiastes 7*

'The end of all things is near. You must be self-controlled and alert, to be able to pray. Above·everything, love one another earnestly, because love covers over many sins.'
From *1 Peter 4*

'Then the end will come; Christ will overcome all spiritual rulers, authorities, and powers, and will hand over the Kingdom to God the Father. For Christ must rule until God defeats all enemies and puts them under his feet. The last enemy to be defeated will be death.'
From *1 Corinthians 15*

Jesus said: 'I am the first and the last, the beginning and the end.'
From *Revelation 22*

Jesus said: 'I will be with you always, to the end of the age.'
From *Matthew 28*

PRAYER
The grace of the Lord Jesus Christ, the love of God and the fellowship of the Holy Spirit be with us all, now and to the end. Amen

Acknowledgements

The material listed below is copyright and is reprinted by kind permission of the following copyright-holders:
Victor Gollancz Ltd and David Higham Associates Ltd for extracts from *The Man Born to be King*, by Dorothy L. Sayers (6 Jan,12 Apr,14,16 Dec); Steve Turner for his poems (7 Jan,25 Sept,10 Dec) included in his anthology, *Nice and Nasty*, published by Marshalls; William Collins and Sons Ltd for extracts from *Letters to Malcolm, Chiefly on Prayer*, by C.S.Lewis (10 Jan), *A Vicarage Family*, by Noel Streatfeild (18,19 Jan; also A.M.Heath and Co.Ltd), *Barchester Towers*, by Anthony Trollope (24 Apr), *Jesus Rediscovered*, by Malcolm Muggeridge (5 May), *Mere Christianity*, by C.S.Lewis (16 June); Hodder and Stoughton Ltd for extracts from *My Life With Martin Luther King*, by Coretta Scott King (16 Jan,4 Apr), *Which One's Cliff?*, by Cliff Richard, co-author Bill Latham (10 Mar), *Christ and the Media*, by Malcolm Muggeridge (24,26 Mar), *The Space Between the Bars*, by Donald Swann (20 Dec); Macmillan Publishers Ltd and David Higham Associates Ltd for 'Jack O'Lent' from *Collected Poems*, by Charles Causley (23 Feb); J.M.Dent and Sons Ltd for 'The Donkey' from *The Wild Knight and Other Poems*, by G.K.Chesterton (27 Mar); Sidgwick and Jackson for the extract from 'Ducks', by F.W.Harvey (1 Apr); Penguin Books Ltd for extracts from Nevill Coghill's translation of *The Canterbury Tales*, by Geoffrey Chaucer (3 Apr,24 Oct), *Resurrection*, by Leo Tolstoy (16,17 Apr), *Childhood Boyhood and Youth*, by Leo Tolstoy (7 Nov); Gill and Macmillan Ltd for 'Green Blackboards' from *Prayers of Life*, by Michel Quoist (10 June); Faber and Faber Ltd for extracts from *Markings*, by Dag Hammarskjöld (26,27 June), *Murder in the Cathedral*, by T.S.Eliot (29 Dec; also Harcourt Brace Jovanovich Inc.); John Murray (Publishers) Ltd for 'Diary of a Church Mouse' by Sir John Betjeman (29 Aug); the late J.B.Phillips for extract from *Letters to Young Churches* (17 Sept); Prideaux Press for extract from *What I Believe*, by Leo Tolstoy (8 Nov); The Bodley Head for extract from *Perelandra*, by C.S.Lewis (30 Nov); Cassell and Co Ltd for extract from *The Blue Cross*, by G.K.Chesterton from *The Father Brown Stories* (29 May).
All Bible quotations are (unless otherwise stated) taken from *Good News Bible*, copyright 1966, 1971 and 1976 American Bible Society, published by Bible Societies/Collins.
The author wishes to record her particular thanks to the following individuals and organizations for their courteous help so willingly given: Leonard Barnard, Ian Bolton, Brian Booth, Denis Burkitt, Kathleen Cann (Bible Society), Fred Catherwood, Leonard Cheshire Foundation, Church Army, Ray Davey (Corrymeela), Paul Davis *(New Christian Music)*, Desmond and Grace Derbyshire (Wycliffe Bible Translators), Mary Endersbee *(Today* magazine), the late James Fairbairn, Steve Goddard *(Buzz* magazine), Alan Hart, the Jamaican High Commissioner, Tony Jasper, Douglas Johnson, Keston College, Ronald Lancaster, Alan Millard, Missionary Aviation Fellowship, Malcolm Muggeridge, National Christian Education Council, National Trust, Mary O'Hara, Nick Page, Nigel Perrin, the late J.B.Phillips, Norman Richardson (Corrymeela), Norman Rotherham, Samaritans, Save the Children Fund, Delia Smith, Geoffrey Smith, Donald Swann, Jan Taylor (formerly of Bible Society), Peter Timms, Steve Turner, Alan West, Gerald Williams.

Sources

The author wishes to acknowledge the following sources which she found particularly helpful during her research for this book:

3 Jan	Humphrey Carpenter, *The Inklings*, Unwin
8 Jan	Elisabeth Elliot, *Shadow of the Almighty,* Hodder and Stoughton
11 Jan	Alan Paton, *Instrument of Thy Peace,* Fontana
20 Jan	(also 26 Feb,19 Apr,26 May,22,30 Aug,22 Nov) *New Music* (now *New Christian Music*) magazine
22 Jan	Pat Seed, *One Day at a Time*, Pan
24 Jan	William Barclay, *Prayers for Young People,* Fontana
28 Jan	(also 29 Jan,16 July,2,22,23 Aug) *Crusade* (now *Today*) magazine
31 Jan	Bernard Dixon, *Journeys in Belief,* Allen and Unwin
3 Feb	Ramon Hunston, *Order, Order,* Marshalls
6 Feb	Robert Laidlaw, *The Story of the Reason Why,* Pickering and Inglis
7 Feb	*Joyce Grenfell Requests the Pleasure;* (also 8 Feb) Reggie Grenfell and Richard Garnett (eds.), *Joyce, by herself and her friends,* Futura
9 Feb	Fyodor Dostoevsky, *The Brothers Karamazov,* Penguin Books
15 Feb	(also 16 Feb) Jean Roblin, *Louis Braille,* Royal National Institute for the Blind
17 Feb	Dan Wooding, *Uganda Holocaust,* Pickering and Inglis
18 Feb	(also 18 Apr,31 Oct) Edith Simon, *Luther Alive!,* Hodder and Stoughton
21 Feb	(also 11 July) Sally Magnusson, *The Flying Scotsman,* Quartet Books
24 Feb	Mary Craig, *Blessings,* Coronet Books
25 Feb	(also 2 Apr,30 July,29 Oct) Keston College
27 Feb	Corrie ten Boom, with John and Elizabeth Sherill, *The Hiding Place,* Hodder and Stoughton
1 Mar	Eunice Diment, *Kidnapped,* The Paternoster Press
8 Mar	Story from Stuart King, General Director, MAF
9 Mar	(also 11 May) Gilbert White, *The Natural History of Selborne,* J.M.Dent and Sons
17 Mar	*Scott's Last Expedition,* from the personal journals of Captain R.F.Scott, John Murray
23 Mar	(also 28 Mar) Susan Chitty, *The Woman Who Wrote Black Beauty,* Hodder and Stoughton
30 Mar	G.W.Target, *The Nun in the Concentration Camp,* Religious Education Press
6 Apr	(also 7 Apr) George Otis, *Eldridge Cleaver: Ice and Fire,* Lakeland
10 Apr	(also 24 June,2,20 July) Cyril Barnes, *God's Army,* Lion Publishing
15 Apr	Sybil Dobbie, *Faith and Fortitude,* P.E Johnston
22 Apr	(also 23 Apr,15 Sept,22 Nov) *Buzz* magazine
28 Apr	(also 1,8 Oct) Georgina Battiscombe, *Shaftesbury: A Biography of the Seventh Earl,* Constable and Co.
1 May	(also 11 Oct) Clyde Binfield, *George Williams and the YMCA,* Heinemann

6 May	(also 7 May,12,13 Oct) Story from the Bible Society
8 May	(also 18 May) Brian Peachment, *The Red Cross Story*, Religious Education Press
10 May	Pam and Peter Cousins, *The Power of the Air*, Hodder and Stoughton
12 May	(also 21,25 Oct) Cecil Woodham Smith, *Florence Nightingale*, Constable and Co.
14 May	(also 14 Nov) Story from the Jamaican High Commissioner
16 May	(also 13 Dec) Wain (ed), *Johnson on Johnson*, J.M.Dent and Sons
20 May	Story from the United Bible Societies
4 June	Brian Greenaway with Brian Kellock, *Hell's Angel*, Lion Publishing
6 June	(also 12 Aug) Michael Davis, *William Blake: A New Kind of Man*, Elek
9 June	*Elizabeth Garrett Anderson*, Jo Manton, Methuen
12 June	Charles Kingsley, *The Water Babies*, Allen and Unwin
14 June	(also 15 June) Harriet Beecher Stowe, *Uncle Tom's Cabin*, J.M.Dent and Sons
17 June	(also 8 July) Charles Colson, *Born Again*, Hodder and Stoughton
18 June	(also 23,24 Sept) William Plomer (ed.), *Kilvert's Diary*, Jonathan Cape
20 June	(also 28 June,24 July) Percy Parker (ed.), *Journal of John Wesley*, Moody Press
25 June	Hesketh Pearson, *The Smith of Smiths*, Hamish Hamilton
1 July	(also 16 July,3 Sept) E.E.Reynolds (ed.), Thomas Stapleton's *Life of Sir Thomas More*, Burns and Oates
5 July	George Borrow, *Lavengro*, Oxford University Press
10 July	(also 15 Aug) Cyril Davey, *Kagawa of Japan*, Epworth Press
12 July	(also 13 July) Phyllis Thompson, *Mister Leprosy*, Hodder and Stoughton; the Leprosy Mission of England and Wales
17 July	(also 18 July,18 Sept) Gillian Wagner, *Barnardo*, Weidenfeld and Nicholson
23 July	From an epilogue on Irish Television
3 Aug	(also 4 Aug) *The Practice of the Presence of God*, Fleming H.Revell
8 Aug	Izaak Walton, *The Compleat Angler*, Harrap and Co.
9 Aug	(also 10 Aug) Fred Lemon, *Breakout*, Lakeland
14 Aug	Joseph Williamson, *Josephine Butler: The Forgotten Saint*, Faith Press
15 Aug	*Keir Hardie*, Kenneth O. Morgan, Oxford University Press
17,18 Aug	Mary Drewery, *William Carey*, Hodder and Stoughton
21 Aug	Paul Hunt, *Inside Iran*, Lion Publishing
26 Aug	John Beresford (ed.), *Woodforde's Diary*, Oxford University Press
2 Sept	(also 19 Nov) *The Autobiography of Richard Baxter*, J.M.Dent and Sons
7 Sept	(also 8 Sept) From a programme on BBC Radio 2
9 Sept	(also 10 Sept) Story from the Far East Broadcasting Corporation, Singapore
11 Sept	(also 13 Sept) Joni Eareckson, *Joni;* Joni Eareckson and Steve Estes, *One Step Further*, Pickering and Inglis
16 Sept	J.B.Phillips, *Ring of Truth*, Hodder and Stoughton

19 Sept	(also 20 Sept) Walter Stranz, *George Cadbury*, Shire Publications
27 Sept	(also 5 Dec) Roger Steer, *Delighted in God*, Hodder and Stoughton
29 Sept	David Sheppard, *Parson's Pitch*, Hodder and Stoughton
9 Oct	*Simple Faith?*, Lion Publishing
15 Oct	Diana Dewar, *All for Christ*, Oxford University Press
19 Oct	Malcolm Muggeridge, *Something Beautiful for God*, William Collins and Sons
3 Nov	Delia Smith, *Frugal Food*, Coronet Books
12 Nov	*The Poems of Wilfred Owen*, Chatto and Windus
13 Nov	Sherwood E.Wirt, *The Confessions of Augustine in Modern English*, Lion Publishing
25 Nov	(also 27 Nov) Brian Peachment, *An Aeroplane or a Grave*, Religious Education Press
29 Nov	C.S.Lewis, *Surprised by Joy*, Fontana
4 Dec	(also 7 Dec) Sheila Cassidy, *Audacity to Believe*, Fontana
9 Dec	(also 22 Dec) Brian Peachment, *The Tiger of Naples*, Religious Education Press
18 Dec	Douglas Hare, *Escape from Death*, Religious Education Press
23 Dec	Adapted from material originally written by Anthea Cousins for The Paternoster Press
25 Dec	Geoffrey Trease, *Days to Remember*, Pan
27 Dec	(also 28 Dec) Rene Dubos, *Pasteur*, Heinemann

The author also wishes to acknowledge her indebtedness to *The Penguin Dictionary of Saints*, by Donald Attwater.

Index

People
Biblical characters indicated by (B) *after entry.*

Abraham (B) 84
Adams, John 319
Alfred, King of Wessex 308
Alliluyeva, Svetlana 364
Anderson, Elizabeth Garrett 169
Augustine of Hippo, St 249, 326
Aylward, Gladys 10, 20

Barclay, William 32
Barnabas (B) 171
Barnardo, Thomas 207, 208, 270
Baxter, Richard 254, 332
Bede, Venerable 156, 157, 226, 330, 331
Betjeman, John 250
Blake, William 166, 233, 341
Bolton, Ian 248
Bonhoeffer, Dietrich 43, 44, 217
Boniface of Crediton, St 366
Boone, Pat 28
Booth, Brian 228
Booth, William 109, 184, 192, 210
Borrelli, Mario 352, 365
Borrow, George 135, 136, 195, 216
Boswell, James 145, 356
Braille, Louis 54, 55
Brown, John 345
Browne, Stanley 202, 203
Burkitt, Denis 67, 68
Bunyan, John 94, 252, 253
Butler, Josephine 235

Cadbury, George 271, 272
Caedmon 331
Campion, Edmund 344
Carey, William 238, 239
Carlile, Wilson 278
Cash, Johnny 65
Cassidy, Sheila 347, 350
Castle, Roy 243, 244
Catherwood, Fred 197
Causley, Charles 62
Cecilia, St 335
Charles I of England 38
Charles, Thomas 138
Chaucer, Geoffrey 102, 306
Cheshire, Leonard 259, 260

Chesterton, Gilbert Keith (G.K.) 95, 158, 287
Christian, Fletcher 31
Christian, Thursday October 31
Christopher, St 215
Cleaver, Eldridge 105, 106
Coggan, Donald 291
Coleman, John and Audrey 233
Colson, Charles 177, 198
Cooper, Anthony Ashley *see* Shaftesbury
Copernicus, Nicholas 154
Coverdale, Miles 286
Cowper, William 110, 333, 339
Craig, Mary 63
Cromwell, Oliver 119, 120, 124

Dana 121, 122
Daniel (B) 211
Darling, Grace 337
Diment, Eunice 69
Dixon, Jessy 335
Dobbie, William 114
Donne, John 99, 229
Dostoevsky, Fyodor 48
Dunant, Henry 137, 147
Dylan, Bob 155

Eareckson, Joni 263, 265
Eliot, Thomas Stearns (T.S.) 372
Elliot, Jim 16

Fairbairn, James 354
Faraday, Michael 246
Flynn, John 338, 340
Foreman, George 312
Fox, George 21, 199
Francis of Assisi, St 285, 287
Fry, Elizabeth 150, 151

Galileo Galilei 50, 154
Gill, Eric 61
Graham, Billy 12, 39, 241
Greenaway, Brian 164
Grenfell, Joyce 46, 47
Guy, Thomas 360

Hammarskjöld, Dag 186, 187
Handel, George Frederick 112
Hanway, Jonas 257
Harvey, Frederick 100
Herbert, George 71, 72, 229
Hilda, St 330, 331
Hill, Octavia 234

Hunt, Paul and Diana   242
Huntingdon, Selina, Countess
   of   245

Ignatius of Antioch, St   40
Ignatius of Loyola, St   221
Irwin, James   206

Jasper, Tony   165
Jebb, Eglantyne   144
Jenner, Edward   75, 81
Jerome   282
John XXIII, Pope   163
Johnson, Samuel   145, 356
Jones, Mary   138
Joni   see Eareckson

Kagawa, Toyohiko   200
Kaguru, Andrew   297
Keble, John   124
Keir Hardie, James   236
Ken, Thomas   87
Kepler, Johannes   328
Kierkegaard, Søren   134
Kilvert, Francis   178, 275, 276
King, Martin Luther   23, 24, 103
Kingsley, Charles   172, 173

Laidlaw, Robert   37, 45
Lancaster, Ronald   318
Laurence, Brother   224, 225
Law, William   107, 108
Lemon, Fred   230, 231
Leonardo da Vinci   131, 132
Lewis, Clive Staples (C.S.)   11, 18,
   176, 198, 342, 343
Liddell, Eric   60, 201
Lincoln, Abraham   51, 52
Livingstone, David   88, 89
Luther, Martin   57, 117, 313
Luwum, Janani   56
Lyte, Henry Francis   161

Maguire, Barry   251
Maria, Mother   98
Markee, Dave   267
Mary Magdalene (B)   212
Mercator, Geradus   73
Millard, Alan   264
Milton, John   323
Mohr, Joseph   367
More, Thomas   191, 196, 255
Muggeridge, Malcolm   92, 94, 134,
   301
Müller, George   279, 348

Newton, John   74, 110
Nicholas, St   349
Nightingale, Florence   141, 303,
   307, 327
Nightingale, Rita   36, 37

Oates, Titus   73, 85
O'Hara, Mary   213
Oswald, St   226
Owen, Wilfred   324, 325

Page, Nick   12
Pascal, Blaise   179
Pasteur, Louis   370, 371
Paton, Alan   19
Paul (B)   33
Penn, William   296, 309
Perrin, Nigel   317
Peter (B)   189, 190
Phillips, John Bertram (J.B.)   268,
   269
Polycarp   34

Quoist, Michel   170

Raikes, Robert   104
Richard, Cliff   78, 165, 240, 241
Rinkart, Martin   351
Russell, Ron   149

Sayers, Dorothy L.   14, 111, 357,
   359
Schweitzer, Albert   22, 256
Scott, Captain Robert   85
Scriven, Joseph   153
Seacole, Mary   143, 327
Seed, Pat   30
Sewell, Anna   91, 96
Shaftesbury, Earl of   127, 283, 290
Sheppard, David   281
Sheraton, Thomas   304
Shippam, Ernest   39
Sidney, Philip   274
Simeon the Stylite   13
Simpson, James   167, 168, 300
Singh, Sundar   361
Smith, Delia   316
Smith, Geoffrey   80
Smith, Sydney   185
Snell, Adrian   118
Spooner, William   218
Stalin, Joseph   364
Stalin, Svetlana   see Alliluyeva
Stanley, Henry   89
Stapleton, Thomas   191, 196, 255
Stephen (B)   369
Stowe, Harriet Beecher   174, 175
Streatfeild, Noel   26, 27

Swann, Donald   363
Swithun of Winchester, St   205

ten Boom, Corrie   66
Teresa, Mother   92, 299, 301
Thomas à Becket   102, 372
Thomas à Kempis   282
Thomas, George   42
Timms, Peter   336
Tolkien, J.R.R   11
Tolstoy, Leo   115, 116, 320, 321
Toplady, Augustus   232
Trollope, Anthony   123
Tuke, William   86
Turgenev, Ivan   310
Turner, Steve   15, 277, 353
Tyndale, William   286, 288, 289

Utchunu   128, 129

Valentine, St   53

Vallotton, Annie   294, 295
Varrah, Chad   315
Vins, Georgi   353

Waddell, Jean   242
Walton, Izaak   71, 229
Washington, George   194
Wenceslas, St   280
Wesley, Charles   97, 245
Wesley, John   70, 107, 180, 188, 245
Wesley, Susanna   70, 214
West, Alan   148
White, Gilbert   77, 140
Wilberforce, William   219
Williams, George   130, 293
Williams, Gerald   183
Woodforde, James ('Parson')   247
Wren, Christopher   302
Wyclif, John   133, 288

Topics

Bible passages indicated by (B) *after entry.*

All Fools' Day   100
Angels   93, 180, 233, 343
Anger (B)   266
Animals   71, 91, 95, 96, 140, 180, 219, 256, 332, 339, 356, 373
Apartheid   19
Arbitration   125, 126(B)
Archaeology   29, 264
Art/Artists/Craftsmen   61, 131, 132, 166, 233, 294, 295, 304, 341

Beginnings (B)   9
Bible Translators/Translations   57, 69, 117, 129, 133, 135, 136, 146, 156, 169, 195, 216, 239, 268, 269, 286, 288, 289, 294, 295, 308, 313
Birds   77, 81, 100, 108
Bounty, Mutiny on the   31, 319

Childbirth   167, 168
Chimney-sweeps   172, 341
Chloroform   167, 168
Christmas tree   366
Cold   73, 85, 348, 361, 373
Conciliation   125, 126(B)
Conversion stories   39, 74, 91, 106, 179, 220, 224, 238, 240, 248, 249, 252, 278, 312, 321, 335, 342
Craftsmen   *see* Art

Dead Sea Scrolls   29
Death   38, 98, 99, 156, 196, 341, 356
Depression   315, 333
Disability   54, 55, 63, 263, 265
Disease, Fight against   30, 67, 68, 75, 128, 143, 173, 202, 203, 210, 300, 359
Diaries/Journals   178, 180, 186, 187, 188, 247, 275, 276, 368
Drugs (illegal)   36, 354

Education/Educationalists   11, 104, 150, 151, 169, 214, 218, 326
Endings (B)   374
Enjoyment (B)   90
Entertainers   46, 47, 78, 243, 244, 282, 363
Envy (B)   49
Evening   44, 87
Explorers   85, 88, 89

Factories   210, 271, 272
Faith   83(B), 84, 279, 348
Fire   70, 166, 254, 255, 287
Fireworks   318
Food   58, 82, 185, 316
Foretelling (B)   355, 358, 362
Forgiveness   18, 35(B), 66, 199, 230, 231
Friends (B)   258
Furniture   304

Generosity   59(B), 285, 360
Gold   72, 237(B), 264, 349
Good News Bible   294, 295

Great Bible 286
Gypsies 135, 195

Happiness (B) 193
Honesty (B) 292
Hospitals 30, 141, 164, 299, 300, 303, 307, 360
Human Rights' Day 353
Humility 40, 187
Hymn-writers 71, 72, 74, 87, 97, 110, 124, 153, 161, 232, 333, 339, 351, 367

Ingratitude (B) 162
Inklings, The 11
Ireland 305

Jack o'Lent 62
Jealousy (B) 49
Journalists 46, 89, 92, 94, 104, 165, 185
Journals *see* Diaries

Laziness (B) 25
Leasehold reform 42
Letters 16, 18, 214
Listening 142(B), 213
Living Bible, The 164
Love 48, 53, 98

Martyrs 16, 34, 40, 43, 44, 56, 133, 191, 196, 255, 288, 289, 297, 344, 366, 369, 372
Mayflower, The 322, 345
Medical men/women 22, 67, 68, 75, 81, 88, 89, 141, 143, 167, 168, 202, 203, 256, 300, 327, 347, 350
Mental illness/Mental hospitals 86, 101, 283, 333, 339
Missionaries 16, 88, 89, 169, 202, 203, 221, 223, 239, 361
Money 79(B), 360
Morning 44, 87, 108
Music/Musicians 28, 65, 71, 78, 112, 118, 121, 122, 155, 165, 182, 184, 213, 240, 241, 243, 244, 251, 267, 282, 317, 335, 363, 367

Natural history 77, 80, 81, 88, 140, 275, 276
Negro Rights (*see also* Slavery *and* Racism) 23, 24, 103, 105, 106, 345
Nobel Prize, Winners of 22, 92, 256, 299, 301

Peace efforts 182, 305, 324, 325
Photography 78, 270
Pilgrim Fathers 322

Poets 15, 38, 62, 71, 72, 95, 99, 100, 102, 110, 155, 158, 166, 233, 250, 274, 277, 287, 306, 323, 324, 325, 330, 331, 333, 339, 341, 353
Politicians 42, 119, 120, 127, 177, 186, 194, 197, 198, 219, 283, 290
Praise 184, 334(B)
Prayer 32, 110, 170, 204(B), 242
Pride 176, 227(B)
Prison/Labour camps 24, 36, 37, 43, 44, 60, 64, 65, 98, 150, 151, 164, 166, 191, 198, 217, 220, 223, 230, 231, 252, 311, 336, 347, 350

Racism 19, 23, 24, 103, 105, 106
Radio/Television 12, 80, 92, 94, 139, 165, 183, 213, 261, 262, 316, 357, (338), 340
Rain 173, 205, 257
Red Cross 137, 147
Revised Version (of Bible) 146
Russian Orthodox Church 15, 115, 116

St Paul's (Cathedral) 99, 254, 289, 302
School 170, 282, 326
Scientists 50, 131, 154, 179, 246, 328, 354, 370, 371
Sea voyages/Storms 74, 149, 309, 322, 337
Sharing 298(B), 350
Slavery, Fight against 174, 175, 194, 219, 345
Social reformers/Reform 42, 86, 104, 127, 130, 137, 144, 147, 150, 151, 172, 173, 174, 184, 192, 200, 207, 208, 210, 219, 234, 235, 236, 257, 270, 278, 283, 290, 352, 365
Space 160, 206
Sport/Sportspeople 60, 148, 183, 201, 228, 229, 248, 281, 312
Stars/Planets 50, 154, 157, 328, 329
Suffering 291
Sunday schools 104, 271

Tact (B) 17
Thankfulness 107
Tongue, The (B) 273
Town planning 272, 296, 302

Wales 138, 216
War 114, 137, 147, 178, 274, 303, 308, 324, 325, 327, 351
Worry (B) 209

Events

American Civil War   52
American Independence,
   Declaration of   194
Balaklava, Battle of   303, 307
Constance, Council of   133
Crimean War   303, 327
Criminal Law Amendment
   Act   235
Diet of Worms   117
Fire of London   99, 254, 302, 332
First World War Armistice   324
Fugitive Slave Act   174
Geneva Convention   147

Gettysburg Dedication   52
Gordon Riots   97, 166
Great Exhibition of 1852   130
Long Parliament expelled   119
Penny Post   18
Pilgrim Fathers sailed   322
Second World War ended   236
Solferino, Battle of   137, 147
Sunday School Movement
   begun   104
Thirty Years' War   329, 351
Watergate Affair   177
Waterloo, Battle of   178, 300
Westphalia, Peace of   351
Zutphen, Battle of   274

Church calendar

Unless otherwise indicated,
saints' Feast Days fall on date
of extract. *Biblical characters
indicated by* (B); *Feast Days
indicated by* (FD).

Abraham (B)   84
Advent/Advent Sunday   346
All Saints' Day   313, 314, 318
Ascension Day   152, 156
Augustine of Hippo (FD 28
   August)   249, 326
Barnabas (B)   171
Bede, Venerable (FD 27 May)
   156, 157, 226, 330, 331
Boniface (FD 5 June)   366
Candlemas   41
Cecilia   335
Christmas   15, 231, 280, 349, 363,
   367, 368
Christopher   215
Church calendar   157
Daniel (B)   211
Easter   12, 15, 64, 111, 113(B),
   115, 116, 212
Epiphany   14
Francis of Assisi (FD 4
   October)   285, 287
Harvest Thanksgiving   250, 284

Hilda (FD 17 November)   330, 331
Ignatius of Antioch   40
Ignatius of Loyola   221
Jerome   282
Lady Day   93
Lammas   222
Lent   58, 62, 82
Luke (B)   300
Mary Magdalene (B)   212
More, Thomas (FD 9 July with St
   John Fisher)   191, 196, 255
Mothering Sunday   82
Nicholas   349
Oswald, King of Northumbria (FD
   9 August)   226
Palm Sunday   95
Paul (B) (FD 29 June with St
   Peter)   33
Peter (B)   189, 190
Polycarp, Bishop of Smyrna   34
Red Letter Days   124
Shrove Tuesday   58
Simeon the Stylite   13
Stephen (B)   369
Swithun   205
Thomas à Becket (FD 29
   December)   102, 372
Valentine   53
Wenceslas   280
Whitsun   159

Organizations and societies

ACAS (Advisory Conciliation and
   Arbitration Service)   125
Australian Bible Society   295
Barnardo's Homes   207, 208, 270
Black Panther Movement   105

British and Foreign Bible
   Society   135, 136, 138
Carmelite Order   224, 225
Cheshire Homes   259, 260
Christians in Sport   148
Church Army   278, 317
Civil Rights Movement   23, 24,
   103

Corrymeela Community   182, 305
Countess of Huntingdon's
   Connexion   245
EEC (European Economic
   Community)   197
FEBA (Far East Broadcasting
   Association)   139
FEBC (Far East Broadcasting
   Company)   261, 262
Flying Doctor Service   338, 340
Gideons International   160
Hell's Angels   164
MAF (Missionary Aviation
   Fellowship)   76
Mau Mau Movement   297
Mother of God Community Centre
   (House of Scugnizzi)   352
Müller's Homes   279, 348
National Trust   234
Pasteur Institute   371
Red Cross   144, 147

Royal Society   81, 246
RSPCA (Royal Society for the
   Prevention of Cruelty to
   Animals)   96, 219
Salvation Army   109, 184, 192
Samaritans (Befriending
   service)   315
Sisters of Charity   92, 299, 301
Society of Friends (Quakers)   21,
   86, 91, 120, 150, 151, 199, 271,
   272, 282, 296, 309
Society of Jesus   221, 344
Tear Fund (The Evangelical
   Alliance Relief Fund)   78
United Bible Societies   149
United Nations Organization   186,
   305, 353
Wycliffe Bible Translators   16, 69,
   128, 129
YMCA (Young Men's Christian
   Association)   130, 236, 293

Countries

Africa   88, 89
Albania   92, 299, 301
Australia   228, 295, 338, 340
Austria   367
Bangladesh   78
Brazil   16, 128, 129
Canada   153
Chile   347, 350
China   20, 60, 135, 136, 261, 262
Cyprus   171
Czechoslovakia (Bohemia)   280
Denmark   134
France   54, 55, 170, 179, 224, 225,
   370, 371
Gabon   22
Germany   22, 43, 44, 57, 112, 117,
   217, 256, 313, 328, 351
Holland   66
India   92, 169, 239, 299, 301, 361
Iran   223, 242
Israel   29
Italy   50, 131, 132, 154, 163, 285,
   287, 352, 365
Jamaica   143, 327

Japan   200, 236
Kenya   297
Malta   114
New Zealand   45, 149
North Africa   249, 326
Philippines   69
Pitcairn Island   31, 319
Poland   154
Seychelles Islands   139
South Africa   19
Spain   221
Sudan   76
Sweden   186, 187, 373
Switzerland   137, 147, 294
Thailand   36, 37
Uganda   56
USSR (includes old Russia)   48,
   64, 98, 101, 105, 115, 116, 136, 220,
   310, 311, 320, 321, 353, 364
USA   16, 23, 24, 28, 39, 51, 52,
   65, 89, 103, 105, 106, 109, 143,
   155, 160, 174, 175, 177, 194,
   198, 206, 251, 263, 265, 296,
   309, 312, 322, 335, 345, 353, 364
Yugoslavia   92, 299, 301
Zaire   202, 203
Zanzibar   88